FAC

A Million Jews to Save

Check to the final solution

André Biss

SOUTH BRUNSWICK
NEW YORK: A.S. BARNES AND COMPANY

First published in Germany as Der Stopp der Endlösung 1966

© Seewald Verlag (Stuttgart) 1966
Translation © Hutchinson and Co. (Publishers) Ltd., 1973

First American Edition published 1975 by
A.S. Barnes and Company, Inc., Cranbury, New Jersey 08512

Library of Congress Catalogue Card Number: 77-146779

ISBN 0-498-07877-9
Printed in the United States of America

To my friends Otto Komoly, Rezsö Kastner, Szulem Offenbach, and all the heroes of The Budapest Committee of Jewish Assistance who died in the struggle.

Despite the indifference of those who lived safe from danger, despite the treachery that decimated their numbers, despite the constant threat from outside, they had the courage to fight to save the last survivors of their people threatened with annihilation – and to win. History will honour their victory and will engrave it for ever on the memory of future generations.

Contents

Preface 9

1 The Background 13
2 The Waada 20
3 Between the Acts 33
4 Brand's Mission in Turkey 43
5 First Negotiations Between Kastner and Eichmann 48
6 Arrested by the Hungarians, Released by the Germans 52
7 I am Saved by a Trick 62
8 The Grey Eminence 69
9 Strasshof 74
10 Kurt Becher 82
11 The Test-Convoy 91
12 Horthy, The 'Saviour' of the Jews 99
13 The Explanatory Note 109
14 News from England 117
15 The Evacuation of the Test-Convoy 122
16 Himmler Asks for Proof 127
17 The Events of September 1944 133
18 Three 'Couriers' from Palestine 143
19 The Arrow Cross in Command 147
20 Kastner Goes to Switzerland 156
21 Budapest in November 1944 165
22 New Trends 176
23 New Enterprises, New Difficulties 180
24 The Last Four Weeks before the Investment of Budapest 185

25 The Columbusgasse Camp   191
26 Various Actions   197
27 The Test-Convoy Finally Arrives in Switzerland   202
28 The Ghetto   205
29 In Budapest Besieged   213
30 After the Liberation   220
31 Conspiracy of Silence   228
32 The Freeing of the Camps   235
33 Epilogue   247

Chronology   261

Index   267

Preface

'The efforts made unceasingly by the representatives of the Joint
Distribution Committee at Budapest from the spring of 1944 were not
in vain. They secured in October of that same year that Himmler gave
orders for the arrest of the "final solution".'

DIETER WISLICENY[1]

At the beginning of October 1944, Otto Clages[2] *Hauptsturmführer* of the SS and commissary of criminal police, in his
capacity as chief of a special section of the Budapest SD, communicated officially to his Jewish interlocutor that Himmler
had, at last, given orders that the massacre of Jews still under
the control of the Third Reich, should cease. For more than
four months, through this delegate, the Jewish-American
Joint Distribution Committee had been tireless in demands
that the genocide should be ended.

Almost twenty years have gone by since these events. The
man who faced Clages and who was thought by the
Hauptsturmführer to be delegated with full powers by 'world-
wide Jewry' was myself.

What hard-fought battles had to be engaged before we obtained the success so long hoped for! More than five hundred
thousand people – that is to say the whole Jewish population
of Europe which had, up to then, escaped massacre – were at
last saved!

1. From a hand-written confession made, before his execution, by one
of Eichmann's principal lieutenants, and the organizer of the deportations
of Jews from Slovakia.

2. At the time Otto Clages wrote his name with a 'K' and I thought it
was a pseudonym. After the war I learned that his name was written
really with a 'C'. 'Clages' must then be read and not 'Klages'.

9

What effort it had cost to stop the deportations of Hungarian Jews! It had been wrung from Himmler in July 1944.

How many and great were the difficulties and complications to be overcome before we obtained, first of all, the instructions for changing the original destination of five train-loads of deportees – some eighteen thousand persons – who were not to see Auschwitz but who were sent to the Strasshof labour camp.

How many efforts did it cost, in the midst of a war, to send a 'test-convoy' full of deportees, from Budapest to neutral Switzerland via Bergen-Belsen.

How many desperate attempts – hardly credible today – desperate and even hare-brained, were made to widen the divisions existing within the SS command and to make the most of Himmler's secret plans. We had to take advantage of his desire to desert the Führer, a desire that led him to undertake negotiations with the 'International-Jewry' to which he attributed such mighty powers.

When Clages told me of the situation I felt that at last God had come to the help of his people's last survivors, and that now our hopes of rescue were not unfounded. But I did not then imagine how bitter and how long – right up to the end of the war – would be our struggle to attain our ends.

Today, although more than twenty years have passed since these events, public opinion seems to know nothing about them. And the same is true of the historians.

We have been able to hear or to read comments on this period which betray a tragic ignorance about the facts and the events. Hannah Arendt's book on the Eichmann trial is not free from such ignorance.[1]

Hannah Arendt, indeed, has analysed with clear-sighted intelligence the Eichmann trial held at Jerusalem in 1961. With a critical sense that is all to her credit, she has given her opinion on the obvious defects in the proceedings. But when she denounces bitterly the inadequacy of the Jewish resistance leaders, it is obvious that those who organized the trial threw

1. Vide *Eichmann In Jerusalem or The Banality of Evil*, 1966.

no light upon the most important phase of the Resistance and that indeed, they intentionally left this in the dark. Most of the articles written about Hannah Arendt's book are not only by writers who are not very competent, but also all of them adopt a moral or philosophical point of view. They reinforce the impression that the subject dealt with is examined only partially and is very imperfectly understood. The object of this book is to fill in the gaps in the record.

I hope that the youth of Germany may learn, in the light of the facts reported here, that whenever injustices are committed, one can, indeed one must resist in the interest of one's own nation. By letting so many opportunities of revolt pass, their parents failed in their duty. However, among the Germans who did realize their duty at that time, we must mention especially a brother and a sister, Hans and Sophia Scholl. With their friends at Munich University these young people organized the 'White Rose' network and they have a place of honour in the German resistance movement. Despite their youth (and when the end of the war was still distant, and it still looked as though Hitler might win) they did not hesitate to follow the dictates of their conscience. If the majority of the German people had followed their example, how many horrors would Germany and the rest of the world have been spared. Let us hope that the heroism of Hans and Sophia Scholl may not fade from the memory of today's young Germans.[1]

Jewish youth clearly have no reason to keep alive an unjustified assumption. It is not true to maintain that the European Jews (save for the heroes of the Warsaw ghetto and of a very few other Polish ghettos) went to their deaths without resistance. It is a fact that the great mass of Hitler's victims had no arms with which to resist him, but they did possess that intelligence their ancestors knew how to use more cleverly than they did, as we can see in the history of the Hebrews from Moses to David.

1. Hans and Sophia Scholl were arrested on 18th February 1943, were condemned to death by a 'people's court' and executed on 22nd February following.

I hope that the young people of Israel may learn from this account that there existed in 1944 a daring resistance movement of insuperable spiritual resources – and that it was crowned with success. It was a Resistance of which the Jewish people will one day be proud, even if now there exists a generation of old and pusillanimous men who do not want to hear about something to which the majority of them owe their lives. This generation is only too well aware that they were unworthy of their task.

1. The Background

In June 1941 the Hungarian government, then under the Prime Minister Bardossy, broke off diplomatic relations with the Soviet Union. A few days later the Hungarians announced they had joined the war on the side of the Axis Powers.

On March 19, 1944, the country was occupied by the German SS. During these troubled times Admiral Nicholas Horthy, the Hungarian Regent, was in Germany. Hitler, having first received him, then put him under temporary arrest. By this time the Red Army had reached the Carpathian mountains and was threatening the Hungarian frontiers. Horthy had made it abundantly clear that he would not carry on with the struggle.

At the same time that they seized power the SS took on the job of settling the Jewish problem. Ever since the years 1938–1939, anti-Jewish laws had been applied in Hungary; while as from 1941 the radical measures adopted involved, for those affected by them, loss of employment, social discrimination, restrictions on bank accounts, confiscation of property and deprivation of liberty. Tens of thousands of Jews who were unable to produce proofs of nationality although they might have been resident in Hungary for several generations, were deported across the frontiers. And that meant that they were handed over to the tender mercies of the Gestapo and met with an inevitable fate. However, up to March 19, 1944 most of the Hungarian Jews had hoped, which seemed reasonable enough, that they would see the end of the war without having to pay too heavy a tribute of blood.

We must present in their historical context the Hungarian anti-Jewish laws. These were, at first, comparatively moderate but later on became much more severe. These laws were not only promulgated under Nazi pressure but they were also due to the anti-semitism of a great part of the population. I would like to stress that I do not attribute to anti-semitism the importance now given it to explain the history of our times, as is the case in Germany. I consider anti-semitism more as the symptom of a widespread disease – racial intolerance for any minority. Our mass civilization, the modern methods of communication we enjoy easily provoke such intolerance. Today all peoples are threatened with the evil of racial intolerance whose extreme form may lead to wholesale extermination.

In Hungary, an independent kingdom and then, through the interplay of alliances and inheritance, a Hapsburg province, the principles of the French Revolution dominated during the first half of the last century, as they did in the rest of Europe. The abdication of the Emperor Ferdinand the First in favour of his nephew, then aged only eighteen, led to the 1848 revolution. The Hungarians would not recognize the new emperor and Kossuth proclaimed a republic. But the Hapsburgs called on the help of the Russian Emperor Nicholas I and the revolt was drowned in blood. The poet of liberty, Petöfi fell fighting, Kossuth had to flee to the West and Count Batthyányi and a dozen of his ministers were executed under martial law.

Within the Hapsburg empire Hungary remained a rather poor province but some fundamental reforms in the social order could not be abolished – such as the suppression of serfdom. The Jews among others benefited by the new state of things. Up to then Jews might engage only in certain despised trades such as those of old clothes merchants, horse copers . . . they accepted this situation with resignation just as the poorer classes bore their lot.

The decisive change however took place only in 1869. After their defeat by the Prussians, the Austrians sought a conciliation with the Hungarians. Francis-Joseph mounted the throne as King of Hungary which from then onwards had its own parliament and ministers. A commercial and customs agreement was signed renewable every ten years. Hungary became to all intents and purposes an equal partner in the empire. The country henceforth was linked with Austria only by the person of the King-Emperor and by common ministers of Defence, Finance and Foreign Affairs. This relative independence brought a land sparsely populated, though one fertile and rich in raw materials, a spurt of commercial and industrial prosperity. This was in a measure favourable to both partners. The standard of living rose and the demand for commodities increased. This development was due mostly to the Jewish community. Owing to their knowledge and experience the Jews occupied key positions in the most important spheres of activity (commerce, banking, small-scale industry) in some of which the Jewish interest amounted to as much as 90 per cent. The gentry, on the other hand, continued to hold such occupations in contempt.

From the social point of view Hungary was composed essentially of four classes. At the top of the social pyramid came the higher nobility, not very numerous but wealthy, cultivated and possessing immense domains. Its members spent most of their time in Vienna, in Paris and also in England. Then came the gentry, the lesser nobility, uncultivated, even in some measure primitive but owners of land. The younger sons who could not inherit the family properties went almost automatically into the civil service and government offices. The poorer peasants and the agricultural labourers who formed the most numerous class of the population were ill-educated and under-privileged for although in theory free, they lived in a state of degrading serfdom side by side with the landed classes.

The fourth class comprised the Jews who since 1867 had been, legally, first-class citizens. Nevertheless, practicably speaking, the doors of the civil service were shut in the face of the Jews as also was the case with the poorer peasants, and the agricultural labourers. Except in the areas inhabited by German minorities there was not in Hungary any prosperous middle class moulding in many respects the public life of the country such as for instance developed after the end of the Middle Ages in Germany, France and England. Such a class however began to form in the second half of the 19th century and the Jews played the leading part in this formation. They exercised their intelligence in the domains of art and literature in a privileged fashion since the gentry considered such occupations as unworthy of them.

The Jewish community's prosperity aroused envy. It was an envy which if examined closely was more directed to the prosperity itself than to those who enjoyed it. This is a fundamental reaction; even a reflex one. Active minorities are exposed to it at all periods and everywhere in the world. Neither the Chinese in India, Malaya and Indonesia nor the Germans in eastern Europe and America, nor the Greeks and Armenians in Turkey escaped from it.

The development of hostility towards the Jews had then first of all as a cause economic considerations and had little to do with racial questions. An indirect confirmation of this may be seen in the growing hostility towards Germans at this same time, a hostility that developed in comparable proportions and for the same reasons as anti-semitism.

At the beginning of the First World War there were some half a million Germans living in Hungary. Some of these were the so-called 'Saxons' of Transylvania whose ancestors came originally from the Rhineland and Luxemburg. About a third of them had been called eastwards by King Geza II about 1150 so as to constitute a frontier population opposed to the Kumans and Tatars. In 1224 the *privilegium andreanum* of King Andrew II conferred a number of privileges on these 'Saxons'.

Then there were the Swabians of the Banat who came originally from southern Germany, Austria and Lorraine. At the invitation of the Empress Maria Theresa and the Comte de

Mercy they emigrated to regions south of the Carpathians and round about Temesvar.

Finally Austrian Germans, descendants of civil servants, soldiers and tradesmen protected by the government, were scattered about all over the country.

Industrialization, as it did everywhere else, caused the appearance of an industrial proletariat in Hungary which engaged in social agitation. In these ranks were also some Jews, but the part they played was insignificant. On the other hand some Jewish intellectuals did take a decisive part in the creation of Bela Kun's soviet republic in 1919. For reactionary Hungarian society a Jew (politically speaking) must belong to the Left opposition.

Therefore during the first two years of Horthy's dictatorship the 'white terror' was mainly directed against the Jews as the supposed instigators and organizers of the brief interlude in 1919. The fact was ignored that the Hungarian Soviet Republic had inflicted much harm on Jewish industry and commerce. Once again it was considerations of a political and social sort much more than religious or racial prejudices and resentments which were at the origin of this wave of anti-semitism. The years that followed afforded proof of this. The extreme right-wing policy which prevailed after the fall of Bela Kun was no doubt responsible for various social discriminations against the Jews but it did allow them nevertheless to keep their predominant position in commerce, industry and banking.

However in 1933 the position changed very considerably. The rapid and apparently successful rise of Germany aroused enthusiasm for National Socialism among the great majority of the Germans in Hungary and especially among the younger people. The pro-German clubs which then slipped into a predominant place on the Hungarian political scene, bore on their banners Nazi, anti-semitic slogans. (Favourite themes with the new brown-shirted masters.) Was not Hungary included within the zone of Nazi political influence? Class differences greater in Hungary than in Germany (where non-Jews controlled the upper and middle bourgeoisie) favoured the growth of anti-semitism among the public. Propaganda stressed the inequalities, especially in the domains where Jewish influence was pronounced. On the other hand the administration and the big landowners were treated kindly, despite the numerous abuses of which they had been guilty.

The real bane of Hitlerism came from the gentry and the bourgeois sprung from it, that is to say the civil servants and the young officers. On the other hand the Nazis came up against the scepticism of the greater nobility and the corps of the higher officers who had a good idea of what belonging to the Great German vital area would mean. Horthy himself, who was an opportunist and an unscrupulous politician, always abandoned at the decisive moment the enterprises of Hungarian patriots who attempted to preserve the independence of their country. The Regent was afraid of the Nazi bosses, whom moreover he regarded as inevitable allies because of their much advertised opposition to communism.

One must also consider this Hungarian anti-Jewish legislation from another point of view. Hitlerian Germany had supported the Hungarians for the partial restitution of territories lost in 1920 by the provisions of the Trianon Treaty. After the First World War the Hungarians had had to relinquish Slovakia to the Czechs (capital Bratislava) and the Ruthenian part of the Carpathians – with the towns of Ungvár and Munkács. After this arrangement the Czechs called their country Czechoslovakia.

The Rumanians annexed Transylvania (capital Koloszvár), towns with a population in majority German such as Kronstadt, Hermannstadt, Schässburg and Bistritz as well as a part of the Banat including the town of Temesvar. Slovenia, Croatia with the town of Zagreb as well as a large part of the Banat, called Batschka, were attributed to Serbia and the state thus constituted took eventually the name of Yugoslavia. Finally the Bürgenland situated on the western borders of Hungary was assigned to Austria much to the bitterness of the Hungarians.

Hungary thus stripped represented only 40 per cent of the area and population it had before the war of 1914–1918. But after eighteen years of vain efforts to secure a revision of the Trianon Treaty, here was the Third Reich which actually did give back to Hungary some of the lost territories. In 1938 Czechoslovakia had to return several areas in the north and the Russian Carpathians. In that same year the first anti-Jewish law was promulgated and the second in 1939. The next year thanks to an arbitration effected by Ribbentrop and Ciano in Vienna, Hitler divided Transylvania between Hungary and Rumania both of which countries he wanted to conciliate. Rumania, a direct neighbour of the USSR was in a delicate position and had to accept. In 1941 Yugoslavia retroceded the Batschka to Hungary where further anti-Jewish laws were enacted.

From then onwards the number of Jews living on Hungarian territory once more reached a total of almost 800,000. The figure, if one can believe official statistics was in 1930 440,000 but this did not at all correspond to the real state of things since many Jews converted to Christianity kept silent about their origins. Although they had practically speaking, no political role, the Jews had to put up with their position as scapegoats in all affairs concerning the destiny of Hungary. Thus it was that Horthy's very moderate war effort and later on his very insincere attempts to shake himself free of the Axis, were attributed by the Germans to Jewish political influence.

The general picture then presented some curious anomalies. The Nazis, bludgeon in hand, proceeded to teach anti-semitism to a people really far more 'racialist' than the Germans themselves. This German anti-semitism, serving as a pretext for the most varied measures of internal policy, had first of all to be advertised. Later on, however, it was thought indispensable to hide from the German people the monstrous enterprise of Jewish extermination. It was forbidden, on pain of death, to listen to foreign radio programmes which revealed among other items of information, what was happening in the concentration camps. In Hungary this recourse to clandestine eavesdropping was superfluous but in Germany anti-semitism was not the expression of hatred felt for a minority or to an explosion of rage due to a state of passionate excitement, but the result of cold-blooded calculation. The murderous paroxysm to which it led is therefore to be condemned the more – if such distinctions are permissible or even conceivable.

2. The Waada

As soon as the SS had taken over command in Hungary, Adolf Eichmann himself arrived in Budapest in order to settle as soon as possible the 'Jewish problem'. The extermination of more than 900,000 human beings (for since the beginning of 1942 many Polish and Slovakian Jews had taken refuge in Hungary) presented a very complicated task. Up to then, Eichmann according to his own expression had put more than 4,000,000 Jews 'through the mills' (that is to say murdered in the gas-chambers at Auschwitz, Maidanek, Treblinka and other extermination-camps). To this total must be added that of 1,500,000 Jews assassinated by other means. For his staff at the Bureau of Jewish Affairs Eichmann had at his disposal a group, small in numbers but pitiless. His 'Jewish commando' consisted of Krumey, Hunsche, Dannecker and Wisliceny.

A section of the SS under the command of *Hauptsturmführer* Otto Clages was put at the disposal of the Bureau. His job was to support Eichmann by ensuring that the whole operation and the real destination of the deportees should remain well-guarded secrets. Clages's section belonged to the special counter-espionage branch of the SS whose rivalry with the equivalent branch of the *Wehrmacht* (under Admiral Canaris) was becoming more and more pronounced.

When Clages replaced Canaris's men at Budapest with his own he discovered a curious situation. Canaris's people in Budapest, as in all neutral or semi-neutral countries, depended on the German embassy. For a long time past they had been in contact with Jewish circles and especially with the Zionists and the representative of the American Jewish welfare organization known as the American Joint Distribution Committee. In their favour Canaris's men had obtained from the German diplomatic authorities safe-conduct passes allowing trains full of Jewish children to cross occupied countries such as Bulgaria and Rumania and proceed to Palestine. Owing to these convoys of children many adults – political adversaries of National Socialism and Jews from Poland and Slovakia had been able to find refuge in Allied territory. Canaris's couriers also arranged – in return for an appropriate commission – for the smuggling in of money and letters from abroad. They even undertook to deliver such remittances to their destinations in Auschwitz, Theresienstadt and other camps.

The SD arrested all the men of the Wehrmacht secret service, including their chief Dr. Schmidt and they admitted the facts. They were, however, careful to conceal that in acting as they had done they had in mind, since the war looked like being lost, the creation for themselves of alibis against the day when they might have to account for their deeds to the Allies. What they did claim was that there had been no other means of establishing relations useful for counter-espionage activities in neutral countries especially in Turkey and that their contacts with the Zionists led in fact right up to Washington. And, it was added, in this manner there was obtained foreign exchange essential for their activities abroad. Clages reported to Himmler himself the results of the cross-questioning. To the surprise of everyone Himmler set Canaris's men free and even took on some of them into the counter-espionage branch of the SS – under the command of Clages.

In January 1943 there was set up in Budapest a Zionist Committee for Mutual Assistance – the Waada – whose primary task was to assist Jewish refugees from Poland and Slovakia. The complete Hebrew name of the organization was *Waadat Ezra Bö-Hazza lah Bö-Budapest* which means 'Jewish Committee of Mutual Assistance in Budapest'. The leading members of this committee – and among them were the engineer

21

Otto Komoly, Dr. Rezsö Kastner and Samuel Springmann – had almost all executive functions within the Hungarian Zionist organization. Because, indeed, of their belonging at one and the same time to both the Zionist and the Waada groups, these persons maintained contacts with Canaris's agents who often supplied precious help for the accomplishment of Zionist and Waada activities.

During the fifteen months before the German occupation, the Waada managed to get into Hungary many refugees from countries under Nazi control – especially from Poland and Slovakia. The Waada protected these refugees from prosecution by the Hungarian authorities and furnished them with clothing and food since most of them were completely destitute. And the Waada allowed many of these refugees to flee clandestinely from Hungarian territory and to reach Palestine. Such an operation was called in Hebrew *Tijul* that is 'excursion'.

In the Waada Joël Brand was responsible for the aid to the refugees. He had not only an obvious natural disposition for this illegal and often adventurous activity, but he had also experience since just after the First World War he had worked underground for the German Communist Party. Then he had also been entrusted with the Waada's contacts with Canaris's men.

As soon as the Germans had occupied Budapest they began to make arrests right and left. Most of the victims of these raids were Hungarian members of parliament, highly placed, but anti-German civil servants, industrialists, Jewish bankers or outstanding politicians belonging to the socialist party. The members of the Waada had to carry on their activities in secrecy since their names were on the Gestapo's black lists as leaders of the Zionist movement. So they must expect reprisals especially as, since the arrest of Canaris's men, the Gestapo possessed excellent information about Waada's work.

From the day that the SS made their entry into Budapest I was plunged into a whirlpool of events. To begin with I was hiding in my Budapest apartment members of the Zionist Committee for Mutual Assistance. A short time later I was occupying a key-post within Waada.

Perhaps the reader will allow the author to devote a few lines to his own life since this book is mainly composed of his own observations, his experiences and of notes he jotted down as events occurred.

I was born in Budapest on May 31, 1904. My father, a lawyer named Dr. Cornelius Samuel Biss, was like my mother Dora (née Brecher) of purely Jewish origin. A short time after my birth my parents moved to Bistritz in Transylvania. Then before the First World War they were divorced and my father took as his second wife a Transylvanian German[1] who brought me up as a Protestant and taught me German. After having been at the German high school in Bistritz I matriculated at Vienna University where I studied law and economics. I also assiduously attended lectures in Protestant theology. Then I was attracted to scientific disciplines. I began with chemistry, after that I spent a year at the Technical High School at Berlin-Charlottenburg. Finally I went to France where in 1925 at Toulouse University I took my degree as a chemical engineer – and that was the end of my studies.

When I got back to Transylvania I took a job as a chemist and ceramist in a factory at Bistritz which specialized in pottery products and in faience stoves. My father had an interest in the business and later on I became part-owner and manager of the undertaking. When in 1940 in order to avoid quarrels between two of his allies, Hitler by the Vienna arbitration divided Transylvania between Hungary and Rumania, Bistritz and the north of the province were returned to Hungary.

My enterprise, that was the largest of its kind in either Hungary or Rumania, had to be adapted to a new market. For professional reasons I had to stay frequently in Budapest. Since I was sure that, as the war went on, the Hungarian government would stiffen its anti-Jewish attitude I took up a second residence in the Hungarian capital and there opened a sales office which was to serve also as a refuge.

1. That is to say a *Volkadeutsche* a term that describes one of the members of the German minorities in various European countries.

I greatly needed such an office where I could centralize my business and also of a few rooms where I could receive my customers. This screen was all the more plausible and unsuspicious because of the difficulty of finding hotel rooms in the state of semi-war conditions then prevailing. My police card for the apartment I occupied at 15, Semsey Andor utca was made out thus – 'Protestant, Transylvanian German'. I belonged then to a class of people much respected and even feared in the Hungary of those days. The idea that I might be Jewish would not have occurred to anyone.

In accordance with the anti-Jewish laws of 1941 it was forbidden, in any business, to employ beyond a certain percentage of Jews. I considered these provisions as contrary to the Hungarian constitution and therefore illegal. I welcomed in my factories – where up to then they had been very few in number – numerous Jewish employees and especially those who because of the new laws had just been dismissed. Officially these figured in the list of workmen or even simple unskilled labourers, but in reality each one of them was an employee paid according to his ability and qualifications. Although I was under no illusions about the possibility of keeping up for long this 'personnel policy' I was convinced that no opportunity must be lost for helping those who were persecuted. Furthermore I was quite aware of the alternatives facing us: either the Allies would soon be victorious and the Nazi regime would collapse or the Germans would occupy Hungary and that would mean an end to half-measures and the Jews would be totally exterminated.

SEMSEY ANDOR UTCA, 15, THE WAADA H.Q.

When after March 19, 1944 the Hungarian Regent Horthy who had been summoned to Germany by Hitler was for a time held prisoner and the SS had seized the country, many members of the Waada and of the Zionist organizations came, with their families, to take refuge in my apartment. Among these were Reszö Kastner and Ernst Szilagyi. Although up to then I had not belonged to the Zionist organization I had admired its leaders' determination to resist with all their strength. Thus it was that I had given financial assistance to various Zionist activities. A few weeks later the chairman of the organization, Otto Komoly, came with his wife to join my other guests. As all were hunted by the police, they dared not leave their hiding-place, so I got provisions for them, furnished them with newspapers and gave them the latest news.

The day the SS entered Hungary, Joël Brand had found a refuge in the flat of a ballerina who was the mistress of one of Canaris's counter-espionage agents called Joseph Winninger. Madame Brand, for a short time lived at the Hotel Majestic in the Schwabenberg district. This place was soon to serve as Eichmann's HQ. Moreover, suddenly in the Press there started up attacks against well-to-do Jews living in hotels, attacks that became more and more numerous and violent. So, I at once became convinced that action was imminent against Jews in hotels, and I went off to fetch Madame Brand and her two children at the Majestic and put them up in my house. My presentiment was well enough founded, on the very next day the papers reported that a raid had taken place at Schwabenberg during the night. All the Jews in the hotels had been arrested and deported. And not one of them was ever heard of again.

A few days after this Joël Brand himself came to join us.

Originally I had thought that my Budapest home might one day serve as a refuge for myself and a shelter for my family. So when about the middle of March I telephoned to my wife at Bistritz and asked her to come and live with me in the capital she was convinced she would there find herself in complete security. A recent decree had forbidden Jews to travel but nevertheless she set out for Budapest despite the urgent pleading of her father who felt sure she was going to her doom.

Like most Hungarian Jews my father-in-law still believed firmly that the government would protect Jews whose forbears had been settled in the country for centuries. He thought one must be crazy to abandon one's belongings and disappear underground. This opinion which was very widespread (and not only in Hungary) prevented right away any attempts at rescue and cost the death of many Jews some of whom were rendered more vulnerable because of their great age. A personal experience, but a very characteristic one, will illustrate the state of mind I refer to.

Some weeks before the German occupation I had put with my wife's family a Polish refugee called Kirschner, he managed to escape from extermination and today lives in Israel where he raises chickens. In Poland he had been the owner of a ceramic factory. After the entry of the German troops, he had been able to keep his job. He had been recognized as indispensable in his factory. He was considered as one of those Jews who were 'particularly useful to the economy' so he thought he and his family were safe. When the German retreat began he was suddenly informed that his family would be evacuated and that they must leave at once. He learned a little later on that his wife and children had been slaughtered when only a little way out of the town. The author of this crime was none other than the SS *Scharführer* who had up to then lived with this family, who had assumed a protective attitude and who treated the children with kindness and sometimes even going so far as to spoil them.

By abandoning at once his job and his factory Kirschner managed to get through both German and Russian lines, to cross the Carpathians and take refuge in Hungary. I had invited him to my factory at Bistritz partly in the hope that the terrible and heart-rending story he had to tell might at last open the eyes of my family as to the fate awaiting all of us if Hungary was occupied by the SS. Kirschner's evidence fully confirmed my own repeated warnings that no one would take seriously. His story was listened to and aroused the compassion of his hearers but no one would admit that such things could ever happen in Hungary. Once the first impression had worn off I was even blamed for having imposed such a guest upon them and for having allowed him to tell us a tale that could only make the atmosphere still more oppressive.

Several of my friends had similar experiences when they

mentioned this subject in the hope that it would serve as a warning.[1]

During her train journey which, in the circumstances, was not devoid of danger, my wife was accompanied by a foreman from my factory. His task was to keep an eye all the time on the next compartment and to inform me at once if she was arrested. At the instant that I entered Budapest station to meet the two travellers, the police were conducting a raid against Jews who had not obeyed the order to stay where they were. Our little group was lucky enough to escape this operation.

To my wife's surprise I took her companion to an hotel and told him to take the first train the next day back to Bistritz. She did not understand why I put him into an hotel since I had several guest rooms free in the Semsey Andor utca house.

When she heard that I had there put up persons who according to the newspapers were among the most sought after by the Hungarian police and that therefore our apartment had become the most dangerous place in Budapest, she was certain that her last hour had come. As it was she sacrificed herself for the welfare of our companions and showed herself a loyal collaborator in our rescue work.

As soon as Komoly, Kastner and Brand and the others dared to leave my apartment and got into contact with the members of the Jewish communities, it appeared clearly enough that in these circles it was expected that the Waada should also come to the aid of Hungarian Jews and concern itself with their fate. In fact, it was at least partly known what the Waada had already done for Jewish refugees and that it had contacts with the German authorities. But these latter had now unfortunately been changed, the SS newcomers were a very different set from the Abwehr men of Canaris.

The leaders of the Budapest Jewish community thought

1. In this connection it may be mentioned that the reproaches made against Kastner after the war were devoid of any foundation. Unhappily, with all the means at his disposal it was in vain that he attempted to tell people the truth.

they would be able by money payments to ameliorate the condition of their coreligionists and ward off the threat of deportation from them. The old remedy of ransom had often enough, in past centuries, proved its efficacy, it had even worked miracles. And now it seemed to be the only recourse available to a people reduced to slavery and indeed condemned to death.

The great majority of the more prosperous sections of the Hungarian Jews was not Zionist. They thought ransom was their only hope of salvation and to such an extent that the Jewish communities suddenly disposed of considerable financial resources. They invited the Zionist leaders hidden in my apartment to collaborate with them. They knew of the former's contacts with the staff of the German counter-espionage and were of the opinion that the time had come to make advances.

I was, at first, opposed to such a step. I was persuaded that money offers could be but the starting-point of a long string of lying promises and blackmail. My Zionist friends were not fooled. They did not believe in the power of money in such circumstances. Among them however was one exception, Joël Brand who had been in the habit of handing over large sums of money to the agents of the German counter-espionage. The Zionists were well pleased to know this since for two years past they had made ceaseless efforts to make the Jews in Allied countries understand that if Eichmann's HQ accepted the money and property of Jews, while making lavish promises and comforting words, it was only to send them the more surely to death.

It was thus that in Poland first of all, then in Holland, France and Belgium numerous rich Jews had brought out their belongings from hiding-places to hand over to Eichmann as ransom. They hoped in this way to save at least, their lives. But the wretched people were not spared for as much. Special convoys carried off the victims to Maïdanek. When the trains set off this name meant nothing to the passengers. It was only very slowly, and first of all among Polish Jews, that the terrifying significance of Maïdanek was spread abroad.

One of these Jews, a refugee in Hungary, had lost all his

family and owed his own survival only to his peasant-like appearance. He told me how he had managed to pass himself off as a plate-layer working on the line and to approach a convoy of Jews travelling in complete liberty. He got into conversation with the travellers who asked him if he knew whereabouts the Maïdanek labour-camp was. They had no suspicions at all. He urged them, in God's name, since they were travelling in 'normal' conditions, to seize the first and slightest opportunity to flee, for Maïdanek was in reality an extermination camp. Those who heard the man were so indignant that they got ready to call the SS guards and the man had to take off as fast as his legs would carry so as not to fall a victim to his good intentions.

But in 1944 and at the same time that the SS arrived in Hungary, we got some news from Slovakia making us think the ransom method might prove efficacious. My friends thereupon changed their attitude and began to hope again.

Rabbi Weissmandl of Bratislava was one of the main leaders of the Slovakian Jewish communities. In letters addressed to various Jewish personages in Hungary he had informed them that, to a certain extent, deportations from Slovakia had been held up owing to the payment of sums of money to SS *Hauptsturmführer* Dieter Wisliceny, Eichmann's representative. The Rabbi in conclusion suggested that his correspondents follow his example since the Hungarian Jews were being more and more threatened with extermination. He added that Wisliceny asserted that deportations in European countries occupied by the Germans, could be stopped on the payment of a ransom of $2,000,000. The operation was called *Plan-Europa*.

It is interesting to note that Wisliceny made a great to-do about this correspondence which he considered as his 'credentials' so to speak. He himself had brought the letters to Hungary where they were handed over to their addressees on the very day the Germans invaded Hungary. But the way in which Rabbi Weissmandl depicted the situation in Slovakia (though his good faith was evident) was based on assumptions both inexact and misleading – as we were to find out later. At this period there were no more than about 30,000 Jews in Slovakia for some 55,000 persons had already perished by application of the 'Final Solution'. It was true that deportations had ceased but not because of ransoms paid. Furthermore this stoppage was very temporary as events were soon to show. Tiso the Slovakian Prime Minister (who sincerely believed at first that the Jews deported to Poland were drafted into labour-camps) had himself intervened to obtain the immediate stoppage of the transportations to the death-camps. It was said that he acted as he did after having seen a secret memorandum from the Pope. The Germans would have given way, for a time, and for political reasons, to Tiso's demands (see p. 133).

But a short time after he had got secret orders from Himmler to end deportations from Slovakia, Wisliceny had been informed of a ransom offer emanating from the Jewish centre in Bratislava, which was directed by Gizi Fleischmann. The sum mentioned was £50,000 which Wisliceny accepted and assured the Jewish delegates that in exchange they could count on deportations being stopped. In reality, as we have shown above, the whole affair was quite different.

The news from Slovakia made a good impression in Budapest. The military situation seemed to be getting more and more calamitous for the Germans. So it came to be hoped that, at the price of financial sacrifices further deportations could be effectively prevented and the survivors of the Jewish people could be saved. From then on, Komoly, Kastner and other Zionists took part in the meetings of the councils of the Jewish communities and did all they could to collect subscriptions for the ransoms.

The first contacts, between members of the Waada and representatives of the Jewish communities on the one side and *Hauptsturmführer* Wisliceny with the most important members of Eichmann's staff on the other side, were arranged through former agents of Canaris's counter-espionage network. Although they had lost all influence and went in fear for their own security these former agents agreed to begin the preliminaries of the negotiations.

30

During the conversations that followed, Wisliceny, who was accompanied by *Hauptsturmführer* Klausnitzer, promised to hold up provisionally the deportations of European Jews on payment of $2,000,000.

As a condition for the continuation of the negotiations the SS demanded the immediate payment of 10 per cent of this amount that is to say about 6,500,000 Hungarian pengös. The chairman of the liberal Jewish community in Budapest, Samuel Stern, and the chief of the orthodox Jewish community, Philipp von Freudiger, got together the greater part of this sum that is to say about 5,000,000 pengös. The Waada put up the rest.

When this 'payment on account' was handed over, there appeared instead of Wisliceny who had been transferred by Eichmann to the provinces, *Obersturmhannführer* Krumey and *Hauptsturmführer* Hunsche. Both of them were on Eichmann's staff. But now there was no longer any question of delaying the deportations, especially as Wisliceny had already begun to prepare them in the provinces. Furthermore, without express instructions from Berlin Eichmann would not have been empowered to hold up the progress of the 'Final Solution' of the Jewish question in Hungary.

Krumey and Hunsche just declared to the Jewish delegates that they were prepared to negotiate the emigration of 70 persons in possession of permits and to discuss some matters of minor importance. They also demanded that payments should continue.

In the meantime Eichmann had had set up in Budapest a 'Council of Jews' composed of eight members depending directly on him or his staff. These had been chosen on the nomination of the Bureau of the Jewish Community (liberal tendency). The president of this community – which was composed of about 80 per cent of the Budapest Jews – was Samuel Stern. Besides Stern and the two presidents of the orthodox Jewish community, Philipp von Freudiger and Samuel Kahan-Frankl, there were also on the council Dr. Karl Wilhelm – whom we shall have occasion to mention often – Dr. Ernst Petö, Dr. Ernst Boda, Dr. Samuel Csobadi and

31

lastly Dr. Nisson-Kahan, the last the only representative of the Zionist movement. All of these men were lawyers. Later on Dr. Imre Reiner was added to their number.

The Waada differed essentially from this Council of Jews since it had not been created at the behest of the Germans but had existed clandestinely before the occupation. Thus the Waada did not have to play the part Eichmann had assigned to the Council of Budapest Jews (as to all those set up at his command) that is to say to see that calm reigned and order was maintained during the deportations.

This difference between the Waada and the Council may perhaps explain why later on the Germans treated the members of the Waada with a certain amount of respect since they believed that the latter were the representatives of world Jewry who had got into contact with them; on the other hand the Germans had nothing but contempt for the members of the Council of Jews. It must be said, however, in all fairness that this Council of Budapest Jews did all it could to bungle the task the Gestapo had imposed on it, and this was all to its honour. When their action became impossible the principal members took to flight or rather went underground.

I did not myself, as yet, take any part in these conversations, but my Zionist friends kept me informed about all the details of the negotiations. While the Jews were asked to pay larger and larger sums if only to secure that the talks went on, the Germans just made promises and took engagements which all, without exception, were never kept. All the same, I managed to secure that, later on, during my own negotiations, these millions (collected with enormous difficulty) should not have been paid over entirely in vain. I was able, indeed, to have them taken into account with Becher when we arranged for the payment of the ransoms demanded for the Bergen-Belsen convoy, the Strasshof camp and the Budapest ghetto. But we will return to this a little later on.

Our position became more and more intolerable and was not to change until Himmler, at the instigation of *Hauptsturm-führer* Clages, ordered Eichmann to negotiate with qualified representatives of the Budapest Jews for the delivery of

10,000 lorries. Joël Brand was thus summoned to Eichmann's office on April 25, 1944.

3. Between the Acts

This proposal that one million Jews should be allowed to reach neutral countries in exchange for the delivery of 10,000 trucks, made by Eichmann to the Budapest Waada, has been much discussed. There are, indeed, few chapters in the history of the 'Final Solution' about which so much has been written and concerning which so much discussion has taken place during the last decade. But this chapter still remains today, very largely, dim as far as its real development is concerned, and this despite the numerous depositions made by witnesses at the various trials of war criminals, despite the copious literature, both political and historical relating to the affair and despite the detailed accounts published by two of the main Jewish actors in the drama.

That the depositions given before the courts by SS accused of war crimes hardly served the cause of truth is natural enough, the principal object of such evidence was to exonerate. As regards the historians' failure, it can be explained by the fact that there exists, practically speaking, no document relating to the affair.

The first of the two accounts given by Jews does not lack historical probability and the honesty of the author is not in question. All the same he did not possess the perspective necessary for the evocation of such events.

The Kastner Report[1] appeared as early as 1946 and was

1. Roneotyped under the title *Rapport du Comité juif d'assistance de Budapest, 1942–1945, presented by le Dr. Rezsö Kastner*. This report was published in book form, with some modifications, at Munich in 1961 as *Rapport Kastner*. This was edited by Ernest Landau.

33

written in a few weeks and was primarily intended for the information of the members of the Zionist Congress held at Basel in the spring of 1947. For more than a year Dr. Kastner had accomplished at Budapest a task that daily drove him almost to the limit of his endurance. In 1946 the memory of this effort was still too fresh in the author's mind for him to be capable of delivering a general judgement on this affair, to define the relative importance of its diverse facets and to present them in a manner which did not expose him to criticism. The impression caused was that a brilliant journalist and an excellent writer had failed in the presentation of his own case.

The second account is lacking in what was so admirable in the first that, is to say honesty and the desire to give the facts in accordance with the truth. The account was not drawn up by the protagonist in the drama, Joël Brand, but by a well-known writer who took down Brand's evidence and his view of the facts. The fault lies entirely with the reporter and not with the author of the book, Alex Weissberg. It was especially after the death of his contradictor, Rezsö Kastner, that Joël Brand managed quite admirably to 'sell' in Israel, in Germany and other Western countries, his version of the facts, intentionally rearranged. And Brand did not hesitate to declare to a curious and receptive public that his account was the only valid one. His success was all the easier since he burst out into a paean of praise to the glory of the brave man whom regrettable circumstances alone prevented from becoming a hero.[1]

This present book, then, has among other aims that of replacing this mutilated version of the facts with a version establishing the truth. The German TV in November 1964 took possession of the *Story of Joël Brand* and presented it to several million spectators in a version which disarms criticism.

1. Die *Geschichte von Joël Brand* by Alex Weissberg, Cologne, 1956. *L'Histoire de Joël Brand. Un troc monstrueux: un million de Juids pour dix mille camions.* Editions du Seuil, Paris, 1957. As a matter of fact Brand was overcome by the task imposed upon him and from a purely subjective point of view one must admit that he could hardly have acted otherwise.

Certainly every author and every playwright is free to stress, at the expense of historical truth, certain elements of a drama. But the manner in which this work was presented and the documentary character attributed to it must be condemned.

The 'Trucks Affair' has risen in importance, almost to an Affair of State, because of this build-up and presentation. In fact it was only an episode, though owing to Brand's incompetence it had tragic consequences. It represented only one incident in a much more important and general activity which had multiple aspects. Despite Brand's declarations, it did not end in a defeat, but when all is said and done, in a remarkable success. This book's main object is to describe this activity. So it has seemed to be necessary to refer once more to the story of Joël Brand which was really his only in its negative phase.

A TROUBLED LIFE

Joël Brand was the man whose collaboration with the Waada and then his flight had the most lamentable effects on the survival of the Jewish people in a Europe occupied by Hitler. He was by origin a Transylvanian from a province which at the time belonged to Hungary. He was born in 1907 at Naszod, the native town both of his mother and of mine. We were indeed cousins. His father was in easy circumstances and owned, at Erfurt in Germany, a business of telephonic material rental which had several branches even abroad.

The young Joël, although bright and intelligent, had very little taste for learning. He wanted as soon as possible to free himself from school discipline. He managed to do this when his father died for then his education and that of his three sisters became the responsibility of his mother alone. He never finished his studies and devoted all his energy to what interested him most – adventure and politics. He joined the Communist Party and was such a successful combatant that a short time before the Nazis' seizure of power, he became a member of the Party's central office in Thuringia. By then he had already travelled far and wide, thanks to the Party and

35

maybe on its orders. He had been not only in the United States and in Russia but also in Japan and in the South Sea islands. As soon as he got back to Germany he rushed into the partisan struggles which took on more and more violent forms during the last months of the Weimar republic. It was then that the SA (assault sections of the Nazis) carried on a pitiless warfare especially against members of the Communist Party.

On Hitler's assumption of power Brand was in hospital after having been knifed during a row between Reds and Browns.[1] Hardly had he got out of hospital than he was arrested, thrown into jail and then a little later condemned to several months' imprisonment. But, as he was lucky enough still to be of Hungarian nationality, he was considered as 'an undesirable foreigner' and at the end of his prison-term, was expelled from the Reich.

So, at the beginning of 1934 Joël Brand came back to Transylvania. He was completely without resources and there was nothing to make him think he could make a new start in life. In fact, in 1918 Transylvania had become Rumanian territory and the native population had acquired a new nationality. Joël Brand, at the time of this change-over, was with his parents in Germany, so he had retained his Hungarian citizenship. But now he was only a foreigner in his own country. His birth-place had been renamed and was now known as 'Nasaud'. No member of his family now lived there nor did he know anybody there. He could then count on no one for help. His mother and her two daughters had remained in Erfurt where she made desperate efforts to keep the paternal heritage intact for her children. Her eldest sister lived in Klausenburg, the capital of Transylvania. She had married a Jewish engineer who had an important job in the Rumanian administration. In view of the anti-semitic prejudice so prevalent in Rumania this brother-in-law could not dare to have Brand under his roof even for a night, especially as this Jewish relation was burdened with a notorious past as a Communist. Rumania was then governed by ultranationalist

1. The SA wore brown shirts and were commonly called 'Brown Shirts'.

and anti-Communist regimes such as those of Cuza, Goga and Vaida who even before the beginning of the Hitler regime had made anti-semitism an integral part of their political programme.

For all these reasons Joël Brand came to me in Bistritz where he found lodging and work in my factory. But difficulties soon arose and they were not only due to the working permit required of every foreigner who wanted to take a job in Rumania. The fact was that Brand had had no real professional training, had never regularly exercised any calling and could not get accustomed to organized activity. He was too fond of rushing about, social life and above all frequenting cafés and night-clubs. He soon found the staid existence of the Bistritz bourgeoisie intolerable. I tried to ease his way into a new existence by taking him, for instance, as often as possible with me on business trips, but I was not very successful. Finally he persuaded me to let him take on in my name, the job of agent for the Citroën works in Transylvania and the Banat, that is to say, for about half of Rumania. As he remained my employee I had to get him a working permit.

For some time everything seemed to go on smoothly enough. Then suddenly alarming news reached Klausenburg. Under the influence of drink, Brand (who was rather addicted to the bottle, something rare among Jews) had let himself go and had boasted to his colleagues of his exploits with the Communist Party. Then a little later he had quarrelled with his boon companions and had been denounced to the Rumanian secret police, the Siguranţa. In the Rumania of those days nothing worse could happen to a foreigner than to be recognized as a Jew and, in addition, to be accused of being a Communist.

Twice I managed, for a price, to get the expulsion order against him annulled. Luckily enough the officials with whom decisions rested were corrupt as were most of the members of the Rumanian police. All the same the note 'Communist' could not be removed from the identification card in the Siguranţa files. When he was finally expelled after a third order, everything happened so quickly that when I was informed by a telephone call Brand had already reached

Budapest – he had not been able to contact me sooner. His Hungarian citizenship had entitled him to be, without any formalities, sent out beyond the frontiers.

Alex Weissberg's book makes no mention of this Transylvanian interlude in Brand's life although it is quite characteristic and revealing about the hero of the work. Likewise Weissberg is silent about several similar episodes.

A NEW BEGINNING IN HUNGARY

In the Hungarian capital Brand found a *joie de vivre* atmosphere which pleased him so much that he decided to stay there. It was all the easier for him to take this step since I had guaranteed him a monthly allowance; but, at Budapest, as elsewhere, his praiseworthy desire to start again from scratch ran up against difficulties of a professional nature. But Brand set out seriously to get a job and finally found one as an assembler in the telephone enterprise which, after the death of his father, had taken over the branch he had owned in Budapest. However, this employment did not last long.

For Brand took it into his head to emigrate to Palestine. Emigration certificates were highly prized and only very sparingly accorded by the British authorities of the Mandatory Power. These certificates were, at least, in theory reserved for young agriculturalists trained for work on a kibbutz. It was quite exceptional for Zionist leaders who had belonged to the party for many years to get the benefit of a visa. So Brand joined the Hungarian Zionist Party and then took a crash-course in agricultural training, the *Hachscharah*, rising to the grade of '*Haloutz*, 'young agricultural pioneer', which enabled him to become a candidate for an immigration certificate.

As these precious certificates were valid for a whole family, the Palestinian civil servants wanted to utilize them to the utmost so as to allow the greatest number of people to get into Palestine. Young '*Haloutzim*, therefore, often married among themselves to get a permit. Such marriages of pure convenience were dissolved without any difficulty as soon as the young couples got to Palestine. During his time at the agricultural school Joël Brand had made the acquaintance of a girl called Hansi Hartmann, and they contracted a marriage of this sort. However, as their immigration certificate was long in coming through, they took and furnished a lodging in Budapest. I contributed towards the expenses of setting up house and increased Brand's monthly allowance.

Hansi Hartmann came from the working class and had been simply but decently brought up. Until her marriage she had earned her living by repairing ladies' stockings. In a side street she rented the front of a small shop where passers-by could see her at work. Then she had an idea that proved quite profitable. She would buy a knitting-machine and manufacture those half-leather, half-wool gloves which began to be fashionable in the thirties. With my help she was able to buy the machine and a good stock of raw materials. Shortly afterwards she took on several girls who worked mostly at home. The business developed rapidly and gave Brand scope. So there began for the young couple a bourgeois life, modest enough but assured. There was no question now of the couple emigrating, especially as their first child, a boy, had already been born.

At the beginning of the war the little business became still more prosperous, despite the rationing of wool and leather, which were proclaimed 'rare articles'. But Joël Brand had good friends among the black-marketeers who often transacted business in the cafés where he spent part of his time. Thanks to these friends he managed not only to acquire larger and larger quantities of raw materials but also to sell the end-products at a good profit. Despite the arrival in Budapest of his mother, two sisters and a niece (all of whose property had been seized in Germany) the Brands, having taken them in, were still able to live very comfortably and without any financial worry.

The emigration to Palestine – constantly put off because of the success of their business – grew still more doubtful as the part played by Joël Brand within the Hungarian Zionist party became more and more useful. No one from then on, would have thought of urging him and his family to emigrate. In 1941 the Hungarian gendarmerie undertook a large-scale operation against several tens of thousands of Jews whose families had been settled in the country for several decades, in some cases even for several generations, but who had neglected to become naturalized. Among the victims of this monster round-up were Hansi Brand's sister and her husband. In the night they were all driven out to German-occupied Poland and Russia, and thus condemned to a fate about which there could be no doubt.

As soon as the news of the deportation was known Joël Brand started to look for someone who, with support from the military authorities, could discover his relations and help them return to Hungary. It was impossible to do more since Hungarian civilians had no right to cross the borders of the deportation zones and not, above all, to remain there.

In Brand's favourite cafés there congregated a number of shady characters always ready to engage in a more or less suspicious business. Here Brand met a certain Joseph Krem who belonged to the Hungarian counter-espionage service and possessed a safe-conduct allowing him into the military zone. After some discussion Krem agreed to look for Brand's relations and to bring them back secretly into Hungary. How did he succeed? How did he procure the necessary papers for his travelling companions? Did he forge the papers himself? That was his business after all and Krem got richly paid for bringing off this exploit.

After this, men-smuggling quickly became a flourishing industry. Among the deportees whom Krem would meet in Poland and in the Ukraine, many still had bank accounts and valuable property in Hungary which they were ready to sacrifice in whole or in part. The essential thing for them was to escape, before it was too late, and to get back to Hungary and relative peace.

It was obvious to everyone that Brand had important contacts with Krem, which explained his increasing influence within the Mapai (the socialist faction of the Zionists) and also his nomination as a member of the Jewish Assistance Committee (the Waada), where he was concerned with aid to refugees.

There is no doubt that he did good work for this organization. Many of those he was able to help have retained a feeling of gratitude towards him. Those who succeeded, thanks to the 'transports of children' or other means put at their disposal by the Waada, in reaching Palestine or free countries, spread among the Jews of the West the story of the Brands devotion. Many leading Jewish people had relations in Poland or in other occupied countries of whom they had had no news – often for as much as several years. Increasingly often the Brands got letters, sums of money and messages that came, in part, from the most prominent Zionists of the free world.

These expressions of gratitude strengthened Joël Brand's self-confidence, which was already marked enough.

In 1943, Samuel Springmann, who was Kastner's closest collaborator, got an invitation from his friends in Palestine to go and see them and to make a detailed report on the situation. It was he who had established and kept up the contacts already mentioned between Zionists and the members of Canaris's German counter-espionage network. Springmann, through discreet and efficient work, had obtained important results. But he was overworked and seriously ill. He accepted the invitation and thus took advantage, as we were to find out later, of one of the last opportunities for leaving Hungary before its occupation by the SS. His successor was Joël Brand, who had up to this time been his assistant. The post was exactly suited to him.

Even before the occupation of Hungary by the SS, Brand was working among the underworld where he kept up friendly relations with the agents of Canaris's counter-espionage. In their company he frequented cafés, night-clubs and brothels, thus obtaining information necessary for our mutual assistance enterprises. When he played cards with these men – as often happened – he was careful to keep them good tempered by deliberately losing large sums. He had plenty of money at his disposal to meet his expenses and to subsidise his new acquaintances. He got on particularly close terms with two of the Canaris agents: Joseph Winninger, whom we have already mentioned, and Bandi Grosz, whom we shall meet again later on.

As time went on Brand became, practically speaking, one of the Waada's managing vice-presidents. Inevitably he came into conflict with Rezsö Kastner, delegate of the president, Otto Komoly. Brand managed to get himself considered by the counter-espionage agents as an important person and the practical chief of the Waada. He gave out that we had influential contacts leading straight to Washington and President Roosevelt. These statements inevitably impressed his hearers, who aided him in his task. In fact, from 1943 the *Abwehr* agents, foreseeing that the war might end unfavourably for the Germans, tried to get condonement of their activities from reliable servants of the American government.

All in all, Brand proved that he was a remarkable successor to Springmann. It must be stressed, however, that neither his position nor his work in aiding refugees put him directly in danger of death. Moreover, the government of Prime Minister Miklós Kállay tacitly tolerated Zionist activities. Furthermore, Brand, since he was a Hungarian citizen, did not – as yet – have any fear of being deported. He had already succeeded in avoiding the compulsory labour imposed on Jews. He had got himself declared diabetic. It is true that diabetes was in his family and that he was later on to suffer from this disease himself.

But Joël Brand was really put to the test after March 19, the day the SS troops occupied Hungary, from which time the services of the *Abwehr* (under Dr. Schmidt) were suppressed. The higher command of the SS looked on Admiral Canaris's activities with a jaundiced eye, and were eager to form, out of their own ranks, an espionage section to replace the Admiral's.

In the Hungarian capital there appeared at the same time as the SS a special commando force of Service IV A 4b of the Gestapo. It was under the personal orders of Eichmann. About the same time another special commando of the SD, commando F, established its HQ in the Schwabenberg section of the city, under the command of *Hauptsturmführer* Clages (or

Klages). Both Eichmann and Clages learned that German counter-espionage agents had collaborated with the Zionists. From the Nazi point of view such activity was highly suspicious, so these agents were arrested, although some of them were imprisoned only for a short time.

Thus Joël Brand, and with him the Waada, lost their most valuable contacts. All the same, some of these agents were re-employed by Otto Clages, and continued later to be of great service to us.

4. Brand's Mission in Turkey

During the cross-examination Clages had inflicted on Canaris's agents he had found out that the chief of the secret Zionist organization was called Joël Brand. Eichmann was informed of this and his close assistant, Wisliceny, revealed to him that he knew Brand well. It was Brand who, with Kastner and in the name of the Waada and the Jewish Council, had often handed over sums demanded as ransoms to Wisliceny.

In the reports he made to Himmler, Clages (who knew his chief wanted to replace Canaris's men with his own) had mentioned the contacts between the *Abwehr* and the Zionists. Clages had insisted that these contacts should be maintained since the Zionists seemed to have a very extensive network. He even proposed to take Canaris's agents into his own service and thus preserve already existing contacts. We were not, however, to learn of these details until much later, and for the moment we were puzzled to explain why Brand was summoned by Eichmann.

The interview between the two men took place on April 25, 1944. Clages and other officers of Eichmann's HQ were also present. Although several different versions have been given of what took place, it seems unnecessary to speak once more about the matter in detail, as all those accounts are based essentially on Brand's own declarations.

When Brand told us that Eichmann had directed him to go to a neutral country – Turkey – and to propose to the Zionist leadership there an exchange of 10,000 trucks and other strategic material for the lives of Hungary's Jews, a violent discussion broke out within the Waada. During the conversation Brand revealed, perhaps inadvertently, that Eichmann wanted Bandi Grosz to accompany him to Turkey, and that it had been impossible for Brand to reject this suggestion. This is what Brand said later on about this individual, then his great friend and one of his intermediaries[1]:

Up to then Bandi Grosz, an agent of the Hungarian Secret Service, had played the Abwehr card, but when he realized that power in Budapest had passed into stronger hands, he changed his policy and tried to get into contact with the S.D. (*Sicherheitsdienst*). The fact that he had to pay for this new friendship by betraying his former associates does not seem to have troubled him at all.

Two days after my interview with Eichmann, Grosz asked me to meet him at the Café Biarritz. He was accompanied by one Klausnitzer, a captain in the river police service of the Danubian Navigation Company. This Klausnitzer played a suspicious role. On the night the Germans came in and even before their troops had reached Budapest, he had joined up with the German parachutists who had landed and formed a shock commando and in accordance with lists which had been prepared long before, had arrested political and economic personalities in the city including many Jews. These people were collected together in the warehouses of the Navigation Company. My name was on this list but luckily I had been warned in time by Canaris's men. Later on I met Klausnitzer during negotiations with Krumey and Wisliceny. At that time he appeared to be a liberal and a pro-semite. Bandi Grosz began the conversation:

Joël, I have a new contact which surpasses in importance all we have had up to now. Let us discard the Schmidt group with whom we are only wasting our time. We will go and see this very afternoon the representative of Herr V. Clages. He is very influential

1. See *L'Histoire de Joël Brand* by Alex Weissberg, pp. 99–100 of the French edition.

and he is often made use of directly by the highest authorities in Berlin. No one must know anything of this meeting, not even Kastner – especially not Kastner in fact. Mr. Klausnitzer will come and fetch you with a car.

This Bandi Grosz was a typical double agent. First he worked for the Hungarians, then for the *Abwehr* and he boasted he was in direct contact with the Intelligence Service. Now he belonged to the SD commanded by Clages. How could one have any trust in such a creature? Kastner, in maintaining that Grosz would only compromise the Waada's representative and imperil the success of this important mission, was merely expressing what we all thought at the time, all of us except Brand.

Furthermore the Waada's members declared unanimously that Brand himself was by no means the man likely to succeed in so difficult a task. Before all, was it not the really important thing to induce Zionists abroad to begin negotiations with the Gestapo and to convince them that such negotiations had some chance of being successful? At least it was necessary that Brand's interlocutors in Turkey should make some promises to his Nazi principals, promises which would perhaps allow us to hold up the deportations. In April 1944, the end of the war seemed, in fact, not to be far off. We had received several messages from the free countries assuring us that as *Aschkenas*[1] was gravely ill we should promise him anything. Thus we learned that from abroad the imminent collapse of Nazi Germany was also expected. But after the unsuccessful attempt on his life on July 20, 1944, Hitler's reactions showed how unfounded the idea was, widespread though it was among the Allies, that the Führer, realizing that he had lost the war, would endeavour, as did Wilhelm II in 1918, to find a way out. On the contrary, Hitler declared that he would carry on the war until the 'heroic death' of the last German. In these circumstances Brand's task would be a very delicate one indeed; he had not only to overcome the natural repulsion his Jewish hosts in Turkey would feel at the prospect of contacts with the SS and the Gestapo which they hated so much, but he had

1. The code-name given to the Nazis and taken from the Bible.

45

also to put up a convincing counter-argument to the objection that since the end of the war was near in any case, the German proposals could not be carried out.

To become accredited abroad as representatives of the Hungarian Jews, Brand and Grosz had to carry with them letters of recommendation signed by the leaders of the Jewish communities who composed the Budapest Jewish Council at that time. Kastner, in many conversations, had made no attempt to hide the serious objections to the despatch of Brand and Grosz on this mission. Therefore, Kastner was arrested by the SD one day and Clages warned him energetically to indulge in such talk no longer.

Despite all the hesitation and misgivings the letters of recommendation were at last signed both by Councillor Stern, chairman of the Progressive Jewish Community and by Philipp von Freudiger, the spokesman of the Budapest orthodox Jews. After all, the dramatic situation in which the Jewish people of Hungary found themselves could not be alleviated except by the mission of Brand and Grosz, which alone held out some hope that hundreds of thousands, indeed almost a million men, might still be saved. Kastner was arrested for a second time, on the very eve of Brand's and Grosz's departure, to prevent his doing anything at the last moment to hinder the project.[1]

Between April 24 and May 17 (the date of his leaving for Istanbul), Brand had been summoned three or four times at least by Eichmann who, in the presence of Clages, had given him instructions. He had taken advantage of these meetings to suggest to Eichmann that a test-convoy of from six hundred to a thousand Jews should be sent to a neutral country. The arrival of the train should coincide with that of Brand in Turkey and would prove the Gestapo's good faith and its real desire to negotiate. In this way Brand would more easily gain the confidence of his Jewish hosts in Turkey which, at first sight anyway, appeared difficult.

As a matter of fact it was really the Waada that made the

1. Clages told me later on that these arrests had been made on Brand's. suggestion.

suggestion, since nearly all of its members were at this time persuaded that Eichmann and his chiefs were actually interested in the delivery of trucks and strategic supplies. How else could be explained their desire to get into contact with the representatives of international Jewry?

And, indeed, a few days after Brand had made his suggestion, Eichmann gave his consent to it. It was then agreed that small groups of Jews from Transylvania and northern Hungary should be got together for transport. But Eichmann declared that it was impossible to send the train as far as Turkey and thus put its passengers on the way to Palestine, for this would provoke the irritation of the Mufti of Jerusalem.[1] The train would instead be sent to Portugal where it would be taken in charge by the Americans and its passengers conducted to the USA.

Eichmann himself was, however, not empowered to order the formation of such a test-convoy. It was Clages who had immediately transmitted the Waada's proposal to Himmler and who had got the *Reichsführer*'s agreement to the principle of the undertaking. Eichmann informed Brand of this. Nevertheless Brand left Budapest persuaded that Eichmann had sent him to inform the Jews in Turkey of the test-convoy proposal. Brand and Grosz promised both Eichmann and the Waada that they would be back in a fortnight even if, when this time was up, they had not been able to get a reply. In this case they were to report to their German principals on what provisional results had been obtained. Both Eichmann and Clages hinted that they would, no doubt, be required to go to Turkey a second time in order to continue the negotiations.

The members of the Waada were perturbed. This word of honour given to return to Budapest was dangerous. After all, the chances of Brand's and his companion's success seemed very slender and one might fear the worst, that they would not have the courage to come back empty handed to

1. Shortly before this the Mufti had paid a visit to Germany, been received by Hitler and engaged in negotiations with Himmler and Eichmann.

Hungary. Brand's behaviour on March 19 at the time of his country's occupation, was enough to arouse such apprehensions. Had he not abandoned his family and put himself in security? Everyone knew that. If Brand and Grosz stayed on in Turkey, the Hungarian Jews and all those in the concentration camps would be exterminated. Eichmann had, indeed, announced Gestapo reprisals in these circumstances – and we all knew what that meant.

5. First Negotiations Between Kastner and Eichmann

It was only after Brand and Grosz had left that I began my work in the Waada's service. Up to then I had been only a volunteer helper.

My friends were deeply distressed. They began to fear more and more that if he was unsuccessful, Brand would seize the opportunity to put himself in safety and take refuge in a neutral country such as Turkey. He had left with the ingenuous conviction that he would have little difficulty in finding the 10,000 trucks which were to save a million human beings. He had not thought for an instant about the political difficulties inherent in the operation. The idea that a nation at war would never agree to deliver to the enemy strategic material – especially to help civilians – had not crossed his mind for an instant. The only thing that counted for him was keeping his rival in the Zionist organization, Dr. Rezsö Kastner, from maintaining contacts which Brand had established with the Gestapo, that is with Adolf Eichmann.

Kastner's high culture and intellectual gifts had always kept people like Joël Brand in the background of the Zionist organization; although unpolished, Brand had for a long time aimed at a more important position. Now that he had contacts with those on whom depended the fate of the survivors of the

Jewish community, the time had come for Brand to triumph over Kastner.

It did not occur to him that in a matter where the lives of a million men were at stake, personal vanity had no place, and competence was what counted. At Eichmann's HQ Brand never mentioned that the real chiefs of the movement were the engineer Otto Komoly and Rezsö Kastner. Before he left he had introduced his wife into the Gestapo's new HQ at the Hotel Majestic and it was she and she alone who was to be his representative. He declared to the Waada that he had been forbidden to mention his mission – considered as a 'State [Reich] Secret' – to anybody else, and added that Eichmann would not discuss it with anyone else but him, or in his absence Mrs. Brand. After her husband had left she told us she had promised him to let no one get in touch with Eichmann, especially not Kastner.

A little later on, when she had thought things over, Mrs. Brand came to consider the possibility that Brand might flee. Kastner and the other occupants of my flat kept warning her of such an eventuality. Gradually she realized that her husband's chances of success in this mission abroad were by no means so bright as he had imagined and described. So it was that she came to feel sure that in case of failure Brand would not come back to Budapest.

Thus, under the urging of all of us and especially that of Kastner, who exercised all his charm upon her, she decided to introduce to Eichmann her husband's rival, Kastner himself. It was June 22, 1944. That day opened a fresh chapter in the story of the efforts made to save the Jewish people. As a matter of fact the efforts we are now going to describe were the only ones crowned with success.

Rezsö Kastner was born at Klausenburg, Rumania, and had studied at the Rumanian Language University where he had taken the degree of Doctor of Law. He was the son-in-law of Josef Fischer, a barrister and member of parliament in the Bucharest Lower House, and the chairman of the Jewish deputies' group.

Kastner had been from his young days a zealous Zionist

49

and was an influential member and even chairman of several Zionist organizations among the young people of Klausenburg. When in 1941 the northern part of Transylvania was retroceded to Hungary (in accordance with the Vienna award by Ribbentrop and Ciano), Kastner was elected vice-president of the Hungarian Zionist Union.

Kastner was a journalist by profession and worked for the Klausenburg daily paper *Uj Kelet*[1] which was printed in Magyar. The editorials he wrote when still a student aroused much attention in the whole country and helped to spread his reputation far beyond the town Klausenburg then was. The Rumanian Prime Minister Iuliu Maniu had taken notice of this young Jewish journalist and granted him several interviews which his older and more experienced colleagues had tried in vain to obtain.

We must remember that by May 1944, 5,500,000 Jews in central and eastern Europe had already been massacred. What we had to do was to save the survivors, about 1,000,000 human beings. And it was to this task that, under Kastner's direction, a number of volunteers devoted themselves.

On May 14, 1944, three days before Brand set off for Turkey, Eichmann gave orders for the wholesale deportation of the Hungarian Jews. But the Jewish Councils and the Jewish population were still being hoodwinked by assurances that the Jews would not be expelled out of the country. The operation in fact was prepared in the greatest secrecy and in agreement with the competent Hungarian authorities. Up to July 6, 1944, no fewer than 410,223 Jews were deported.

The first thing Kastner noticed was that Eichmann was in no way opposed to their meeting. Brand's statement on the matter was quite unfounded. I learned later from Clages that Eichmann never had the intention of limiting his contacts with the Waada to those he maintained with Brand and his wife. Brand's attitude then could be explained only by his desire to gratify his vanity and to eliminate a rival.

1. It is interesting to note that *Uj Kelet* is the only Magyar language Jewish daily paper in the whole world. It still appears in Israel and Kastner continued to write for it until his death in 1954.

The second thing Kastner found out was that Eichmann was carrying on most energetically the deportations begun after Brand's departure. Everything was happening as though he feared Brand might be successful, or at least as though he did not wish him to be. In this connection Kastner was able to discover that Eichmann had no intention of keeping his word and forming a test-convoy of Transylvanian Jews. Their deportation had also begun.

However, our only chance of being listened to abroad lay in the existence of undoubted proof of the Gestapo's 'good-will' – a proof it was our business to furnish. The convoy that was to have reached a foreign country at the same time or shortly after would at least convince sceptics among the Jewish communities in allied or neutral countries. It would afford proof that, on the German side, it was firmly decided to negotiate and to keep promises.

Kastner quite soon realized that the payments which the Jews of Budapest and he himself had made, on Brand's recommendation, to Wisliceny, Krumey and Hunsche, had remained quite useless. Eichmann's Bureau of Jewish Affairs had, as always, been indulging in its favourite game of squeezing the Jews like lemons before sending them off to the death camps. It was clear that Eichmann's promises to Brand were far from sincere. Up to then their sole effects was that they had allowed a man – one man only – accompanied by a professional agent – to get abroad.

It remained to be seen why Brand had been allowed to undertake his journey and at the same time be given the opportunity of fleeing. Was he, as an accredited member of the Budapest Assistance Committee, meant to facilitate his travelling companion's job of espionage? Was he just to cover up this task with the authority of the Waada and of the Zionists?

These suppositions seemed rather vague and did not stand up to close examination. Kastner, however, represented the survivors of a people pushed to the extremity of endurance and practically condemned to death. He had not the right to give up all hope – indeed he had hardly time to question himself. He had to act, to put Eichmann and his people to the test, though in full realization that he was exposing himself.

The fortnight's delay set for the two emissaries' return had not yet expired. The position of the Jews, then, regarding the SS was ostensibly unchanged. Later on, however, owing to Brand, this position was to get worse. Meanwhile Kastner was able to point out energetically to Eichmann that the deportations which were being undertaken were in fundamental contradiction to the proposition Brand had been charged to transmit. Furthermore, the latest news did not mention the formation of a test-convoy in Transylvania. On the contrary all the inhabitants of several ghettos had been deported without there having been retained for the convoy those people whose names figured on the lists submitted by the Zionist organization.

Eichmann answered that an authorization was ready for the emigration of 600 persons. But this convoy would not proceed to Palestine; it would have to go through Germany and the occupied zone of France whence it would be directed to Portugal where the emigrants could take ships for Africa or an Allied country.

6. Arrested by the Hungarians, Released by the Germans

In the meantime I had been obliged to leave my apartment. As I had not gone back to Bistritz and had not obeyed the order to join the compulsory labour service, I was considered a deserter by the military authorities and hunted by the police. My behaviour in this matter I considered an act of protest. I thought, in effect, that the compulsory labour imposed on the Jews was in contravention of the article of the Hungarian Constitution which guaranteed equal rights to all citizens irrespective of race or creed. Had I been regularly called up to the army I would have done my duty as my principles would dictate. I would have added that because of my university education I was entitled to be a cadet, that is to say a prospective officer. The idea of being a slave exposed to the arbitrary will of armed guards, was intolerable to me. After having had some experience of this service for some months in 1942–43, I decided to desert rather than obey the call-up order.

My wife and I were living in a furnished room. We gave out that we were non-Jewish refugees who had left eastern Hungary as the Russians were advancing. But every day I managed to slip into my old apartment at Semsey Andor utca 15 which was still occupied by my friends. There I got my mail and the latest news. I had false papers in the name of Andor Kiss.

On May 28, 1944, our house-porter (who had been told our secrets and who backed us up faithfully) informed me that my friends Rezsö Kastner, Otto Komoly and their wives as well as Hansi Brand and Szulem Offenbach had been taken off to an unknown destination by the Hungarian police. The police, in civilian clothes (apparently members of the Hungarian Gestapo under the orders of Peter Hain), had carried off several suitcases and had put seals on the apartment.

Until then I had still hoped, rather inexplicably I admit, that Kastner had a trump card and that by playing it he could stop the deportations, perhaps saving other victims from death. No doubt this hope was based on news broadcasts by British and American radios. These vied with each other in predicting the imminent end of the Third Reich, so that we were convinced it was enough for us to secure the interruption of the wholesale massacre of our people.

I could not bring myself to believe that Brand had been sent on a mission abroad just to let him escape and act as cover for a secret agent. The only man I had thought capable of turning to our advantage the almost desperate situation of our persecutors was none other than Kastner. But now the Hungarian authorities (who by order of the Germans knew nothing of these delicate negotiations) had just arrested him, thus preventing him and his close associates from making any further attempt to proceed with the enterprise already begun.

What could I do? I was the only one of our group who had not been disturbed. At least I was in possession of three important telephone numbers: first that of Eichmann's Jewish Affairs office at the Hotel Majestic (which was the number of the Gestapo, Service IV A 4b); second that of the SD Special Section 'F' under the orders of the commissary of police and *Hauptsturmführer* SS, Otto Clages; finally the number of Canaris's office under the command of Dr. Schmidt.

Brand had given me these three numbers before he left for Istanbul. He advised me to make use of them if, during his absence, the Hungarian authorities should take it into their heads to create difficulties for the Waada or for his family. I could no doubt get some help from these sources. Brand had insisted on the importance of Clages who had promised that the apartment at Semsey Andor utca 15, would be put under the unobtrusive protection of the SD. But the essential thing was that the 'State Secret' should be closely guarded and that the Hungarians should not in any circumstances get any hint of our negotiations or of Brand's departure for Turkey.

So first of all I rang up the Gestapo and then the SD. On each occasion I was told that the chiefs of these offices – Eichmann and Clages – were on leave and not in Budapest. As it was Whit Sunday I could not get in touch with any of the influential people who could have taken effective action. Until March 1944, before the arrival of the SS, Brand had been confidential agent of the Zionists with the *Wehrmacht* counter-espionage organization. But when I telephoned this office I was first of all asked to say exactly what the matter was. As I did not want to give too many details over the telephone and thus betray the 'State Secret', I just asked for support in favour of Dr. Kastner, Otto Komoly and Mrs. Brand. I got what seemed to me an odd reply, in essence evasive and in any case useless. I did not know that at that moment Dr. Schmidt and his men had all been arrested and their offices occupied by members of the SD detached from Clages's section.

Since my telephone calls had proved useless and my efforts to find out where my friends had been taken to in vain, I went to the Hotel Majestic to try to see Eichmann in person. I was received by one of his lieutenants, SS officer Otto Hunsche.

I told him in a few words what had happened to my friends and stressed that no doubt the Hungarian authorities would do all they could to discover the reasons for Brand's trip to Turkey. I insisted on this point since I knew from Brand and Kastner that Eichmann and Clages had taken great care that the Hungarians should know nothing about their negotiations with the Waada. Luckily it did not strike Hunsche that since I had not been a witness to my friends' arrest, I could not have found out the Hungarians' intentions. I had indeed noticed that besides Hunsche there were in the room other SS officers listening, but in my distraction I had not paid close attention to them. It was only later on, when I got into personal contact with Eichmann, that he told me he had been present at this interview. He liked to allow his subordinates, Krumey, Hunsche and Dannecker, carry on alone this sort of discussion, while he remained a silent spectator.

I left Eichmann's office without having been disturbed in any way but also without having obtained any tangible result. I was asked, however, to report my friends' liberation as soon as they should turn up. Thereupon I went at once to the Hotel Mirabel close by where Clages had his office. Formerly this hotel had been a favourite with the well-to-do bourgeoisie of Budapest and the provinces, which young couples and families of older people frequented. Almost nothing was known about Clages's organization except that it was made up of a tiny autonomous commando under the direction of the *Hauptsturm-führer* SS. However, one got the impression that at the Mirabel Clages and his men kept an eye on the more imposing Majestic and Eichmann's numerous staff. Events were, afterwards, to confirm this first impression.

Clages knew me no more than did Eichmann's people. But as soon as I had introduced myself as the friend of Kastner, Komoly and Mrs. Brand, and had told him I was the owner of the apartment at Semsey Andor utca 15, I was immediately shown in.

Clages was a slim, well-dressed man of about forty. He was in civilian clothes, close shaven like an actor, and full of wit, intelligence and sly humour.

55

Of all the SS officers I met he was the only one to be highly cultivated and possessed of an extensive range of information. I never saw him in uniform. He was a specialist in police matters, a criminologist, and even a real gentleman, yet he belonged to an organization dealing in pitiless murder. No doubt he endeavoured to escape from the sequence of events in which he was involved, but in the wake of Eichmann and his gang he was obliged to commit grave crimes and to bear the responsibility for an inexpiable offence. At that time I had not yet heard of Nebe;[1] today I should be inclined to say that his case was very like that of Clages.

I managed both to convince and to interest my interlocutor. Clages promised to take the necessary measures at once. I insisted strongly on the point that certain facts made me think that those responsible for the arrests belonged to the recently established organization of Peter Hain. I added that they had at once enquired where Brand could be hidden.

My guess proved to be right. The Germans did everything to find the prisoners and secure their liberation. Later on we often asked ourselves what the Hungarian secret police must have thought when they saw all the trouble taken by the SD and the Gestapo to liberate Jews found in *flagrante delicto*. Had not gold and stocks of foreign currency been found in their rooms? Had not forms for the establishing of false papers and even a false seal of the German embassy at Budapest been discovered among their belongings? When, to cap all, the German ambassador Veesenmayer was instructed by his government to get my friends freed at once, the Hungarian secret police could no longer doubt that we were in close contact with its opposite number, the Gestapo. This conviction was to have dramatic consequences later on, especially at the moment when Hungarian policy began to break with that of the Third Reich. As a matter of fact the search of my apartment and the arrests of my friends were not to be explained by the desire of the Hungarians to get to the bottom of our relations with the SD and the Gestapo. At

1. Nebe, the chief of criminal affairs of the R.S.H.A. which had taken part in the extermination of the Jews in the East.

this time they knew nothing about these contacts. The matter had quite a different explanation. We have already mentioned that the Waada had endeavoured, by every means, to help Jewish refugees in Hungary and particularly those from Poland and Slovakia, to get to Turkey and thence to Palestine. These refugees were sent through the neighbouring states, Rumania, Yugoslavia and Bulgaria. On several occasions young people furnished with false papers had managed to get across the Rumanian or Yugoslav borders and some of them arrived safe and sound in Palestine. A Budapest printing works turned out forged papers in quantities. We had baptized this operation by the Hebrew name *TIJUL* that is 'excursion'.

In the spring of 1944 a group of eighteen young people, *'Haloutzim,* was arrested on the Rumanian frontier. The Hungarian secret police had taken these people into custody and then tortured them. But no information could be extracted as to the origin of the false papers or the money in the refugees' possession.

In addition to this group, several isolated travellers had been arrested. They were also in possession of false papers delivered by the printing works, though the Waada had not been informed of this. The Hungarian secret police's methods broke down the resistance of these refugees and extorted from them the name of the owner of the printing works who, in his turn, gave my address as that of the Waada at Budapest. A search of my apartment was therefore ordered. The discovery of large sums in dollars, Swiss francs and in Hungarian money had as its consequence the immediate arrest of all persons present. But there was something more compromising still – the seizure of forged papers, of various stamps and seals all very well imitated from originals belonging to embassies or administrative offices.

In their haste, however, the police did not find a suitcase full of baptismal certificates in blank, these had been carefully camouflaged and during the night following the arrests, some *'Haloutzim* managed to carry off the certificates despite the seals which had been affixed to the apartment.

My friends were not released until June 2. Clages had first

of all arranged for them to be interned in a luxury hotel at Schwabenberg, which the Hungarian secret police had requisitioned near his own. On the pretext that my friends had rendered themselves guilty of the most heinous crime a Jew could then commit, the Hungarians at first refused to release them. Clages had, at last, telegraphed to Berlin, to Himmler in person, who gave orders that the ambassador Veesenmayer should ask to be received by Sztojay, the Hungarian Prime Minister on the subject of this affair. Veesenmayer, who was a member of the SS, did as he was told.

This was an effective intervention indeed. My friends were at once liberated. Mrs. Brand had to be driven back by car since, owing to the torture to which she had been subjected, her feet were so swollen that she could not stand much less walk. She was isolated and treated for quite a considerable time in an apartment requisitioned by the SD but this did not save her from suffering the effects of her internment for several months afterwards. Mrs. Brand had shown herself very brave up to then. She knew that if she revealed the 'State Secret' not only her own life and the lives of her children would be lost but also those of the last surviving Hungarian Jews. She had heroically held out under torture and had been careful to tell her tormentors nothing about her husband's trip abroad. So they left her alone and turned their attention to Kastner and put him the same questions. The SD men made their appearance at the Hungarian secret police offices while the cross-examination of Kastner was just beginning. As the Germans held the orders of release he and Mrs. Brand were able to leave with the others of the group.

Despite the tragedy of the situation the declarations of Eichmann and Clages about Mrs. Brand's courage, which they compared with that of an 'Aryan', were slightly amusing. They regarded Mrs. Brand with a certain amount of respect from then on. They had paid her no doubt the highest compliment these men could make to a woman. Although she was henceforth obliged, owing to the sufferings she had undergone, to be less active within the Waada, she was all the same often used by Kastner. He hoped that Mrs. Brand's presence at his side during the stormy interviews he had with Eichmann would moderate the outbursts of anger of the SS. And, in effect, Kastner's hopes proved to be well founded.

The relief Clages showed, when he found out that neither Mrs. Brand nor any other of the prisoners had mentioned the negotiations outstanding, gave us a precious lesson and influenced our behaviour. For myself, this lesson furnished the key to the action I began to undertake within the Jewish Committee for Mutual Aid.

With the courage of despair Kastner set to work again. The first thing he noticed was that Eichmann was proceeding with and even increasing the volume of the deportations. On the very day of his liberation, June 2, Kastner went to see Eichmann and to show him a telegram received from Istanbul. Brand had been able to conclude a provisional agreement, the primary and sole stipulation of which was that the SS should stop the deportations. But it was just this stipulation which was not observed. Deportations had, in fact, taken place in the Carpathian region forming the most northerly province of Hungary. Each day news arrived from the north of Transylvania announcing that Jews were parked in camps in all the towns of any size: Kolozsvár, Maros-Vásárhely (now Targu-Mures), Nagy-Várad, Szatmár, Beszterce – (Bistritz) and Dés. Convoys for the concentration camps were being speeded up. Kastner asked that the test-convoy of 600 persons be formed at once. But his position was weak as Brand, despite his promises, had not come back, two weeks having already elapsed since he had left Budapest.

His telegram had simply announced that a courier would bring very soon the text of a provisional agreement, that is to say a Jewish proposal to be submitted to German approval. Eichmann was not satisfied. He felt he was justified in carrying on with the deportations and gave it to be understood that the formation of the test-convoy would be compromised if Brand did not return at once. On June 3, Eichmann told Kastner that he considered nothing decided at all. The persons who were to be passengers in the special train and who came from Transylvania, especially Klausenburg, would not arrive at

Budapest where they should have been assembled. He had sent a telegram forbidding their departure for the capital.

Once again he justified himself by Brand's absence. But as a matter of fact the special convoy should have reached foreign soil while Brand was still in Istanbul so as to lend weight to the proposals the Waada's envoy was to make to the representatives of international Jewry. It was obvious then that Eichmann's 'justification' was not valid at all. To explain his refusal Eichmann also pointed out the very real irritation in Hungarian government circles. The Hungarians had been provoked by the agreement concluded by the SS authorities and the family of Baron Manfred Weiss. [By the terms of this agreement forty members of the family had been able to take refuge in a neutral country.]

The story of this agreement is worth telling. Kurt Becher was at this time *Obersturmbannführer* of the Waffen-SS. He was promoted to *Standartenführer* much later – in January 1945. As chief of an equipment mission he had been sent to Budapest after German troops occupied Hungary. His job was to buy horses and material for the cavalry and service corps of the Wehrmacht and Waffen-SS fighting on the Russian front. This work had put him in touch with the Weiss family chief, the banker Franz Chorin, who had been one of the sons-in-law of the late Baron Weiss. At Chorin's request and with Himmler's authorization, Kurt Becher made an arrangement according to which the SS would control the majority of the shares in the Manfred Weiss factories, the largest industrial group in Hungary. The SS thus acquired a discretionary power over more than fifty enterprises producing mainly arms and war material. In exchange the SS had allowed forty members of the Weiss family to seek refuge in Portugal and Switzerland. The exit-visas had been granted by Eichmann's Bureau of Jewish Affairs – accorded not without hesitation but on Himmler's orders. Since Eichmann had taken no part in these negotiations or their conclusion he had no influence on their results.

When he learned on June 3 from Eichmann himself that the special convoy we were all so anxious for had been simply suppressed, Kastner lost his head for the first time. He threatened to break off the negotiations there and then and swore he would telegraph Istanbul that the discussions, now pointless, should be abandoned.

Kastner's forthright attitude at a time when he was not yet in a position to appreciate how important negotiations with those who were supposed to be the representatives of international Jewry were to Eichmann's superiors, had, in my opinion a decisive influence on our action.

Eichmann, in reality a coward, maintained a threatening attitude towards Kastner but did not have him arrested. Kastner, therefore, after leaving Eichmann was able to have a conversation with *Obersturmbannführer* Krumey and *Haupsturmführer* Clages.

During this conversation Kastner became convinced that Clages wanted the discussions to go on and wanted to satisfy Kastner. Clages asked him to go back to Eichmann the next day, in the meantime he would talk to his chief. Only later did Kastner learn that what he had assumed to be a perfectly ordinary arrangement for a meeting between Clages and Eichmann was, in fact, something entirely different. Clages had made up his mind to inform Himmler himself about the exact course of events.

When Kastner arrived the next day, June 4, at the Hotel Majestic, Clages emerged from the office of the chief of Section IV A 4b. Eichmann received him in the presence of only a few other people: Krumey, Hunsche, Nowack and Wisliceny.

He began at once to haggle. But Kastner obstinately played the same cards and maintained his demands. First of all the 600 Jews from the provinces (whose minimum number had been fixed by common accord) must be brought to Budapest and they must be sent abroad by special train. Eichmann, not much accustomed to so much insistence from a Jew, threatened Kastner with immediate deportation to Theresienstadt or Auschwitz, but he did not put an end to the discussion; Kastner himself did not realize how strong his position was.

After some hours of unequal combat between the two adversaries, Eichmann made some conciliatory proposals which Kastner ended by accepting.

The essential thing for us was that several hundred Jews would reach a neutral country and thus offer proof that we had not made a mistake, that our tactics had been right, and that there was some sense in going on with the negotiations.

Whether this first convoy comprised 200 or 600 Jews was of little importance. What counted was that it should be formed as soon as possible and that it should by the mere fact of its arrival in neutral territory help us in our enterprise.

On that same day Kastner also discussed with Eichmann many details concerning the transport of Jews from their provinces, their provisional encampment at Budapest, the continuation of their journey, and the secrecy which must be observed throughout the whole operation so that the Hungarian authorities would not get wind of it.

As usual Eichmann kept none of his promises. We will tell further on how this convoy was formed despite Eichmann – although much later than had been foreseen – and how it arrived in a neutral country.

7. I am Saved by a Trick

My friends had been released for only a few days when I found out that the Hungarian police were not going to spare me either. About the beginning of June – I have forgotten the exact date – while my wife and I were lunching at a restaurant, she suddenly drew my attention to a nearby table where a man was sitting with his eyes fixed on us. She was sure he was an employee of the Bistritz electricity company who used to check the meters and take the money due for the accounts.

Now he was in uniform and must have been doing his military service. Without any doubt he had recognized us.

The man got up brusquely as if he were going to inform the police, and I knew that my hour had come. I made a sign to my wife and we got up to leave the restaurant as quickly as possible. Then I remembered I had not paid the bill. During the few minutes I had to wait – they seemed like an eternity to me – my wife had time to get away. Therefore I was relieved of anxiety on her account.

When I got into the street I walked rather more rapidly than usual. I glanced unobtrusively behind me and saw the Bistritz employee and a policeman on my tracks. I set off to run as fast as I could, followed by the two men. Several passers-by stopped and I heard cries of 'Catch him, catch him'. I jumped into a moving tram and at that very instant a policeman on a bicycle came pedalling towards it and made it stop. I was caught in a trap. Within a few seconds I was arrested and marched off.

At the police-station I was put in a cell where I spent a few hours with thirty or forty companions in misfortune. I got into conversation with one of them. When I learned that his case had been settled and he was waiting to be let out, I scribbled a few words on a leaf from my diary to tell Mrs. Brand (who was still living with my friends at my old apartment in the Semsey utca) that during my interrogation I would pass myself off as the secretary of the Waada and would invoke Clages's authority. I then asked her to inform my wife and the SD offices at Schwabenberg that I had been arrested by the Hungarian police. I stressed also that Clages should intervene in my favour. Shortly afterwards my companion was set free. I had his promise to do all he could to take my note to Mrs. Brand.

Towards evening I was led to the Budapest Prefecture of Police and there passed the night in a room about twenty yards square in which were already some hundred persons, almost all Jews and guilty of not wearing the Yellow Star. All night long we remained standing jammed against one another. By pushing and shoving as much as we could we managed to clear a space to allow the oldest among us to lie down in turn and take a little rest.

The next morning I was led into a large hall where about thirty policemen, each one sitting at a table, began the cross-questionings. Within the next few minutes either I would secure my release or at least get myself taken to Clages's office, or my number could be up. I would have no chance of escaping deportation to the Kistarcsa camp, the first halt on the way to Auschwitz. So I displayed no hesitation in obeying the order of a warden who pointed vaguely to a queue.

As I had been able to note a few days earlier when my friends were arrested, Clages greatly feared that the Hungarians might find out the secret of our negotiations, so I decided to play that card.

The police officer before whom I found myself began by asking me where I had got permission not to wear the Yellow Star although I was Jewish. Why was I in possession of false papers? He knew quite well I was not called Andor Kiss. Did I not know I had broken the law by not handing over to the authorities valuables in my possession? As he said this he pointed to a small box which contained my valuable gold watch and a signet-ring, inherited from my father, set with a diamond of several carats. I had been stripped of these on my arrest. Then came the final question: Why had I not presented myself for compulsory labour service? Did I know I was a deserter?

I did not give any detailed reply to these accusations but answered in a lofty manner that I was engaged in an activity covered by official secrecy and that I had given my word not to speak about it. If he wanted to know any more he had only to call one of the telephone numbers in my note-book, either that of the Gestapo offices under Eichmann, or that of the SD, and mention my name. Some days before the use of these numbers had liberated my friends. The police officer, obviously impressed by my self-confidence, called one of the numbers. When he got no reply he dialled the other. But I was unlucky. No reply that time either. He seemed to wonder what he should do with me and then I suddenly got an idea.

Politely, but with a self-confidence I was really far from feeling, I asked him to telephone his colleague who was liaison officer between the Hungarian police and the Gestapo and ask him to give information about my case. This time I was lucky. 'My' superintendent not only learned that all the telephone numbers of the German offices in Schwabenberg had been changed and that mine though 'correct' were no longer valid, but was also given the new numbers.

This time the bureau of Jewish Affairs answered at once. As the man at the other end of the line talked very loudly I could catch each word of the conversation. No, neither the name of Andre Biss nor of Andor Kiss was known there. I urged the commissary to say that I was the secretary of the group headed by Drs Kastner and Komoly. Yes, these people were known; they also possessed a permission from the Bureau of Jewish Affairs authorizing them not to wear the Yellow Star. I then suggested he should ask whether I should not be taken to Schwabenberg. He did so and I heard a voice say 'Yes, of course, bring him here at once.'

The officer hung up and gave me a suspicious look. But he did not refuse when I proposed he should take my wallet with the necessary money for a taxi and go with me to Schwabenberg. Apparently the idea of an outing during office hours did not displease him. At the Bureau of Jewish Affairs I had to wait in a corridor while my policeman parleyed. In a short time he reappeared and took leave of me almost deferentially but not without saying, 'You know you've no right to walk about without the Yellow Star, they've just confirmed that.'

I was shown into an office and there before me was *Obersturmführer* of the SS, Hunsche. There was no one else there. 'Oh, so it's you,' he said. I noted with a good deal of relief that he had recognized me. Then after a pause he asked me casually, as though he attached little interest to the question:

'But what can they really want at the Prefecture of Police?'

'They wanted to know why Joël Brand has gone to Istanbul and what my activities were, and those of my friends. In a word they were after the "State Secret".'

Hunsche gave me a stern look.

'And what did you tell them?'

'I told the police officer to apply to you, and that's why I am here.'

'And what do you yourself know about all this business?'

Though the question had been put in a threatening tone of voice, I felt more reassured since I realized I had played the right card.

'I know only what the secretary of the group should know.' My answer seemed to satisfy Hunsche. He called an SS *Scharführer*, telling him to take me to an adjoining room and wait with me.

We waited for hours, how long I cannot say. From time to time my warden gave me a sidelong look, obviously wondering whether this man he was guarding was a visitor or a prisoner. When I got very thirsty I asked him if he could get someone to go and buy me a bag of cherries at the nearest shop. This request convinced him that I must be a visitor. As my pocket-book had been confiscated by the Hungarians I gave him all my spare change I had in my pocket. He told one of his men to go and get the cherries, so that a little later there I was, grotesquely enough, sitting in the HQ of the Bureau of Jewish Affairs and sharing a few cherries with a *Scharführer* of the SS while my fate was being decided a few doors away. I was sure that I had escaped the worst, at least for the moment, but was ill at ease since I had walked about not wearing the Yellow Star quite without permission.

It must have been about five o'clock in the afternoon when Hunsche appeared once more and told me sharply to follow him. We walked from the Majestic to the Mirabel by a way I already knew. Hunsche did not answer when I asked him if we were going to see *Hauptsturmführer* Clages but threw me a quizzical look when I added that the *Herr Hauptsturmführer* usually left his office before this hour. No doubt I managed to give Hunsche the impression that I had visited Clages several times. In fact, the sentinel on duty at the Mirabel's entrance informed us that Clages had just left his office. Hunsche looked at me as though he did not know what to do. I forestalled any decision, by saying:

'Surely the best thing would be for me to go home and come back again tomorrow.'

Hunsche was quite flabbergasted by my impertinence and asked where I lived. I told him and added that the address of my apartment, Semsey Andor utca 15, was also that of Dr. Kastner, the engineer Komoly and other leading Zionists. Hunsche remarked that he knew the address and, after pondering an instant, he ordered me to appear on the next day at the office of *Hauptsturmführer* Clages who would deal with the case. I was free.

When I got home I found to my astonishment that the apartment was empty. After my messenger had delivered news of me, Kastner, Mrs. Brand and my other friends had fled for fear that he had been followed. After a long search I found all the group at the home of a common friend. I was informed that Kastner had as yet done nothing to secure my liberation, either with Clages or with Eichmann. I was energetically reproached for having, through my carelessness, imperilled a movement destined to save thousands of human lives. Why had I sent a note to Mrs. Brand? No one would admit that thanks to my presence of mind I had escaped by a hair's breadth deportation to Auschwitz. The evening before my wife, with tears in her eyes, had implored Kastner to do something to help me. She had been so coldly received and treated in our own home that in a state of the greatest dismay she had gone off to bed in a furnished room we had at the other end of the city.

At the time this attitude seemed shameful in its ingratitude. I had not then realized how unimportant one human life was in our task. Today I know that Kastner had other worries and other duties to preoccupy him, and that he could not concern himself with the fate of one person.

The next morning at 11 o'clock I went to the Hotel Mirabel. Clages did not himself receive me but his assistant *Hauptsturmführer* SS Neugeboren was there. He did not know the reason for the steps I was taking. I told him briefly the facts, my arrest by the Hungarian police who wanted to get information about Brand's trip to Istanbul, and about the activities of our group, then I mentioned my removal to

Eichmann's Bureau of Jewish Affairs. It was *Obersturmführer* Hunsche who had instructed me to present myself before *Hauptsturmführer* Clages. Neugeboren disappeared for a minute or two in order to consult his chief. When he came back he asked what it was exactly that I wanted. Clages seemed to be very busy. The Allied landings in Normandy had aroused feverish activity everywhere.

I replied that I myself wanted nothing, would only like to know what was wanted of me. Thereupon Neugeboren sent me off home. Thanks to a trick and to my own efforts, I had got out of a potentially nasty situation and therefore acquired a strong feeling of personal security and self-confidence. Since I had not been given back either the papers or the valuables I had had on me at the time of my arrest – I missed my ring most of all – I went to the Prefecture of Police to retrieve them. I asked to speak to the officer who had interrogated me the day before and whose name I have now forgotten. I was led almost at once into the big hall where the cross-questionings took place. When he saw me my interrogator of the previous day gave a gasp of surprise and he ordered the person before him taken away. He 'welcomed' me by remarking, 'Oh, there you are, I see you're still not wearing a Yellow Star. I was assured you had no right to go without one. What are you doing here?' I told him I was quite in order, and in fact had no need of written permission as I was employed on a secret mission. If he wanted to see for himself he had only to arrest me and the German authorities would once more insist on my release. I had come just to get back the personal property which had not been returned to me. The commissary went off to consult his chief and returned with my diary, penknife and a few other small objects, but no sign of my watch, signet-ring or cash. My pocket-book had contained rather a large sum. He told me that all these objects had been handed over to the Hungarian National Bank since I as a Jew was obliged by law to surrender such things. Furthermore, since I had broken this law and was going about under a false name and with forged papers, I would be prosecuted and in due time would get a summons.

I had to have a pass in order to leave the Prefecture so 'my' commissary walked with me as far as the entrance. While we were going down the stairs he asked in a low tone of voice whether it would not be possible to get two young men taken on in my department at Schwabenberg. He had two sons who were 'Jews' (no doubt he had married a Jewess and according to the new 'racial' laws applicable in Hungary the children of 'mixed' marriages were considered Jews). He was obviously convinced I had an influential job in the Bureau of Jewish Affairs. Into my hand he slipped a piece of paper with his address. As I did not want to disillusion him I promised to do all I could and to keep him posted. As a matter of fact I never saw the man again.

The Bureau of Jewish Affairs and the Hungarian Police now knew my real name and address, so my wife and I no longer had any reason to lodge in our furnished room. Therefore within the next few days, we went back to our apartment.

8. The Grey Eminence

During his visit to the man, Kastner got the impression that Clages had a certain amount of influence in our affairs (though of a much lower rank than Eichmann or Krumey) perhaps even a decisive influence. We knew hardly anything about the relations existing among the different organizations of the SS, the Gestapo, the SD, the Bureau of Equipment and the economic and military sections. But we felt that there must be links and crossed lines among them which would yield information to our advantage.

No doubt Clages had seemed reserved, but during this interview Kastner had noticed that he spoke of me with a certain liking and even respect. It was through my daring that he had been informed in time of the Hungarian authorities' arrest of Waada members, and was able to take the necessary steps for the release of Kastner, Komoly, Mrs. Brand and Offenbach.

Between Clages and me a very bitter discussion then began. He wanted to find out what I knew and at the same time to discover just how far our influence really stretched. The wrangle was from the start an unequal one. At the time we represented nothing very much nor did we possess the slightest political link with Roosevelt in Washington. And I myself knew little or nothing of what might interest Clages.

Furthermore it was part of the game to hide both what one knew and what one did not know, for we were up against people who under the influence of their own propaganda believed that we must represent 'world-wide Jewish power'. This belief, one of the main causes of the extermination of the Jewish people in Europe, ironically helped save the last survivors.

So I could reveal nothing to Clages, since I knew nothing of importance. All the same, I tried to strengthen his pre-conceived idea that I did know a lot, and in doing so I learned from him many details most useful for our enterprise.

The special section of the SD commanded by Clages was quite autonomous and did not in any way depend on Eichmann's organization. Indeed part of Clages's job was to keep an eye on Eichmann and to see that everything was done to ensure that the secret behind the 'final solution' should be completely guarded. It was therefore necessary that the object of the deportations should remain unknown. Clages, with this end in mind, had to attentively observe the effects, positive or negative, of these measures. He reported directly to Himmler on these matters without going through the usual official channels. This close contact with the *Reichsführer* became still closer after Himmler, having learned through Clages's report that there was co-operation between the Zionists and Canaris's counter-espionage organization, had endeavoured through us to engage in a line of action which he hoped would have consequences favourable for himself.

Relations between the SS secret services (the most important of which was the SD) and the Wehrmacht counter-espionage under Admiral Canaris were, as we have noted, extremely strained. They resembled those between the Wehrmacht and the SS. As from the spring of 1944 many people expected a *Wehrmacht* putsch or rebellion against the SS, and indeed, there was an attempt some months later on July 20, 1944. It could be foreseen several weeks in advance and already poisoned the atmosphere.

During my conversation with Clages I was able to form a character sketch of Himmler, a portrait at first vague and then as time went on more and more precise. After he had tried to get arms and war material through us to increase the strength of his SS, he attempted to get guarantees covering him and his past deeds from Washington, guarantees strictly limited to himself – his chief the Führer being totally excluded, as I was able to assure myself later on. At long last I managed to get the explanation for Clages reserved attitude towards Kastner. Brand and Grosz had denounced Kastner and had recommended that the SD should arrest him. Everything must be done to keep Kastner from spoiling the plans for the Istanbul trip and from denigrating the two men to the Waada, which might then refuse to furnish them with the indispensable recommendations. Brand and Grosz had gone so far as to reveal that Kastner was in touch with the counter-espionage services of the Hungarian army under General Ujszászy, and that since he knew Lt. Colonel Garzoly well, Kastner had no doubt informed him about the 'State Secret'. This, apparently their most convincing argument, was dangerous since the collaborators in the Hungarian military counter-espionage had close contacts with Canaris's agents. Moreover, both groups were convinced that Germany had already lost the war. In these circumstances, Clages feared that private conversations with Kastner might enable the Hungarians to find out Himmler's private intentions. There was the danger that the Hungarians would inform certain persons whose reports would be influential with Horthy who might in time apply directly to Hitler to clear the matter up. But on no account, must Hitler know anything about Himmler's attempts to create an alibi. In such a case Clages had good reason to think Himmler would use him as a scapegoat.

Clages's fears and suspicions about Kastner were not altogether unfounded. Kastner in fact was firmly convinced, or was until October 15, that in order to save the Hungarian Jews the rupture of the alliance between Germany and Hungary must be encouraged, or better still that Hungary should withdraw from the Axis. Rumania's defection in August 1944 had only strengthened Kastner's conviction. I myself maintained an entirely different point of view. I had no confidence in Horthy or in those around him. They were all too lacking in courage to take so decisive a step. We had only one chance of gaining time and that was to negotiate with the SS, to have recourse to ruse and to make, if necessary, a few deliveries of small importance. The collapse of the Third Reich seemed very near and I was much surer than my friends that the salvation of the Jews depended essentially on gaining time.

On the other hand, some Hungarian Zionists thought their only chance of survival lay in following the policy of the Hungarian government, and rejected any idea of contact with the German authorities.

The efforts I also made to find out exactly why Clages had sent Brand and Grosz to Istanbul did not go unrewarded. Gradually I learned to guess which arguments would have the most weight with him and I learned how to handle him. I suggested that Brand would have a great deal of scepticism to overcome abroad and that he would succeed only with difficulty in his mission since he was by no means the Jewish personality best suited for or most likely to accomplish his task. A short time before, the time limit for Brand's return had expired. Brand had not kept his word nor had his travelling companion. The confidence Clages and above all, Himmler might have had in us and in our negotiations was seriously impaired. It seemed to me that the time had come to accustom Clages to the idea that he had sent abroad a man unsuited for carrying out such an important mission. While I was cautiously trying to get Clages to share this opinion, I learned that Grosz had introduced Brand to him by presenting him as the most important executive individual in the Waada. Brand had of course done nothing to persuade Clages otherwise. In reply to a carefully phrased question he explained to me that neither he nor Eichmann had wished that Mrs. Brand alone should keep in contact with them during her husband's absence. They had never pretended that Komoly and Kastner were not qualified for such contacts. It was Brand himself who, a short time before he left, had expressly appointed his wife to represent him with them.

On the strength of telegrams received from Istanbul I pressed Clages more and more to form the test-convoy, a sign of German faith and good-will that had become indispensable. Thanks to Kastner's energetic insistence with Eichmann and his staff, the 388 Jews from Klausenburg who had been chosen for this convoy arrived at Budapest on June 10 and we had put them up in a building in the Columbusgasse which had formerly been a Jewish orphanage. Now the whole scheme appeared to have got bogged down, and after having made us wait in vain, Eichmann was now obviously sabotaging it.

Clages gave me to understand that Himmler was waiting for material compensation in exchange for so generous an action and that he would, on no account, forgo such compensation. He must, in some way or another, justify such an undertaking in the eyes of his staff. This interview took place at a time when my friends and I were still of the opinion that our opponents were thinking only of doing a good piece of business. But it seemed to us impossible to obtain from abroad anything at all in exchange for the convoy. As for the cash and valuables which had been collected in Hungary itself, this could hardly be considered compensation by the very people who, in any case, had disposal of our property and our lives. In this matter Eichmann's attitude was characteristic. He had grabbed millions in exchange for promises which soon proved quite illusory. Jews in any case must hand over to the authorities the property they possessed. Eichmann did not consider his word binding.

Clages mentioned to me that Himmler expected compensation, but said that he himself was not authorized to carry on negotiations respecting the formation of the test-convoy. Eichmann alone had power to do this and Kastner discussed the matter with him in vain. Former experience had convinced us it would be useless to offer Eichmann more money or valuables. So it was that the discussions between Kastner and Eichmann concerning this convoy dragged on their weary way.

9. Strasshof

Eichmann went on deporting the Hungarian Jews as fast as possible. I urged Clages with all my might to do something about the test-convoy and bombarded him with requests that he make Heinrich Himmler understand that Eichmann's deportations would surely have consequences on the discussions taking place with our Western friends. These deportations should cease at once. Clages answered that in view of the rapid advance of the Russian forces, this was impossible. The German command would in no case permit these Jews to be liberated by the Russians. I begged him not to send these deportees to Auschwitz. We knew (and I had not hidden from Clages the fact that we knew) that there they would be immediately sent into the gas-chambers – with the exception of a few who were picked out as soon as they reached the camp.[1]

1. We were informed about what happened at Auschwitz. The Waada's activities long before the occupation of Hungary on 19th March, 1944, had consisted to a large extent of collecting information about the places of deportation and the fate of the deportees from Poland, Russia

I also gave Clages to understand that at this rate in a very short time the last survivors of the Jewish people would be annihilated, and the Germans would soon not have enough bargaining counters in case our present negotiations resulted in agreement.

Without commenting on my allusion to Auschwitz, Clages implicitly confirmed my statements to the extent that he reminded me how critical the food situation was in Germany which was not, like Hungary, an agricultural country. The Hungarian peasants had not been taken into the army except in small numbers, and the population had not had to suffer from the export of agricultural produce. On the other hand, in Germany it had become difficult to feed non-working deportees who because of their state of health or their age were, practically speaking, unproductive.

I at once proposed, in the name of the American Joint Distribution Committee, to buy large quantities of foodstuffs in Hungary and to put them at the disposal of the deportees. I laid down, however, one condition, that they should not be sent to Auschwitz but to special camps and that no more selections should be made. I added that eventually they could be sent abroad as soon as the test-convoy had arrived in a neutral country and as soon as the agreements relating to other convoys has been concluded.

Clages immediately forwarded my proposal to Himmler which was that to start with 100,000 persons should be interned in special camps and without any selection. Two days later Himmler gave Clages his acceptance – in principle – for a first trial involving thirty thousand persons. A short while afterwards Eichmann got a telegram ordering him to form the first convoy that was to consist of six trains, each containing three thousand passengers – a total of 18,000 people.

---

and other countries occupied by German troops. It was first of all through our Waada that people in the West had received detailed reports about the methods of wholesale extermination practiced at Auschwitz. The information on this subject which, to the stupefaction of the world was broadcast by the British and American radios, came mostly from our Budapest services.

At the same time as my efforts with Clages, Kastner had also tried to induce Eichmann not only to send the test-convoys to a neutral country but also to hold up the deportations. As long as Brand did not come back Eichmann had an excellent excuse for not allowing the test-train to leave. And as for stopping the deportations or sending the deportees to other camps than Auschwitz, there was no question of his doing either.

On June 2 a telegram[1] from Brand arrived. In it he announced the conclusion of a provisional agreement and the despatch of its text, but this text never arrived any more than did Brand himself. This was the telegram:

'Provisional agreement concluded stop am leaving as per your instructions Molodet discuss technical details and guarantee meeting place at Schwartz's with Ban myself and Schröder stop sending text contracts stop partner must respect conditions stop look after family stop telegraphic address unchanged stop why no news stop greetings Joël.'

While we were anxiously waiting, alarming news reached us from the provinces. The deportations had reached a figure of ten thousand persons a day and no doubt even exceeded this number. Although we had received only a few telegrams from Turkey, Kastner went almost every day to see Eichmann and to ask him most earnestly to hold up the deportations. Kastner always used the same argument I had employed with Clages: he argued that the capital – the number of human lives he could barter for trucks and foodstuffs – would be reduced so rapidly as to become practically negligible even before the negotiations had been concluded. Kastner, furthermore, did not hesitate to talk in Eichmann's presence of the exterminations which were a State secret and which the majority of Germans themselves were supposed to know nothing about. We who claimed in the name of world Jewry to represent the victims were obliged, all the more, to affect ignorance about the extermination camps. Each time Kastner talked of 'extermina-

1. In this telegram 'Molodet' means Israel; 'Schwartz' was the delegate from Europe of the American Joint Distribution Committee. Schroder was the code name of the German negotiator.

tion' Eichmann angrily declared that these 'atrocities' were a complete invention.

I kept Kastner posted about my talks with Clages but it was clear to me that my friend continued to hope Eichmann would finally accept his argument. But what Kastner did not know yet – or would not admit – was that Eichmann was not the ultimate authority. He was entrusted with organizing the deportations, but his power regarding them was limited to making conditions either harsher or more tolerable. Eichmann so obstinately satisfied his sadistic longing to carry his orders out in the most brutal manner that it became impossible for him to draw back. But he had no direct contact with Himmler, either personally or through official channels. Eichmann's orders were dictated to him by his immediate superior, SS *Gruppenführer* Müller, chief of the Gestapo; the latter in his turn depended on Kaltenbrunner, head of the Reich security organization, who took instructions direct from Himmler, the *Reichsführer* of the SS.

It sometimes happened, however, that particularly important instructions from Kaltenbrunner came straight to Eichmann without passing through the hands of Müller, but such instructions never came direct from Himmler. On the other hand Clages, responsible for a special section of the security services, reported on certain matters direct to Himmler. One of the most important of such matters, of which I later had tangible evidence, was that which held out to Himmler a promise of entering into direct relations with Washington through us.

The telegram ordering Eichmann to send the convoy of 18,000 persons to the Strasshof camp near Vienna instead of to Auschwitz was signed, as were all especially important orders, by Kaltenbrunner. This was an indication that the instructions came directly from Himmler. But Eichmann was careful not to give this information to Kastner. He kept the leading role for himself and declared he had taken the decision to switch this convoy over from its original destination. The practical problems which arose regarding the convoy were no concern of Clages. Kastner had to discuss with Eichmann all the details of the operation, particularly the possibility of the Waada lodging and feeding 18,000 people.

On June 14 (the date of July 14, 1944, given in the Kastner report is incorrect) the two men conferred at length on the conditions of this transport; the food we had agreed to furnish was one of the main subjects of discussion, for Eichmann wanted to be certain we could deliver to him large quantities of lard, meat, bacon and canned goods. Kastner promised everything asked of him so that the original figure of 18,000 would be maintained. Kastner did not know that the discussion concerned an order Eichmann had to obey and that he had taken no part in the decision.

To lay hands on scarce and dear goods such as these was no easy task. Much had to be bought on the black market and handed over to Eichmann's staff. The deportees at Strasshof rarely saw these supplies, for Eichmann had better things to do than hand out such treasures. The prisoners, then, until their liberation got the 'normal' pittance served out in the concentration camps. But the object was achieved – these deportees escaped the Auschwitz gas chambers.

The struggle to get 'concessions' from Eichmann (which could not originate with him and which he gave only unwillingly and on superior orders) prevented Kastner from seeing the real position with regard to influence. The chapters in his report dealing with these negotiations clearly show to what extent he was fascinated, hypnotized even, by the formidable power of his interlocutor. Kastner ascribed to Eichmann and himself the merit of concessions which could be accorded only by very high authority.

One must not forget that even the bravest man, if he as a Jew had to fight step by step with Eichmann, would have been deeply affected spiritually. Once the events had passed and successes had been achieved Kastner could scarcely have been able to react other than in the way he did.

Still, it is regrettable that in his report (dated 1946) Kastner places so much stress on the details of his negotiations with Eichmann, while he leaves the real circumstances which ensured the success of the negotiations totally in the dark. The reader is left with the impression that the success of these discussions was finally due to Eichmann and to him alone. Proof to the contrary was established at the Eichmann trial in the shape of a telegram giving Eichmann orders to send the six trains not to Auschwitz but to Strasshof. In another telegram Kaltenbrunner informed the mayor of Vienna of the arrival of the first five trains containing 12,000 persons in all, a third of whom were fit for labour. Here is the text:

> The Chief of Security and of SD
> IV 4 4b–3 433/42 g (1446)
> Berlin SW 68, 30th June, 1944

SECRET
Express letter to the Mayor of the City of Vienna.
Brigadeführer of the SS Blaschke. Vienna.

OBJECT: Allocation of workers to labour of military importance in the City of Vienna.

Dear Blaschke,

In view of the pressing need you have informed me of and which is also pointed out to me in a letter from SS Brigadeführer Dr. Dellbruegge, I have given orders for some convoys of evacuated persons to be sent to Vienna-Strasshof.

To begin with there will be four trains containing about 12,000 Jews. They should arrive at Vienna in a few days time.

In the light of the experience we have had in these matters, and according to our estimates, there should be in these trains about 30% of Jews fit for labour or in this present case (approximately 3,600 persons) who if they leave here at any moment now could be allocated to the work in question. Naturally only a closed and well-guarded place of labour and quarters in an enclosed camp can be permitted. It is on these conditions that these Jews are placed at your disposal.

As for the women and children of these Jews, who are inapt for labour, they must be kept in readiness for another departure in view of special action. It is obligatory that they be kept under constant supervision even during the daytime.

Please ask for further details from the security services in Vienna, *Obersturmbannführer* SS Dr. Ebner, and *Obersturmbannführer* SS Krumey of the Hungarian special commando who is at the present time passing through Vienna.

I hope these convoys will provide you with the help you need in carrying out your task.

Heil Hitler!

Yours devotedly

(signed) Kaltenbrunner.

There was something odd about this telegram. The Strasshof camp could not make use of more than a maximum of 4000 to 5000 workers, generally selected from the contingent of deportees to Auschwitz who cleared the 'selection' net certified as 'good for labour'. But not only did the convoy prepared now exceed by more than three times the needs of Strasshof, but what was more it was more than two-thirds composed of women, children and men unfit for labour, thus constituting a unique exception to established custom. The telegram merely mentions in passing the possibility of a *later* selection and that the supplying of the deportees would be effected by special deliveries. These different telegrams were signed by Kaltenbrunner on the orders and in the name of Himmler.

The Jews who, thanks to the Strasshof operation, arrived in Lower Austria, came from provincial towns which had never ceased to belong to the Hungarian homeland, such as Székesfehérvár, Komárom and Debrecen. The majority of the Jewish population of Transylvania and Ruthenia, territories in the east of the country, was either en route for Auschwitz or had already perished. In the execution of his orders, in particular the one that was to save the life of thousands of Jews, Eichmann enjoyed great latitude. He considered the Jews who lived in eastern Hungary biologically superior to those who lived in the provincial towns of Hungary proper. The latter had fewer children and their ties to the Jewish community had been severed – in fact they were on the way to being assimilated. So Eichmann preferred to send them to Strasshof and thus protect them against immediate extermination. On the other hand the Jews from Transylvania and other territories in the east, must not benefit from such measures of clemency, for in his fanatical obstinacy Eichmann feared these above all.

What happened to a convoy of 3000 persons from Györ (in German Raab) shows that the life or death of thousands of human beings hung by a thread. The SS *Unterscharführer* who was in charge of the train had already done the trip many times and as usual headed the train for Auschwitz. It was only when it arrived at the Slovenian frontier that he noticed that the number of the convoy did not figure on the lists. He telephoned Eichmann who decided that the train should go on to Auschwitz. Its number was changed for that of another train coming from Debrecen whose passengers, instead of going to die at Auschwitz, waited at Strasshof until the end of the war.

The administration of the Strasshof camp was under the command of one of Eichmann's lieutenants, Krumey, who had had a special office set up in Vienna to carry out his work. The necessary administrative staff was recruited from among the prisoners.

Until then Krumey had controlled the deportations in Hungary under Eichmann's direct supervision, and had managed to accomplish his task with a small number of assistants, among whom were Dannecker, Hunsche, Nowack and Wisliceny. Unlike his chief, Krumey already foresaw the possibility of the Third Reich's defeat. The unprecedented order to send 18,000 Jews to Strasshof without any selection being made strengthened his conviction that very highly placed persons were preparing to follow a less rigid policy in the Jewish Affairs.

In the spring of 1945, as soon as the Russian troops had entered Vienna and while the fighting was still furious, the Strasshof camp was liberated. Eighteen thousand persons, mothers and children, grandmothers, grandfathers and fathers (these latter not numerous since many had been drafted for labour service before the deportation), invalids and the sick, were set free at once. They immediately left this unique concentration camp and went back to Hungary. The return of whole families seemed like a miracle. Those who got back from other camps were most often miserable survivors of what had been flourishing families. Half dead of hunger and devoured with disease, they found it hard to understand how thousands of others could come back, in whole families and in good health, from their deportation at Strasshof.

10. Kurt Becher

The interviews between Eichmann and Kastner from June 7 to 10 had been marked by violent scenes. Indignant at Joël Brand's conduct, Eichmann had threatened reprisals and declared that at the last minute he would prevent the departure of the Klausenburg group, which at that moment had not yet reached Budapest. Wholesale deportations were in any case going on at an increased rate. But although Eichmann gave vent to his anger – mostly by furious shouting – whenever he could, he could not disobey orders. As we have already seen, the Klausenburg deportees at least reached Budapest – on June 10, 1944.

Between June 10 and 20, while we were doing all we could to get orders given for the Strasshof operation to start, I pressed Clages urgently for the test-convoy to leave Budapest for Portugal. Large sums of money could not be collected before the train had got to Lisbon, nor could we pay over any more ransom money, knowing as we did that despite our payments, Eichmann would not keep his word.

About this time our committee learned facts hitherto kept secret concerning the existence of the SS equipment department under the orders of an *Obersturmbannführer* called Becher. He was reputed to have negotiated the transaction whereby the owners of the Manfred Weiss factories had been saved from deportation and to have also helped them to emigrate. We also found out that Becher would have the job of taking delivery of the 10,000 trucks if our negotiations came to a satisfactory conclusion. When asked about this Clages broached a very delicate question, that of Himmler's policy on equipment. The SS *Reichsführer* intended to allocate to the SS units he was in the process of forming any material produced through the agreement he was trying to conclude with us. The sums previously received by Eichmann had served to cover the needs of his own units or had been paid, in the prescribed manner, into the Reichsbank. The SS budget had not benefited at all.

At this period Himmler was already setting up his own State within a State. Under these circumstances I suggested that Clages should put Becher and Kastner in touch with one another. A meeting took place on June 20. Clages and Eichmann were also present. The conversation, however, was fruitless, since Becher was not authorized to take part in negotiations. His job was to receive the trucks and the war material. It was no use for Kastner to point out that we had at our disposal several millions in foreign exchange, gold, jewels and cash. Becher remained reserved. Such valuables were, as yet, of no interest to him. The attempt I had made to bring into our conversations a partner less uncompromising than Eichmann, ended then, for the moment, in fiasco. Eichmann remained in control of the negotiations. Clages played the part of a passive observer and from time to time simply sent to Himmler protests I might make regarding the rigorous measures taken by Eichmann. Contact with Himmler through Clages seemed to hold our only chance of success and I tried all I could to secure, the dispatch of the test-convoy at all costs.

I dangled before Clages's eyes the bait of large payments. I added all sorts of promises though without describing by what means such payments had been made or might be made.

Kastner and I based our arguments on the numerous telegrams which were, at first, sent to Brand's old address (which both he and his family had left) and which we would go and fetch every day. Although his name figured in all the messages only the first really came from him; the others were sent by members of the Istanbul Waada. The telegrams made a great impression on Clages. They showed, indeed, that the Istanbul Jews were very busy and were ready to accept our requests, though on certain conditions. I was able to persuade him that in this affair I really did represent active and influential American personages. Kastner acted in the same way with Eichmann, but the telegrams had much less effect on him since his fixed idea was the extermination of the Jews.

Here is the text of one of these telegrams:

'Accept principle your proposal Irbirah Stephan and Locker working actively stop special messenger arrives tomorrow for interview stop further prolongation stay being refused by central service Bandi leaves tomorrow morning provisionally Szamo stop stay until 4/IV accorded me in view meeting with representative telegraph urgent return or departure for Szamo continue negotiations with Bandi this weekend. Joël.'[1]

Here again are the texts of two other telegrams signed by Wenja Pomeranz, one of the members of the Istanbul Waada:

'Your 3/VI stop regret so late reply several telegrams stop utilization positive reply Erez and Stefan[2] in sense your proposals demanded further journey foreseen by you stop we ask Schröder consider this stop. We continue according your instructions and both arrange meeting quickly before contact Schwarz and Rezsö stop confirm telegram stop cordially Wenja.'

'Awaiting arrival special messengers of Stephan stop telegraph if Gerusch stopped – Wenja.'[3]

We had to strike while the iron was hot. The test-convoy must be formed and despatched before Brand's failure at Istanbul became known, a failure we all feared.

After the first attempt to establish permanent contact between Becher and Kastner had failed on June 20 it seemed

1. 'Stephan' was the code-word for the U.S.A. (from the name of the American Zionists' chief Stephan Wise a friend of Roosevelt's), 'Locker' meant England (from the name of the Zionist leader Berl Locker) 'Irbirah' meant government, 'Szamo' indicated the Palestine of that day because Szamo Springmann lived there. The special messenger in question was Ira A. Hirschmann who as representative both of the Refugee Board and of Roosevelt was in Turkey as McClelland was later on in Berne and Zurich.

2. Erez is Palestine, Stefan the U.S.A., Schröder the German negotiator, Schwarz is Joe Schwartz. The object of this telegram was to justify Brand who instead of having returned to Budapest as he had promised had travelled on towards Syria.

3. The word *Gerusch* signifies 'deportations' – we were asked to tell them if the deportations had already been stopped.

clearer than ever that we could hope for nothing more from Eichmann. During the last days of June, I had begged Clages not only to obtain the departure of the test-convoy but also to make a request to Himmler that further negotiations should be entrusted to Becher unless Clages himself would agree to undertake the assignment.

In this connection we have already mentioned a precedent. The SS had seized the factories of the industrial group 'Manfred Weiss'. In exchange the departure abroad of forty members of Baron Weiss's family had been authorized and facilitated. It was Becher who had carried the business through and with much tact. He had insisted energetically with Eichmann that the Bureau of Jewish Affairs, which Himmler had entrusted with the transport of the Weiss family, should carry out the engagements undertaken. This did not please Eichmann very much.

It was by mere chance that Becher got into touch with the Weiss family. Some members of this numerous family lived in the block of flats where Becher had been lodged; their flats contained a valuable art collection, much furniture, and precious tapestries. In the very first days of the SS occupation of Hungary, the Weiss family, like hundreds of other outstanding Jews or enemies of the Third Reich, had been arrested by the Gestapo and forthwith despatched to a concentration camp in Austria.

Becher, who was in no way connected with the Gestapo's activities, learned of the circumstances in which the Weiss family had been robbed of its possessions. He demanded that an inventory be drawn up which he intended to sign so that later on he might not be accused of theft or considered responsible for what had happened. Thereupon a certain Dr. Billitz, one of the managers of the Manfred Weiss plant, went to see Becher and was at first surprised to find such a scrupulous attitude in an SS officer. After a few interviews he got the impression that perhaps Becher could save his chiefs and their factories.

He told Becher in detail how Dr. Franz Chorin, the son-in-law of Baron Manfred Weiss (long dead) and the present head of the family, had been arrested with others of his relations and carried out of the country. Billitz added that the factories, whose joint managing directors were the young Barons Alphonse and Eugene Weiss, were now deprived of their regular management and were headed for ruin. As for the Hungarian Bank of Commerce, up to then run by Franz Chorin himself, it had never before been in difficulties. Billitz strongly urged Becher to get in touch with Chorin; he hoped Becher would be able to give Chorin some supplies of medicine and at the same time ask him for information about the good management of the works.

Billitz knew what he was doing. He knew Chorin's persuasive powers, and his extraordinary gifts of improvisation. A meeting with Becher would give him an opportunity to find a solution for the difficulties the combine was having, and perhaps something might be done to alleviate the condition of the Baron Manfred Weiss family.

Becher himself had not been very successful in carrying out his job in Hungary – that of finding horses and war material. Hungarian society, composed mainly of aristocrats, did not consider commerce and industry to be occupations worthy of a gentleman. As there was no risen middle-class, it was the Jews who had developed these two branches of modern economy, and to such an extent that commerce, industry and banking came to be almost exclusively in their hands. Most of the Jews who were prominent in these various activities had been arrested, and the laws promulgated by the government had paralysed and panicked Jewish circles so that Becher's men, unable to find many people with whom to discuss business, did not manage to make any deals of importance. Even agricultural business, such as horse trading, had been up to then mainly conducted by Jews.

Billitz gave Becher to understand that through Franz Chorin, who naturally had many contacts in all the branches of Hungarian economy, he could perhaps obtain assistance and advice. Becher then let himself be persuaded to go and see Chorin in Austria whither he had been removed. Chorin seized this opportunity to suggest that Becher should take him back to Hungary; once there Chorin would put himself at Becher's entire disposal to organize a perfectly effective purchasing campaign throughout the country.

Kastner's conversations with Eichmann at the beginning of June concerning the fate of the Klausenburg Jews had revealed further details of the Weiss family history. Every time their name was mentioned Eichmann flew into a fury. It was evident that he was extremely displeased with the way in which the problem of the Weiss industrial empire had been dealt.

Himmler did not give a negative reply to the proposals we made him through Clages, but displayed a certain incredulity about having recourse to Becher for the further conduct of the negotiations. However, we were told to get in touch directly with Becher, as in the case of the Billitz-Weiss affair. If Becher seemed interested he had only to refer to the *Reichsführer* of the SS. Kastner, thereupon, tried to get in contact with Becher and, after several vain attempts, turned to Dr. Billitz who in the meantime had become Becher's confidential adviser and counsellor. The manager of the Manfred Weiss factories showed an immediate interest in the business and promised to help us. He kept his word and one day between June 25 and 27 Becher received Kastner in his office at the Weiss plant.

The offers Kastner made were astounding – under the goading of despair, his proposals exceeded the bounds of the possible. But they were such that the young SS officer, whose influence with Himmler was due to the success he had had in the Weiss affair, declared he was highly interested. He promised to report in Kastner's favour to Himmler and to lay our proposals before the *Reichsführer*.

In view of the general difficulty in obtaining supplies, transactions such as that concerning the Weiss works or that which we were proposing in exchange for human lives could suit the SS only because they would be able to discover sources of revenue which they alone would exploit. Enterprises run directly by the SS exploited the cheap labour furnished by the concentration camps. This brought in considerable sums for the SS which got only a certain percentage of the booty extorted by the German army or administration in the occupied countries. Most of this war-loot was distributed among the army (*Wehrmacht*), the *Luftwaffe* (the air force), the navy and the German economy as a whole.

Convinced Nazis had no doubt whatever that in exchange for the lives of thousands of Hungarian Jews, 'International Jewry' would be prepared to make sacrifices amounting to far more than the sums paid by merely forty members of the Weiss family. Becher himself counted on the determination of foreign Jewish communities to come to the aid of their coreligionists still in Hungary. However, as Dr. Billitz had repeatedly told us, Becher was not deaf to human arguments. Kastner had noticed this at the first long interview he had had with him and I myself realized this when I got to know him better.

Immediately after his discussion with Kastner, Becher went to Berlin to see Himmler and came back with instructions to take the place of Eichmann in the negotiations. As soon as he returned there was a decisive meeting between Becher and his aide-de-camp *Hauptsturmführer* of the SS Grüson on the one side and Kastner, Dr. Billitz and myself on the other. For the first time we were able to discuss facts about the despatch of the test-convoy that had already been formed. Becher said he was ready to suggest to the SS *Reichsführer* that the convoy should be sent abroad as soon as a certain sum, representing a minimum guarantee, had been handed over in Hungary. The payment of the remainder of the whole sum agreed upon was to be made in 'free' currency when the train reached its destination in a neutral country. In this way the sum put up as a guarantee could be re-employed for the following train and so on. This provisional agreement was reached after discussions during which we had explained to Becher that our friends abroad would certainly never accept paying an advance in a free country for a first train before its arrival abroad, while, on his side, Becher maintained that Himmler would never consent to let a whole convoy of Jews depart without the exchange sum having been paid previously. We had proposed a tariff of 100 dollars a person, but we were obliged to pay $1000. Becher moreover did not hide from us that the *Reichsführer* was counting on doubling this figure.

With regard to the question as to how the payment of the guarantee should be effected, Becher declared that not only at his first interview with Kastner on June 20 but also at the second quite recently he had certainly heard mentioned a sum of several million dollars which had already been paid over. But neither he nor his staff had seen this money. Kastner was a Bohemian at heart – he paid little attention to financial matters and did not realize the value of money. He simply told Becher that a committee set up by Otto Komoly and Szulem Offenbach must have already handed over a considerable part of the sums to be paid by the passengers of the special train about a week before; but he did not know to whom.

When Kastner referred to the 6,500,000 pengoes the Waada Jewish Council had collected which, at the beginning of the German occupation, he had handed over to Eichmann's office in Brand's presence, Becher answered that payments made to the Bureau of Jewish Affairs, did not concern him and therefore could not be taken into account. With this statement the interview came to an end.

There was no question of our quickly gathering the objects of value which had been supposedly paid to the Germans on June 20. Quite by chance I managed to discover where these objects were – during an interview with Clages on the subject I learned to my great astonishment that they had been deposited with him. He had even put an office at the disposal of the Waada's treasurer, Szulem Offenbach, and the precious boxes were still locked up in the drawers of the office desk.

When my friends were arrested by the Hungarian police at the end of May, large sums in dollars and securities had been taken from them and deposited, in accordance with the decrees in force by that time, in the Hungarian National Bank; we could not obtain their restitution. Luckily Offenbach had taken his time before paying Eichmann's Bureau of Jewish Affairs the cash and jewellery collected afterwards for the test-convoy operation. He suspected that the promises would not be kept. To be certain that all this money would remain at the disposal of the Waada, Offenbach had applied to Clages's orderly officer, *Hauptsturmführer* Neugeboren (although Eichmann was still at that time entrusted with the negotiations). Neugeboren had taken part in the liberation of my friends who had been arrested by the Hungarians, and this was how Offenbach made his acquaintance and obtained his permission to place the boxes in Clages's offices. In the confusion of events, Offenbach had not had the opportunity to inform Kastner and me of these arrangements.

Now we had to officially hand over to the SS equipment service the valuables collected as an advance and as a guarantee for the first test-train. At a later conversation Becher told us that he could take delivery of nothing without an exact inventory and estimation of the worth of these valuables, since in addition to cash in various currencies there were jewels, gold coins and ingots. Such an estimation would demand a considerable amount of work, so to gain as much time as possible it was decided that the *Hauptsturmführer* and I should agree on the value of each object and base our appreciation on detailed lists drawn up by a committee of four expert valuers.

Each day the four men removed a certain quantity of gold, diamonds, foreign currency and jewellery from the boxes and the same evening gave us a complete list of the objects with the weight of the gold, the number of carats of the precious stones etc. Grüson and I had then to agree on the value in dollars of each object. After I had perceived that my partner was not to be counted among the more dangerous fanatics of the SS, I tried to convince him gradually that it was doubly advantageous to us to be liberal in our estimates. On the one hand each $1000 represented a human life saved, and on the other hand the test-convoy with about 1300 people could not leave Budapest until the sum of $1,300,000 had been obtained; the negotiations now going on – to which the *Reichsführer* attached great importance – depended to a great extent on the early arrival of this train abroad. Grüson let himself be convinced and showed himself very liberal in his estimations. When, after that, I spoke to him of gas chambers in the camps, he first of all refused to believe me. But while he was on leave he heard my stories confirmed by one of his friends who worked at the *Reichssicherheitshauptamt* and was so overcome that he promised all the help he could give. He also rendered us other precious services and exposed himself personally to a good deal of danger (see p. 136).

While the negotiations with Becher went on I persisted in asking Clages to see that Eichmann got orders from Berlin to send off the special train from Budapest, for although Becher had taken his place in the negotiations, Eichmann and his staff remained the only people with authority to get the convoy going.

After all the patience and obstinacy required by our task, the object of our efforts was attained suddenly and in a most surprising way. On June 30 the test-convoy left Budapest for Lisbon – or at least that was what we thought.

11. The Test-Convoy

It was with good reason that in his Report Kastner called this train 'Noah's Ark': it carried a group of 1684 persons whose nucleus comprised the 388 inhabitants of the Klausenburg ghetto who, in being sent to Budapest, owed the good fortune of having at the last minute escaped deportation to Kastner's daring. Originally other similar groups ought to have come from other regions of the Carpathians and Transylvania. The Zionist leaders had drawn up lists and handed them to the Bureau of Jewish Affairs, but Eichmann hastened to cut the ground from under their feet. Several ghettoes had been emptied and their inhabitants deported before a definite order had been obtained from Himmler instructing Eichmann to carry out the transports which had been foreseen for Budapest.

Even the Klausenburg group no longer corresponded with our original lists. When Eichmann had received, through Clages, the peremptory order to transfer the group to Budapest, a good half of those detained in the Klausenburg camp had already been deported, and among these were a good many persons whose names figured on our lists. Other names were put in their place, in part on the orders of the Hungarian, German or Jewish chiefs of this ghetto. It is hardly surprising that this Dantesque tragedy gave rise to feelings of bitterness and hatred – still lively today – among those whose close relations were not allowed on this test-convoy.

Besides the people from Klausenburg the train carried small groups of Polish, Slovak and Yugoslav refugees who had managed to seek asylum in Hungary and whom we were anxious to evacuate first of all since they were obviously the most threatened. The orthodox and the liberal Jews formed two other groups gathered around the respective chiefs of their communities – Philipp V. Freudiger and Samuel Stern. Among them was also the religious chief of the ultraorthodox Jews (Hassidic persuasion), Joël Teitelbaum, who was called the 'Rebbe of Satmar', and also about forty rabbis. Then came the most numerous group, Kastner's pride – the Zionist Youth. These were composed of the members of various organizations of agricultural pioneers, of extreme right-wing 'revisionists' who already possessed immigration certificates, and a number of orphans. There were also some Jewish savants (one of whom was a psychologist of world-wide reputation, Dr. Szondi), artists and writers, all chosen by Otto Komoly and Ernst Szilagyi. Lastly came those who had been able to pay cash for their journey, for we had to collect the sum the Germans demanded. But of the 1684 passengers in the train 300 at the most were in this category.

Moshe Krausz, the manager of the Palestinian office, was Kastner's open enemy and a still more fierce opponent of all policy entailing contact with the Germans. He was convinced the convoy was headed for destruction. He told leading Jews in Switzerland this in letters which a messenger from the Swiss legation in Budapest carried, and accused Komoly,

Kastner and the Waada as a whole of being simply tools in Eichmann's hands and of having sent the convoy to annihilation. Furthermore the unfortunate travellers had had to pay a high price for their place in spite of all the cruel experiences that had been undergone in the matter of ransoms. But the merit of having invested this undertaking with a moral significance is due to Otto Komoly, the chairman of the Waada. He it was who by using all his reputation and his authority in Jewish circles enabled the test-convoy to become a reality.

To prove that he really did believe in this convoy and to convince sceptics, he wanted his only daughter to take part in it. Kastner's mother, his brothers, sisters and other members of his family from Klausenburg were passengers; Brand's mother, his near relations and his sisters – with the exception of his wife and his two sons who remained with us – were also in the train. My own mother was one of the travellers too. Fate had taken charge of those who were nearest and dearest to us, but we did not know whether their destiny was to live or die.

Members of the families of those who had fought for the formation of this convoy formed at the most a group of from forty to fifty persons. It is worthwhile stressing this fact since, after the war, many reproaches were made against us and especially against Rezsö Kastner. He was accused of wanting to save his own family first of all. What blame he would have incurred, we would have incurred, if the enterprise had been a failure! Who would dare to deny Kastner and the other members of the Waada the right to include in this convoy of one thousand six hundred and eighty-four persons (obtained and organized by them often at the peril of their lives) their mothers, brothers, sisters and their nearest relations?

It may be worthwhile mentioning briefly here the 'case' of Szulem Offenbach. He was born at Lodz in Poland and was an enthusiastic Zionist. He, his wife and his two children were already settled in the train when Komoly and Kastner came, literally at the last minute, and begged him to remain with them. The Hungarian decrees that all Jews must on the pain of the most serious punishment, surrender all the valuables

93

they might have in their possession, made it absolutely necessary for us to have an able and reliable treasurer and Offenbach had had on several occasions, the opportunity to show how competent he was in this position. He scarcely hesitated at all, said good-bye to his wife and children, and stayed on in Budapest with us.

On the day of the departure there was at Budapest an air-raid alert lasting four hours. In the confusion that ensued about 380 persons managed to clamber into the train which left Budapest, not with 1300 passengers as expected, but crammed full with more than 1700 travellers.

We went back to my house and rested a few hours. We were thoroughly tired out and our nerves at breaking point. Who could have supposed that a new chapter in our crazy existence was to begin that very night?

The train sped off towards the Austro-Hungarian frontier, territory that was under German control, when a first alarming incident occurred. The convoy halted for three days at Moson-Magyaróvár. It had originally been arranged that the train (whose passengers enjoyed a certain amount of liberty) should first of all be sent to Strasshof, near Vienna, and then, a short time afterwards, on towards Lisbon. But owing to a careless remark of one of the German guards, the rumour spread that the train was going to be switched over towards Auschwitz. What the man actually said was 'Auspitz' but that sounded so like 'Auschwitz' that the gravest fears seemed justified. One of the passengers took advantage of a halt on a siding to jump off the train and hop into another going in the opposite direction and got back to Budapest where he gave the alarm. Kastner at once went to see Eichmann who reassured him. There was no question of sending the convoy to Auschwitz but the temporary overcrowding of the Strasshof camp had made it necessary to send the train first of all towards German territory, passing through the large junction at Auspitz.

After a short stop at Vienna where the passengers were fed, the train got to Linz. There the travellers were told to go into the bathrooms for disinfection. This order caused renewed and violent excitement among the refugees for it was already known that at Auschwitz the gas chambers were camouflaged as bathrooms. But these fears also proved groundless. On July 8, 1944 the convoy reached Bergen-Belsen near Hanover, the location of one of the so-called 'privileged' camps. This but a stage on a journey whose destination was still presumed to be Portugal.

In the night that followed the departure of the test-convoy, the door-bell rang long and loud at the apartment Semsey Andor utca 15. Most of our friends who had sought refuge with me in my house during the early days of the occupation had, in the meantime, either gone back to their own homes or had found new and more comfortable places to live in. Only Mrs. Brand, Rezsö Kastner and Szulem Offenbach were still living with my wife and I when the men of the Hungarian secret police brutally ordered us to get dressed and follow them. While I was getting ready I tried to telephone to Clages. I used my shirt to deaden the sound of my voice. I knew he would do all he could to stop us from being arrested and above all from being subjected to an interrogation which might make us reveal the 'State Secret'. But, alas, the policemen noticed my manoeuvres, snatched the telephone out of my hands and shoved me out of the apartment. A few minutes later we were thrown into cars waiting at the entrance of the block of flats and driven off to the Hadik barracks, HQ of the Hungarian counter-espionage. Kastner alone had remained in the apartment with two of the policemen who had come to arrest us. He seemed to have known them for a long time.

As soon as we got to the Hadik barracks we were separated and led into individual cells, without even any trouble taken to check our identities. I felt sure the door would open at any minute and I should be taken off for interrogation, but nothing happened. After several hours of waiting in uncertainty, we were released in the afternoon of the same day and without the slightest explanation. At the entrance to the barracks Mrs. Brand and Kastner were waiting for us in a taxi. Both of them looked like conspirators and replied evasively to my questions. Did they know what had happened? It was all a matter, they answered, of the internal affairs of the Zionist movement, and connected with the arrival of messengers from Palestine. In the meantime these affairs had been settled.

There were things happening among our people that I was not informed of since I was not a Zionist of long standing. The ignorance I was kept in perhaps did harm sometimes to our enterprise.

The text of the so-called 'Provisional agreement', announced in Joël Brand's telegram which has been cited above, reached us at Budapest very early in July. The chiefs of the Istanbul Waada, Chaim Barlasz, Wenja Pomeranz (Echud Avriel) and Menachem Bader had drawn up the text very skilfully and no doubt the Germans could accept it as a basis for discussions. Here is the text as it is given by Alex Weissberg.[1]

'In the course of a meeting held this day in the presence, on the one hand, of the responsible representatives of the Jewish Agency, and, on the other hand, of M. Joël Brand authorized by the Central Council of Hungarian Jews, it was decided as follows:

(1) The preliminary condition to a valid agreement is the immediate stoppage of the deportations.

(2) Special delegates of the executive of the Jewish Agency are on their way to Istanbul. The Jewish negotiators count on the despatch, by the German negotiators of representatives to Istanbul But the place of meeting could be fixed in another country if it so desired.

(3) The manufacture and delivery of the goods demanded by the opposite party meet with very great difficulties. A solution to these difficulties will be found as soon as the Jewish representatives are convinced that the opposite party takes their offer seriously.

(4) While awaiting the conclusion of a definite agreement, the representatives of the Jewish Agency at Istanbul propose to the opposite party the immediate conclusion of a provisional agreement containing the following clauses:

---

1. In *'Die Geschichte des Joël Brands* (p. 175 f) from which the text of the 'Provisional Agreement' is taken, Alex Weissberg declares that this is not a word for word reproduction of the original but rather a 'reconstitution' and I have had to be content with this since I do not possess the original text either.

(a) The deportations will immediately cease and in exchange for this there will be advanced to the opposite party the sum of one million Swiss francs monthly.

(b) Emigration to Israel will be permitted. A sum of four hundred thousand dollars will be paid for each convoy of a thousand persons designated through us.

(c) Emigration to countries overseas will also be authorized with transit through neutral countries such as, for example, Spain. One million dollars will be paid for each convoy of ten thousand persons.

(d) Authorization will be accorded for the despatch to ghettos and concentration camps of foodstuffs, clothing, shoes and medical supplies. In exchange the opposite party will retain for themselves 50% of the goods sent.

(5) While waiting for the conclusion of a definite agreement, in the sense mentioned in paragraph 2 of this minute, M. Joël Brand is authorized to carry on negotiations and to enter into engagements.

The Representative of the	The Authorized Representatives
Central Council of	of the Jewish Agency,
(signed) Joël Brand	(signed) Chaim Barlasz
	Echud Avriel
	Memachem Bader.

'The representatives of the Jewish Agency empower M. Joël Brand to inform his principals of the following facts:

In Schellenberg's Memoirs we read that Himmler had not himself tried to prevent the July 20 putsch although he had been told about it by the lawyer Langbehn. The fact is that he must have then thought Hitler's death a possibility. He had put the Gestapo in action to execute the 'retaliatory measures' of baleful memory only when he was sure that Stauffenberg's attempt had failed. It was only after Stauffenberg and the principal conspirators had been arrested by the Berlin Guard battalion under the command of Major Remer that Himmler decided to act. To crown all it may be noted that this battalion depended on the *Wehrmacht*, which was itself deeply implicated in the organization of the putsch. Himmler's informant Langbehn was, after the failed attempt, one of the first of the conspirators to be executed on the *Reichsführer*'s orders. Thus

Himmler removed the slightest suspicion which might have attached to himself. But if Stauffenberg's plot had been successful, Himmler would no doubt have tried with the aid of the Gestapo and his personal army (the SS monstrously enlarged) to carry the day. However, at the beginning of June, the SS *Reichsführer* could not foresee how the putsch would turn out. So Brand's return within the fixed delay with proposals for agreement – even fictitious – would certainly have encouraged Himmler to take an active part in the resistance himself. He would have felt sure, from that time, that he had through our intermediary, important contacts abroad. Such contacts were indispensable for his project of succeeding Hitler.

Since our provisional proposal had arrived after more than a month's delay, Himmler scarcely believed any more in the possibility of getting into contact with 'International Jewry' through us. If in spite of everything we were able to carry on negotiations with him, that was due only to the constant worsening of the military situation.

Happily for us our German interlocutors still did not know at the beginning of July that Brand had been arrested by the British in Syria.

This 'Provisional Agreement' was obviously nothing more than a sham, if we reflect on the real opportunities at the disposal of the Jews. The Jewish Agency had, indeed, promised money and foodstuffs, but the Allies had not yet made clear their point of view in the affair. They had decided neither for nor against. Nevertheless this proposal for an agreement was a first success for Clages; for the first time a document intended for the SS carried the signatures of high Jewish officials, men whose names he knew quite well. For Eichmann the question was quite a different one. Such a proposal did not arouse in him the same hopes as in his colleagues of the SD or in his supreme chief, the *Reichsführer* himself. Fortunately, Eichmann's attitude no longer had more than a relatively minor importance in this connection.

When the escapee from Moson-Magyaróvár told us the test-convoy was to be switched over to Auschwitz, Kastner hurried off to Eichmann's office and I went to see Clages. I did not find him but when I did see him a few days later, on July 8, I learned that Eichmann, on his own responsibility, had ordered the whole train to be sent to Bergen-Belsen where he intended to keep it until Joël Brand, whose arrival we were daily announcing, had actually returned.

Eichmann often waxed ironical about the SS themselves having helped Bandi Grosz and Brand to flee by air to a neutral country, and declared, said Clages, that these two were enough. He also told me that Eichmann meant to protect the *Reichsführer* against all attempts made by the Jews to swindle him. There could be no question of letting a whole convoy into a neutral country when the Jews had nothing to offer in exchange.

All the efforts I made after this were in vain. Clages got a reply from Himmler that, after all, Eichmann had acted rightly. Since Brand, in any case, would come back any day, the test-convoy could quite well remain at Bergen-Belsen during this short space of time. The first thing to do was to listen to what Brand had to say and to examine his report.

We had been beaten with our own weapons, for we had known for a good time past that Brand would never come back to Budapest.

12. Horthy, The 'Saviour' of the Jews

The numbers of Hitler's Hungarian admirers went on increasing during the first weeks of the occupation. The lightning operation which had allowed the Führer to grab the country without striking a blow was calculated to impose silence on those who were sceptical about the final victory of the Axis Powers – or at least to oblige them to keep their voices low.

The Regent, Nicholas Horthy, was satisfied with slavishly following the Führer's lead. Not only did he allow the former

Hungarian minister at Berlin, and Hitler's trusty follower, Döme Sztojay, to be imposed on him as prime minister, but he even accepted that a 'Commissariat for Jewish Affairs' in the ministry of the interior should be entrusted to two anti-semites of unsavoury reputation, Lászlo Baky and Lászlo Endre. For their new jobs the two men were promoted to Secretaries of State. They had long been known and feared for their violent antisemitic speeches. Henceforth these two confirmed alcoholics were to enjoy almost limitless powers – they were the equals of Eichmann. They took the opportunity offered by the promulgation of the anti-Jewish laws to intensify these by decrees totally contrary to the Hungarian Constitution. With the aid of the Hungarian gendarmerie – who were entirely at their disposal – they mercilessly applied all deportation measures. They made no exceptions, even in the case of those who had the reputation of being very close to Horthy, such as the big industrialist Goldberger who was the Regent's partner at cards. Horthy himself refused absolutely to do anything to alleviate the lot of the Hungarian Jews.

But as the weeks and months passed it became obvious that the reverses suffered by the Third Reich were not just temporary. Little by little the enthusiasm died down, even among Hitler's convinced partisans. After the German surrender at Stalingrad in February 1943, the Russian forces had advanced on all fronts. They already occupied the larger part of Rumania and had crossed the Carpathians. On June 6, 1944, the Allies landed in France. Hitler's authority and prestige continued to decline. The number of his detractors, which had considerably lessened after the occupation of Hungary, now once more increased.

On June 25 when the deportation of Hungarian Jews from the provinces was practically finished, articles were appearing in the Western press about Hungary. In these Horthy was rightly enough presented as the accomplice of the Nazis. Mgr. Angelo Rotta, the Papal nuncio handed the Regent a message from Pope Pius XII. The Holy Father took up, though in guarded language, a position against the deportations (cf. *The Kastner Report*, pp. 124 *et seq.* and p. 140).

On the next day, June 26, the American Secretary of State Cordell Hull presented to Horthy an ultimatum through the Swiss legation. He announced that the American government would take measures of reprisal against Hungary if the deportations were not stopped. Three weeks later Cordell Hull in a broadcast speech, confirmed these reprisal measures. As the United States was at war with Hungary such a step as this was more than unusual (see Nicholas Horthy, *Ein Leben für Ungarn*, Bonn, 1953, p. 272).

When, in their turn, King Gustavus V of Sweden and the chairman of the International Red Cross, Professor Karl Burckhardt, addressed notes of protest to Horthy, the Regent, who up to then had remained quite passive, was obliged to make a statement. Although as early as April 1944, the Jewish organizations had sent him detailed reports which left no doubt as to the object of the deportations and the fate of their victims, the Regent pretended to be astonished and declared he had learned the truth about the 'final solution' only from the protests received from abroad. After that, Horthy gave public expression to his disapproval of the anti-Jewish measures – especially in the presence of diplomats from neutral countries.

British interests in Budapest were entrusted to the Swiss legation which, therefore, also acted in affairs concerning Palestine, which was under British mandate. When the Swiss transmitted to the Hungarian government a proposal to authorize the departure of a convoy of Jewish emigrants (already in possession of immigration certificates for Palestine), Horthy had this proposal accepted by his minister of foreign affairs. The owners of such certificates would be considered British subjects before they left and consequently placed under the protection of the Swiss legation. The Swiss consul entrusted with the undertaking, M. Lutz, was much impressed by Horthy's goodwill and remained so despite the final failure of the enterprise.

Moshe Krausz, the head of the Palestinian Office who had taken refuge in the Swiss legation, worked with Lutz on the negotiations. He also had placed great hope in the Regent's change of attitude. But such hope was deceived since for the

Hungarian government the whole matter was simply a symbolic act. The convoy never was formed despite the support given the project later on by Ribbentrop, the German minister of foreign affairs, who referred to the oral permission he was supposed to have obtained from Hitler himself for the carrying out of the proposal.

Within the Waada Otto Komoly represented the tendency to seek our salvation through the Hungarians. He had carried on negotiations with certain members of the government and he thought his optimism justified. He had some influential non-Jewish Hungarians as friends – such as the Syndic of the Hungarian Reformed Church, Albert Berecky and Mester, the secretary of State in the Ministry of Cultural Affairs. Komoly clung desperately to a fiction, that of the autonomy and the sovereignty of the Hungarian government. He remained convinced that when all was said and done only recourse to Hungarian authorities would save the last surviving Jews of the country. My point of view was diametrically opposed to his. I considered that only direct negotiations with the Germans, through Clages, Becher and Himmler, would give results. From the beginning I was convinced that Horthy and his government were unscrupulous and as cowardly as the other Hungarian parliamentarians who from March 1944 had given clear indications of what could be expected of them.

At that time (and thus shortly before Horthy's visit to Hitler), these deputies had almost unanimously passed a vote of confidence in the then prime minister Kállay, who always protested he was not under German control. 'We must have the courage to remain Hungarians,' he had shouted amid the plaudits of an enthusiastic House. However, a little later on, after the country's occupation and the arrest of some Jewish deputies and other socialist or monarchist parliamentarians, this same chamber had voted unanimously its approval of Sztojay, the new prime minister imposed by the Germans. The words of Kállay were completely forgotten and he had to seek asylum in the Turkish embassy. Later events were to show still more clearly how justified was my point of view when in October 1944 Horthy was forced to resign and was replaced by Szálasi. Then this same parliament broke with the Regent and put its confidence in a man who was his mortal enemy.

So Komoly's hopes of an independent Hungarian policy were definitely dashed to the ground. But the hopes that Kastner had placed in the 'new conjuncture' were to have much more serious consequences for our activities. In reality Kastner shared my opinion, but he was sometimes weak enough to think that one day the Hungarian government would dare to break with the Axis Powers, as the Rumanians had done. Unfortunately the Hungarians never had enough courage.

During the month of June we had succeeded in securing the transfer of the Klausenburg refugees to Budapest and their later despatch to the Strasshof camp near Vienna. Thus we saved from certain death at Auschwitz the 18,000 people occupying the six-train convoy. But while I was negotiating with Clages for the departure of the test-convoy, it became clear that he (then our only means of contact with Himmler) was very suspicious of Kastner. Despite all the precautions of the German representatives and their obvious effort to keep the 'State Secret' from the Hungarian officials, the Budapest government got wind of our negotiations. Kastner's contacts with the Hungarian counter-espionage and his attempts to fan the flame of the latent Hungarian feelings of revolt against the Third Reich were not without relevance to Clages's changed attitude. For instance, Kastner was in close contact with Lt.-Col. Garzoly of the Hungarian counter-espionage. His double agents kept Clages fully informed about this 'friendship', and it irritated him. He was convinced it was the loophole through which the 'State Secret' was reaching the Hungarians. I tried all the time to calm Clages down, first by denying the contacts and then by minimizing their importance – but without much success. During these interviews, which mainly concerned the maintenance of the 'State secret', it appeared that Clages had two reasons for his efforts to forestall indiscretions possibly of advantage to the Hungarians. First of all he feared the demoralizing effect that would be produced on the Hungarian ally by the revelation of plans for saving what remained of the Jewish community by selling it for a good price to the Western Allies or to neutral states – this would mean that after the war the Jews would come back. Their return was feared by the Hungarian extremists since the property of those deported had for the most part passed into their hands.

On the other hand – and this I noticed only little by little – Clages did all he could to leave both the name and the intentions of his own chief, Himmler, in the dark so as to protect himself from the results of possible indiscretions (cf. p. 97).

As the Hungarian government and the Regent got wind of certain measures by Himmler which indicated a change of policy and the beginning of a moderate line regarding the 'Jewish Question', Horthy also began to preach moderation and to act as one opposed to the deportations. On June 26, when through the Swiss legation he had received Roosevelt's ultimatum threatening Hungary with reprisals and announcing air raids on Budapest, Horthy demanded of the German government that the deportations should be stopped.

One consequence of Horthy's *volte-face* was the conspiracy of Lt.-Col. Ferenczy who with Baky and Endre began to prepare a *coup d'état*. Besides Eichmann and Hunsche, who were informed of it and backed it up as much as they could, certain authorities in the German government at the highest level knew about Ferenczy's intentions of which they approved since they were beginning to find Horthy a nuisance.

It was a favourable time for a *coup d'état* since there were then almost no more German troops in Hungary, and the Germans were, for the most part, relieved from taking part. On the other hand, Horthy had on his side most of the Hungarian army which was still in the country since he had sent to the Ukrainian front, where the Germans were urgently in need of troops, only the Jewish labour battalions – in effect practically all the male Jewish population.

Under pretext of the imminent deportation of the Budapest Jews, the Hungarian gendarmerie was concentrated in the capital during the first week in July. In reality these dispositions were to lead to the overthrow of the Head of the State and his replacement with Eichmann's personal friend László Endre, secretary of State. When Horthy was informed at the last minute what was afoot, he ordered into Budapest some detachments of infantry and armoured cars. Relying on these, he ordered the gendarmerie to leave the capital immediately. He also asked the German government to recall Eichmann at once. The same day and on the Regent's orders (it was July 8, 1944, the date when the test-convoy Eichmann had diverted arrived at Bergen-Belsen) Baky and Endre were dismissed from most of the posts they held in connection with the Hungarian government's Jewish policy.

This sudden change in the situation was hailed unanimously among the Jews as an event of happy augury for the future, but the news that filtered through filled me with an intense anxiety shared to a great extent by Rezsö, though he never admitted as much openly.

In view of the doubts I have already expressed as to Horthy's strength of character and steadfastness I was sure the Regent would give way as soon as the German government or Hitler again took up an energetic stance. Horthy took as the immediate pretext for his resistance the Jewish policy of the Nazis, though up to then he had hardly taken any interest in it. His change of front would benefit the survivors of the Hungarian, and therefore European, Jewish community, only if he remained firm in his new attitude. If he did not, then the whole affair would surely end in a catastrophe for the Jews.

Since the Hungarian government had taken away their extensive powers from Baky and Endre the gendarmerie could hardly take any further part in the deportations, and the Germans, having no troops available to overthrow him, dealt gently with Horthy. But the Jews who were made responsible for Horthy's ever more obvious defection were soon to feel the unleashed fury of the Gestapo.

First of all Eichmann decided to deport the Jews shut up in the Kistarcsa camp. There were about 1450 of them and on July 14, 1944 Eichmann had them sent off to Auschwitz. The local authorities and units of the Hungarian gendarmerie assisted the Germans as before and without paying any attention to Horthy's orders.

The Council of Budapest Jews was informed by telephone what was happening and at once told Horthy, who in the meantime had resumed his contact with outstanding Jewish notables. The Regent, extremely annoyed by the disobedience of certain Hungarian departments, had the convoy stopped by his troops before it reached the frontier and brought back to Kistarcsa. The Jews, however, were not liberated since the Regent obviously had not enough courage to take more radical measures. His new-found friendship for the Jews did not go as far as liberating them.

Now Eichmann could counter-attack. Inspired (as far as I know) by the advice of Otto Hunsche, his aide-de-camp and legal expert, Eichmann managed to get hold of these Jews again and this time sent them off without difficulty to Auschwitz.

While the Council of Budapest Jews celebrated with satisfaction and joy the first apparent success obtained by Horthy's will to resist, and the news of the Gestapo's first evident defeat spread quickly, Eichmann was preparing another convoy. A few days later, on July 19, all members of the Council of Budapest Jews were summoned to the Bureau of Jewish Affairs where they were received by Otto Hunsche who showed himself particularly affable and stated that he had plenty of outstanding affairs to discuss with them. The interview lasted several hours. These people, who had been abruptly summoned in the morning, were not permitted to leave the room for an instant the whole afternoon. It was only towards evening that they were allowed to go – after Hunsche had received a mysterious telephone call.

When they got home the members of the Jewish Council learned that the 1450 prisoners in the Kistarcsa camp had in the meanwhile been deported in trucks and that the convoy had already passed the Austrian frontier. The Waada (where I, in the absence of Kastner, was the only one to defend the policy of 'direct contacts with the Germans') had not even been informed by the Jewish Council who thought themselves sure of Horthy's support.

The effects of Horthy's new policy were then felt on the Waada's line. Himmler obviously did not want any stopping of deportations to lower the prestige of departments depending on him, and was not prepared to leave to the Hungarian Regent credit for a more moderate Jewish policy. Once again he gave Eichmann a free hand, as the Kistarcsa affair clearly showed. Any credit from abroad for stopping the deportations had to accrue to Himmler so that he could later hope for some acknowledgement from the Allies.

This is why, for a time, we lost control of events and Kastner, whom I had never yet seen weep, told me on July 17, with tears in his eyes, that all was now lost. Eichmann had just informed him that the passengers in the test-convoy then at Bergen-Belsen would in a week be transferred to Auschwitz and 'put through the mill' without any previous selection being made, if Joël Brand did not come back to Budapest by that time. Kastner and I knew only too well that Eichmann had the habit of keeping *that* sort of promise. Now the convoy was lost. It seemed as though our opponents in the Jewish camp had been right in predicting the failure of our undertaking. Now it was we who had got the train off from Budapest and who in addition had paid the assassins.

The news affected us all the more because we had been able of late, to count some partial successes. Not only had Becher taken the place of Eichmann in the negotiations, but I had also been lucky enough to induce *Hauptsturmführer* Grüson to adopt a generous attitude. The evaluation of the ransom was not yet complete but it amounted to considerably more than we had expected. That meant that with the sums realized we could pay the price of other convoys in addition to that of the deportees at Bergen-Belsen.

As soon as his interview with Eichmann was over, Kastner got into touch with Becher and begged him ask Himmler to thwart Eichmann's plans. Becher refused. In view of the *Reichsführer*'s great nervousness since the recent events in Hungary, and since Joël Brand as well as the payments from abroad were still awaited, Becher did not think the moment was propitious for irritating Himmler.

In the evening of that ill fated day, my wife, Rezsö Kastner, some other of my 'guests' and I got back after an absence of some hours to Semsey Andor utca. As we crossed the threshold my wife whispered to me that she had seen some suspicious individuals who, according to all appearances, had been waiting for us. She had been struck with the rapidity the people had disappeared into a side street as soon as we arrived. When we had got into our apartment what my wife had said induced me to go down to the portress and ask her whether anything had happened while we had been away. As soon as I got to her she appeared flurried and told me that several policemen in civilian clothes had asked for me and Kastner and that they insisted on knowing what our 'activities' were.

Then the bell rang. The portress showed me into her room and quickly nipped out into the hall to see who had come in. I heard muffled voices, but I could make out that she was being sharply told to go up to my apartment and fetch Dr. Kastner. A few minutes after she came back to me and whispered she had been told to go into her room, but that Kastner was now talking to the two men in the dim corridor. As they were speaking in low tones we could catch nothing until Kastner suddenly burst out: 'Help, help, murder, murder.' The words echoed through the silent house. Then we heard the confused noise of a scuffle. The portress clung to me and begged me not to show myself as they would kill me also. I shook myself free of her, wrenched the door open and ran to Kastner's assistance.

Two burly men in civilian clothes were dragging him by the arms to the front door trying to stop him yelling. Kastner fought back as best he could but he was of slender build and had no chance of shaking free of the two giants. As I flung myself on them in order to free my friend, three other men, just as hefty as the first two, appeared in the hall. They pulled me away from Kastner whom I had got hold of, twisted my arms and hustled both of us towards the empty street now plunged in complete darkness. In front of the house was a powerful car. Kastner who tried in vain to cling to the door was the first to be hoisted into the automobile. Then I managed to get free. I ran a few paces, then stopped and called for help. But Budapest had by then become a city of terror. No one even dared to open a window much less come out into the street. Then my pursuers suddenly abandoned me, turned round, ran to the car, jumped in and shot off at once. The number of the car – it was stamped on my memory – was not registered with the Budapest police as Clages soon found out.

The car vanished. Then all the windows suddenly flew open and the portress came out. As I had no interest in giving too much publicity to the incident, I went back to my apartment and found my wife and friends terror struck. From the brutal way Kastner had been kidnapped we must not hope to see him again alive. Now I alone must assume the task of attempting to save what I could in a catastrophic situation, since Kastner and I alone had up to then carried on the talks with the Germans. Otto Komoly was less inclined than ever to take an active part in the negotiations. During the preceding few weeks he had come to hope more strongly than ever that the stoppage of the deportations could be obtained through the Hungarians and especially through the Regent himself.

13. The Explanatory Note

It was not until July 19, 1944 that I was able to see Clages in his HQ at Schwabenberg. I told him of Eichmann's threat to send the Bergen-Belsen train to Auschwitz in a week's time. I begged him to persuade Himmler to oppose this plan. Since Becher had refused Kastner's request to interfere in this business, it seemed to me that it was only through Clages that I might achieve my object.

Furthermore, Clages knew that Kastner had been kid-napped by unknown persons. If we had a chance of seeing our friend once more alive it would only be because Clages sought him out in order to keep the 'State Secret'.

Before I went to Schwabenberg I called at the Majestic Hotel, the offices of the Bureau of Jewish Affairs, but I was not able to see either Eichmann or his personal representative, Hunsche. From this I gathered that Eichmann's staff considered they had said their last word about the test-convoy and that they were not disposed to any further discussion. What, however, was unusual was that I had not even been able to speak to Hunsche, who never let slip any opportunity of pressing me with questions as to whether we had received any fresh news from abroad regarding our activities.

I was not to guess that it was just that day the Council of the Budapest Jews was meeting in Hunsche's office to discuss 'current affairs' with him. It was only much later I learned that Eichmann and his assistant responsible for the transportations, Nowack, were at Kistarcsa to supervise the deportation – definite this time – of the 1450 Jews whom Horthy had had brought back to the camp.

In Clages's office the atmosphere seemed favourable for my purposes. It was the day before Count Stauffenberg's attempt on Hitler's life, and on looking back today, one might be inclined to think there was 'a certain something in the air'. Clages received me, but was obviously nervous and in a bad temper. But as each hour was precious for us, I had no right to let pass a single day without some action, and therefore I explained to him what Kastner had told me about his interview with Eichmann two days before. I also mentioned that Becher was very reticent and would not undertake to approach Himmler anew because of the *Reichsführer*'s present state of irritation. For this reason, I said, I was appealing to him, Clages, for Himmler *must* be informed of this affair. It was a matter not only of the fate of the people in the test-convoy, but also of the 'State Secret', and of the possible success of all that enterprise. Our friends and principals abroad would at once break off all negotiations if the Bergen-Belsen train were sent to Auschwitz.

Clages roundly refused my request. As I went on insisting

he became more friendly and finally advised me to write a memorandum without mentioning either the addressee or the address and especially not his name or that of his office. He would undertake to see that this memorandum was sent by air to Himmler. Since all our negotiations, he added, had hitherto been carried on orally, the different reports which then existed – those of the Gestapo, of the Bureau of Jewish Affairs, of his own office and of the SS central office for equipment – had given Himmler only a 'somewhat blurred' and contradictory picture of the situation and of our declarations. In this way only might there be a chance of re-kindling Himmler's dampened confidence. Clages made a short note of the second reason for my visit – Kastner's recent kidnapping. Then I was dismissed.

The task facing me was no easy one. Kastner and I in our distress had more than once promised miracles, and these constant changes in our promises – adapted to each situation – were not in accordance with the slender reality of our payments and our possibilities.

However, in the memorandum I could allow myself to mention points and advance arguments which had no doubt never been transmitted by his subordinates to Himmler, even though I had made allusion to them, very openly, during our interviews. For instance I had made plain reference to the annihilation of the deported Jews. Under the Third Reich this matter (with that schizophrenia characteristic of the Nazis) was kept a great 'State Secret' and was always officially and indignantly denied. Furthermore, I now had an opportunity to give an explanation of Brand's absence and to present the problem of his return as something of minor importance.

Before I went home I called at Becher's office where I discussed the whole matter with Grüson. This *Hauptsturmführer* was then replacing his chief who had, I knew, left for a few days travelling.

The next day was July 20 and I again went to see Clages. I had with me the rough copy of the 'Explanatory Note' which I had drawn up during the night. For psychological reasons I thought it better first to ask Clages's advice. Again, and this was much more important, I wanted to act in this grave affair absolutely in agreement with him. Our conversation was interrupted by an SS *Scharführer* who handed Clages a paper that was obviously a message by teleprinter. After having glanced through it, Clages usually so calm, leapt up, whistled through his teeth, and ran off to the office of his aide-de-camp. He came back after a couple of minutes and asked me to return in two or three days time. As an important event has just taken place; we must break off our interview.

A little later, I heard over the radio what had so upset Clages – it was Stauffenberg's attempted assassination of Hitler and the abortive putsch of July 20, 1944 conspirators.

On July 22 I handed over to Clages the 'Explanatory Note' in its final version, as follows:

Budapest, 22nd July 1944

EXPLANATORY NOTE

Following on an interview today with SS. *Hauptsturmführer* Grüson we define our requests on the following points with the motives indicated below:

(1) We ask most urgently that the complete train which left the privileged camps of Budapest on 20th June should be sent on to the Spanish frontier. The passengers in this convoy are now at Bergen-Belsen, near Hanover, and it is extremely important that they should all pass into a foreign country at the same time that your representative and ours arrive. Thus will be established the psychological conditions necessary for a rapid and favourable conclusion of the negotiations.

(2) We beg you to fix a date for the journey to Lisbon so that we can inform our friends at Lisbon, Madrid and Istanbul whose telegrams reached us yesterday and which we have presented today. At the same time we ask your assistance in obtaining the passports and visas necessary for our representative at these negotiations.

(3) We should like, if possible to send to Lisbon Dr. Kastner R. as delegate, but we need your powerful assistance in order to discover his whereabouts since about three days ago he was forcibly carried off by individuals who wish to hamper or to wreck our accords, it would seem, and we do not know where he is. But

obviously the disappearance of Dr. Kastner must not hold up for a single day the course of the negotiations, therefore, should it be necessary, we reserve the right to name another delegate in his place.

(4) As we have many times repeated a very important preliminary condition for a favourable conclusion at Lisbon is, in our opinion, that the deportation of Jews from Hungary should cease until the emigration of those who remain, organized with our collaboration, takes the place of the deportations when the agreement is concluded.

(5) Here is an opportunity to recall our very first request – which we have continued to repeat in the most urgent manner, namely that the Jews already deported from Hungary should be saved from extermination. Indeed, on the one hand, the persons fit for work represent a real asset itself, while, on the other hand, person, not fit for work will be the first to be exchanged in accordance with our agreement. This category includes children of less than 12 years of age, old men, and mothers not fit for work. Even if this group entails, for a certain lapse of time unproductive expenses, it represents nevertheless a potential economic asset which could be utilized in a very short time.

We are, moreover, prepared to aid, on a greater scale, in the feeding of these deported Jews with supplies bought in Hungary and we will, should occasion arise, take care of their other needs. On this point we would again mention that during our last negotiations with SS *Obersturmhannführer* Becher and Eichmann not only was the economic value of this solution agreed upon but it was also recognized that the counterpart payable by us – and especially the trucks – would result in an economy of German blood. Thanks to us you would spare, indirectly, German lives in exchange for Jews not even fit for work. The wastage of Jewish substance at present in your hands, whether for ideological reasons or because of possible utilization would be a mistake, according to us, a mistake which might cost the German people itself dear.

The arguments in support of the five points indicated above are the following:

(1) The first special train which is, so to speak, the prelude to a large scale politico-economic transaction, was constituted on the basis of our preliminary discussions and with the authorization of your highest officials. In commercial terms the matter is a despatch of samples that one sends to a customer before the forwarding of a

larger stock. The figure of about 1600 men out of a total number of some 6 to 700,000 does not amount, in any case, to more than a very small sample. In principle the total amount payable in exchange must be delivered in raw materials, in manufactured goods and above all in trucks. Despite the extremely serious politico-military obstacles which hamper the carrying out of this plan (especially in the Anglo-Saxon camp) our friends abroad have managed to obtain an agreement in principle from the adverse party. This is based on information from our representative Brand. You have the proof of this in the positive telegrams that have been laid before you. As far as the quotas per head which are to be paid for the emigrants in dollars or goods we have as yet concluded nothing definite with you. *Your* own evaluations were indeed not concordant. While on the one side SS *Obersturmbannführer* Eichmann had spoken on one occasion of a hundred Jewish lives for one truck, on another side a minimum was mentioned of a price between $1000 and $1200 and this of course exceeds the financial possibilities of our friends who nevertheless are prepared to make the heaviest sacrifices. The news we get from Lisbon indicates that there one could obtain a price of from $300 to $400 a head. We repeat we would exchange first of all the children under twelve years of age, mothers and older men unfit for work, while the others could continue with their tasks in Germany until their turn comes.

Although a definite agreement regarding the quota per head, had not been concluded, at the departure of the first train it had been agreed that we would collect with our own resources, a sum in raw materials, in money and in other valuables, that would cover about the highest demands you made during the negotiations. However this contribution was to be reckoned, when the whole transaction is concluded, as covering a number of emigrants at the rate finally agreed upon per head, at Lisbon.

However, we have, up to now paid about $1,100,000 in foreign exchange, gold, diamonds and Hungarian currency. The value of the goods already delivered or being now delivered amounts, as we can prove to about $800,000 according to the list communicated. It is then a total of some $1,900,000 which had already been paid or which is on the point of being paid. Several million pengoes which Joël Brand paid over earlier are not counted in this total but they will be taken into account with you after Joël Brand's return.

When the first train left, we informed our friends abroad that it would arrive in a neutral country before your delegates and ours got to Lisbon, since, according to the above account, even on the basis of the inacceptable demand of $1200 a head, we have got together, by our own means, the price of about 1600 persons. This sum, however, taken in connection with the whole transaction must represent enough to cover a number of men three or four times greater. But for the moment it represents a guarantee for the first convoy until the conclusion at Lisbon of a complete agreement. We have then announced this abroad on the strength of the assurances you have given us and since your highest authorities have given their approval.

Now that the train has left and we have come to the question of payments, we are informed that the convoy has first of all been held up near Hanover and that it will not continue on its way to Spain until the conclusion of the agreement at Lisbon and until the delivery of the trucks begins. This new demand on your part would have an unfavourable influence on the conclusion of an agreement at Lisbon. It would indeed perhaps imperil the whole business. The moral credit of our information regarding the agreements made with you, which has already been doubted on several occasions, could become completely destroyed.

Our foreign friends have several times called us Utopian – and not without cause – since the various informations we have received concerning the deportation of Jews from Hungary, again, regarding the treatment and the protection of the deportees until the conclusion of our negotiations, have been rapidly proved to be false. Now, on the strength of your assurances and of the consent given by your highest authorities, we have begun to proceed to payments in goods and money. Now we await from you a generous acknowledgement which should be the promised despatch of the first convoy to Spain.

Our friends abroad who will take part with you in the transaction consider this despatch as quite natural. A check to our hopes in this matter would for obvious psychological reasons, prevent, on the other hand, an accord and would render impossible the opening of the credits indispensable for the transaction. Today we are fighting against a degree of scepticism among our own friends and financial backers abroad. We would lose at once the first round in this fight to gain their confidence, if our reports on the continuation of the journey of the 'samples' were not confirmed despite our payments.

We have been informed that the prolonged absence of Joël Brand would have an unfavourable influence on the final stage of the convoy near Hanover. We have already often pointed out that this delay is due to passport and visa difficulties for which neither J. Brand nor myself is responsible. Furthermore, at the time of the despatch of this first convoy, the question of the return of Brand (who had already outstayed the time fixed for his visit to Turkey) had not been taken into account. In no case was it ever maintained, when we began to make our payments in kind that the despatch of the first convoy linked with the immediate return of Joël Brand.

We would like to stress, once again, that all of us of the Hungarian Jewish community – whether in part already deported to Germany or still resident in Hungary – remain in your power. We are, consequently hostages who guarantee the observance of the engagements entered into. The delivery abroad of the first convoy amounting to about 1600 persons would have not any noticeable effect on the numbers who remain – from 600,000 to 800,000 – but it can however be enough to bring the whole transaction to a successful conclusion. But delay in sending the convoy might be enough to cause insurmountable obstacles to arise.

(2) As is proved by the telegrams mentioned, my friends Schwartz and Dobkin are, as from today, in Lisbon and a meeting with them can lead to immediate agreements. We should make use of this opportunity as soon as possible since we should have to lose much time later on, in order to reassemble such decisive factors.

Dipl. Ing. Andre Biss. (signed)

As regards the telegrams mentioned in paragraph two, the reference is to communications we had received from Istanbul. According to these messages, the director of the American Joint Distribution Committee for Europe, Joe Schwartz, and the chief of the emigration department of the Jewish Agency for Palestine, then Elijahu Dobkin, were ready to meet Becher and negotiate with him. It was also stated in the telegrams that Joël Brand would take part in such meetings.

My allusion to Kastner in paragraph three was expressed in a particularly 'pressing' way since I hoped I should thus get the search stepped up to find him.

My remarks about the high sums in dollars which we

alleged we had already paid over, and about the value of the goods delivered, could be questioned since they were based on unilateral estimates accepted by Grüson in the name of the adverse party, but which Becher had not yet definitely ratified. As a matter of fact, the objects in question had a real value that was only a fraction of the sum I indicated. Likewise, the 'goods being delivered' never reached their destination – with the exception of a few compensatory deliveries of relatively small value which I had to effect later on since they were absolutely necessary to get the test-convoy on its way.

When I handed this 'Explanatory Note' to Clages he assured me that the Bergen-Belsen train was perfectly safe and that I had nothing more to fear from Eichmann's threats.

As the delay fixed by Eichmann was to expire in two days, this important assurance reached us at the eleventh hour so to speak.

14. News from England

According to the German official account the uprising had drawn the people still closer to their Führer, whom Providence had miraculously saved once more from death. This 'miracle' clearly showed that Destiny would ensure the final victory of the Germans.

In reality the situation worsened daily. The Russians were rapidly advancing on the eastern front, and it was becoming evident that in the West the British and Americans, who had already occupied Brittany and Normandy, were not going to be held up.

On July 19 the BBC, and on the 20th *The Times* of London, had made public an article on the mission of the Jewish emissaries in Istanbul declaring categorically that neither the

British government nor the Western Allies would deliver 10,000 trucks or any other war material to save from extermination those Hungarian Jews who had not yet been deported and whose numbers were estimated to be between 400,000 and 450,000.

The Times article which threatened to put us in a desperate position with the Germans, ran as follows:

A MONSTROUS 'OFFER'

German Blackmail

BARTERING JEWS FOR MUNITIONS

It has long been clear that, faced with the certainty of defeat, the German authorities would intensify all their efforts to blackmail, deceive, and split the allies. In their latest effort, made known in London yesterday, they have reached a new level of fantasy and self-deception. They have put forward, or sponsored, an offer to exchange the remaining Hungarian Jews for munitions of war – which, they said, would not be used on the Western front.

The whole story is one of the most loathsome of the war. It begins with a process of deliberate extirpation and ends, to date, with attempted blackmail. The background is only too well known. As soon as the German army occupied Hungary in March of this year, anti-Jewish measures were applied with a brutality known, until then, only in Poland. At the end of last month 400,000 of the 750,000 Jews in Hungary had been 'liquidated' – which means that the younger ones had been put into labour camps, where they work under conditions of appalling harshness and the older ones were sent to the lethal camps in Poland. After reports had come that more than 100,000 had already been done to death in the gas chambers which are known to be there, both Mr. Eden and Mr. Cordell Hull expressed the horror of the civilized world and promised punishment for the guilty.

A short time ago a prominent Hungarian Jew and a German official, whose job obviously was to control his actions and movements, arrived in Turkey and managed to get a message passed to British officials. The Hungarian Jew said he had 'every reason to suppose' that the German authorities were prepared to spare the lives of the remaining 350,000 Jews in Hungary, and even let them leave for abroad, if the British would send Germany important war stocks, including 10,000 army lorries. These stocks, he said, would not be used on the Western front.

THE ONLY ANSWER

Such were the terms of the offer as reported to London. The British Government know what value to set on any German or German-sponsored offer. They know that there can be no security for the Jews or the other oppressed people of Europe until victory is won. The allies are fighting to achieve that security; and they know, as well as the Germans, what happens when one begins paying black-mail. The blackmailer increases his price. Such considerations provided their own answer to the proposed bargain.

Whether the German authorities seriously believed that Britain would heed the offer cannot be known at this stage. Probably even before making it they had decided for one reason or another – perhaps for transport difficulties – to drop the deportations to Poland; yesterday, in fact, the International Red Cross announced that the Hungarian Government had agreed to put a stop to the deportations and even allow some Jews to leave. In the light of that announcement (which will be judged by events) the German 'offer' seems to be simply a fantastic attempt to sow suspicion among the allies.

Fantastic though it was, London made sure that Moscow and Washington were quickly in possession of all the facts.

So the Allies refused 'to yield to blackmail'. They were not even ready to negotiate. We were full of bitterness at the lack of political instinct displayed by the broadcasting of such news; it was clear that London thought all we had to do was wait patiently for the arrival of the Allied troops in Budapest, whereas at the rate of 10,000 people exterminated each day there would not be a single Jew left alive at the end of the war.

Luckily Himmler seemed disposed to resume negotiations. I explained to Clages that the radio comments and *The Times* article were necessary to reassure the Russians, who refused any sort of negotiation, even if the lives of millions of innocent people were at stake. This justification was not illogical since the Germans had given an anti-Soviet character to the pro-posed operation by declaring explicitly that the famous trucks would be used only on the eastern front. The Germans also knew that Stalin was extremely irritated[1] by the long delay in the Normandy landings. So my explanation might seem quite plausible. In any case, Clages listened with interest and soon we noted that, despite the news from England, Himmler did not appear to have changed his mind.

On July 26 Clages informed me that my memorandum had been favourably received in Berlin and that Himmler had ordered the deportations from Hungary stopped once more. Clages furthermore assured me that Eichmann had been forbidden to take any steps regarding the convoy at Bergen-Belsen. As for his journey to Switzerland, that would be decided in the next few days when Himmler had discussed the matter with Becher.

A MYSTERIOUS ARREST

It was already nine days since Kastner had disappeared and he was still hidden from the SD. Clages's statements indicated that his department had discovered no trace of Kastner in spite of all the efforts made. In the morning of July 26 Becher telephoned my house. He had to discuss an urgent matter with one of us. If Kastner had not reappeared 'before the next day' I was myself to go to his office.

I did not have to keep this engagement for on July 27 Kastner suddenly reappeared when our hope of ever seeing him again had lessened by a day. He replied with confused and mysterious remarks to our questions as to who had carried him off, where he had been so long and how he had been liberated.

It was only later on we learned the truth. Kastner had been arrested by the men of Ferenczy, the gendarmerie Lt.-Colonel who managed the deportations on the Hungarian side. He wanted to learn more about his German allies' negotiations with the Zionists. To win over Ferenczy to Horthy, then 'inclined to swap horses', Kastner had told the colonel about

1. Ribbentrop had tried to take advantage of this irritation in order to secure a separate peace and Stalin had not failed to brandish this menace so as to put pressure on the Allies.

the 'State Secret'. He had said that the handing over of the Jews in exchange for ransoms was explained because the Germans had for long known they had lost the war and wanted to save their skins. As this affair would surely be concluded (here Kastner had purposely exaggerated), the Hungarians would alone incur heavy responsibility if they persisted in their uncompromising attitude. They would have to pay for it one day. Ferenczy, indeed, soon afterwards did move over into Horthy's camp, though he remained there only until the failure of the Regent's attempt at a putsch.

As Clages had said to me several times that he wanted to talk to Kastner as soon as he got back and in any case before he visited the Bureau of Jewish Affairs or Becher, we went to Schwabenberg on the morning of July 27. Clages received us at once and asked Kastner where he had been so long. Kastner replied briefly that he had been held by unknown Hungarian authorities. Clages, in an irritated tone unusual with him, demanded more precise explanations. All the Hungarian authorities to whom he had applied had answered they knew nothing at all about the matter. Kastner insisted he could not say who had arrested him nor where he had been kept for the ten days. He said that his eyes had been at once blindfolded in the car and he had no doubt been taken out of Budapest since the drive had taken more than an hour. He had also been blindfolded for the return journey and it was only shortly before reaching Budapest that the bandage had been taken off and he was left alone in the middle of the road. He did not know where he had been detained. Clages remained calm though obviously annoyed. He then asked Kastner what information he had given the Hungarians, since in any case they must have cross-questioned him. Kastner replied he had been asked what we were doing. He said the Hungarians particularly wanted to know why and at whose instigation Brand had gone away in May. According to Kastner, however, he told Clages no more than had been revealed by the British press and radio. There was nothing more to be got out of Kastner, and Clages dismissed him. Kastner hurried off mentioning that he was going at once to Becher. I was relieved and beginning to breathe again when Clages asked me, 'What do you think of that story?' To calm him I answered that Kastner had certainly told the truth since he had no interest in betraying our cause.

Clages snapped back, 'Well, your cousin M. Brand was not at all of your opinion.'

15. The Evacuation of the Test-Convoy

THE FIRST INTERVIEW AT SANKT MARGRETHEN

Directly after he left Clages' office, Kastner called on Kurt Becher. When he got back he informed us that Himmler had summoned Becher to Berlin in connection with our affair. Becher, who only ten days before had such a non-committal attitude towards Kastner, now gave us to understand he had received information from Berlin that a favourable outcome to our enterprise might be hoped for. But he had not been able to indicate the real reason for this happy change in Himmler's attitude.

On August 2, 1944, Becher got back with good news from Berlin. Himmler had agreed first of all to let 500 persons from the test-convoy into Switzerland, and to permit the 1200 or so others to pass as soon as Becher and the American Joint Distribution Committee had concluded a firm agreement about the payment of the 'exchange fee', even if it was only partly paid abroad. Furthermore, by that date the estimation of our valuables, made by Grüson and me, must be complete and definite, and the deliveries from within the country promised in addition must be effective and reckoned at their value.

The decision to continue negotiations not at Istanbul but in Switzerland had been preceded by numerous telegrams in which we had asked our friends to change the meeting-place from Turkey to another country more easily accessible. Chaim Barlasz, the chief of the Istanbul Waada, had finally informed us that Dr. Joseph J. Schwartz, the director of the American Joint Distribution Committee for Europe, and Elijahu Dobkin, managing member of the Jewish Agency who were then both at Lisbon, were ready to negotiate there with representatives of the adverse party. A telegram sent to Schwartz at Lisbon had got us a reply confirming again, in his own name, that he was at our disposal. This exchange of telegrams had visibly raised the hopes of our German opponents and had confirmed in their eyes our position as plenipotentiaries and representatives of the 'International Jewish Power'.

Although we asked ourselves, with some anxiety, how we could fulfil the conditions laid down by Himmler regarding the second convoy, we were happy enough to have succeeded in making its departure depend no longer on Joël Brand's return to Budapest. Becher himself seemed satisfied with the provisional results of the negotiations which he had conducted courageously and without troubling himself about the risks he was running.

It was once more the Bureau of Jewish Affairs that had to carry out Himmler's orders. As usual, Eichmann – obviously little impressed by the decisions of the *Reichsführer* – dragged things out although Kastner spent his time at the Bureau of Jewish Affairs where he urged Eichmann to take the necessary measures. On August 10 I applied once more to Clages and asked him to complain to Himmler that Eichmann was clearly indulging in passive resistance.

At last we reached our goal. Eichmann's second-in-command, *Obersturmbannführer* Krumey, left for Bergen-Belsen to supervise the departure of the train. Kastner had already agreed with Eichmann that the first transport should be organized on the spot by the Jewish leaders of the group, and we had at once asked them to make a fair selection by taking into account the various categories of passengers. When Kastner had asked outright whether there was any objection to members of his own family leaving by the first train, Eichmann had said 'no' and even promised to give Krumey orders to this effect.

On August 21, 1944, the convoy arrived at the frontier post of Sankt Margrethen. There it was taken in charge by Saly Mayer, the Swiss banker who, as chairman of the Swiss section of the American Joint Distribution Committee, had been assigned to take care of the group of passengers and to negotiate at once with Becher.

The Swiss government had been helpful in granting entry-visas and, later on, adopted a friendly attitude towards our activities. Joseph J. Schwartz and Elijahu Dobkin, citizens of a belligerent Allied Power, had not been able to engage in discussions in Lisbon as had been arranged, and so had delegated their powers to Saly Mayer.

On the German side the negotiators were Kurt Becher and Max Grüson. Becher was also accompanied by Dr. Billitz, manager of the Manfred Weiss concern, thanks to whom we had got in touch with Becher. Kastner, as representative of our Waada, had left for Sankt Margrethen where he was to meet Saly Mayer.

Our first great disappointment was the news that the convoy consisted, not of 500 persons, but only of 318. Later, Eichmann justified a smaller number than that agreed upon, by alleging 'lack of means of transport'. Though he had trains enough to deport from 10,000 to 15,000 Jews to Auschwitz every day, he pretended he could not find enough rolling-stock for another 200 persons in the convoy even with almost three weeks in which to make preparations.

As we learned afterwards, he had sent Krumey to Bergen-Belsen with orders to send only 300 persons to Switzerland and *not* to let them be chosen by the Jewish leaders of the group. Furthermore, on Eichmann's express orders, Krumey had excluded from the convoy both Kastner's relations and the family of Joël Brand. All this was personal vengeance on Eichmann's part since he had been forced to execute orders which ran counter to his own plans. Finally, however, Krumey, without reference to Eichmann, had allowed eighteen extra persons to leave.

Our second great disappointment was the attitude of the

Swiss Jewish representative. It was without many illusions that Kastner started for the Swiss frontier, and at the Budapest Waada we all knew we could hardly count on large sums from abroad. But we had hoped that our desperate situation would have at least induced Becher's Swiss interlocutors to make offers, and possibly even false promises, and that they would thus create a foundation for continued conversations, for as long as the negotiations dragged on we should gain precious time

It is not Saly Mayer's fault that he did not prove equal to this task. He was a Swiss banker, an honest man, perfectly upright and whose word given over the telephone was as good as his signature on a cheque. He neither wished nor was able to bluff or to make offers he knew he had not the authority to honour. He did not understand that, in such desperate circumstances as ours, hundreds of thousands of lives could be saved by empty promises and vague engagements; nor did he see that the fate of the last Jews in occupied Europe depended on him – the honourable and pacific citizen of a neutral country.

As we look back, we must admit that the real tragedy was this: influential Jews in the Western countries were concerned to remain loyal to the Allies, to participate in the boycotting and destruction of the Third Reich and had too soon judged that we, the last survivors, were lost. Without any doubt the negotiations should have been entrusted to a younger man than Saly Mayer, one endowed with sharper wits and more able to adapt himself to the situation. Another negotiator – even if he also had come with empty hands – would probably have dared to go beyond the strict letter of his instructions in order to help us gain time. Rendering us this inestimable service would have, moreover, harmed no one. I am thinking of a man who played, a little later on, an important part in this story, Boswell D. McClelland, President Roosevelt's personal representative who, in just as difficult a position, showed admirable initiative and thus saved the lives of numberless people.

The first conversations between Saly Mayer on the one

side and Becher with Grüson on the other took a very un-
promising turn. As the Swiss customs officials would not
allow the German delegates to cross the frontier and as Saly
Mayer refused Becher's invitation to follow him to the German
frontier post, the meeting took place on the small Sankt
Margrethen bridge on the actual demarcation line between
Austria and Switzerland. The first surprise for Becher was
that Saly Mayer presented himself not as a delegate of 'International Jewry' but as the representative of Jewish humanitarian organizations. Neither would he agree that he was sent
by the American Joint Distribution Committee. Saly Mayer,
sincerely shocked being the moralist he was, and without
realizing that the situation hardly lent itself to such statements – branded as infamous, the Nazi policy towards the
Jews and especially the massacres in the gas chambers,
demanding they be stopped. He would not hear of delivery of
goods. Finally he did admit that ransom might be considered
one day but only after the slaughter had ceased and when all
the members of the test-convoy still at Bergen-Belsen had
arrived in Switzerland.

Such a beginning left Becher of course disappointed, since
we had assured him that the western countries were ready to
make enormous sacrifices in order to save the five hundred
thousand or even a million persecuted persons, and this
sacrifice would represent a very considerable sum. Owing to
this promise Becher had been able to get permission from
Himmler to carry on with the negotiations and to meet Saly
Mayer on the Swiss frontier.

And now he learned from Saly Mayer himself that what we
had dangled before his eyes at Budapest, in the name of 'the
Jewish World Power', was only a lot of vain promises –
an expression of the despair of thousands doomed to extermination.

He violently upbraided Kastner, since he had the impression
we had lured him into a trap, and he saw only one way out –
to explain to Himmler we had fooled him. That might have
unforeseeable consequences for him.

During long discussions Kastner and Billitz tried to hold

him back from taking such a disastrous course for us. Finally they persuaded him not to forward at once an entirely negative report to Himmler.

As Saly Mayer had, all the same, asked Becher to fix another date so he could consult his 'principals' in the meantime, a second meeting was arranged for a week later. In referring to these remarks, Kastner and Billitz endeavoured all the same to present the Swiss banker as the delegate of the American Joint Distribution Committee. According to them Saly Mayer had not been permitted, at the request of the Americans, to admit this, however, his 'principals' were nevertheless the 'American Joint'.

16. Himmler Asks for Proof

As soon as Kastner got back we both went to see Eichmann and to protest that only 318 persons, instead of the 500 promised, had arrived at Sankt Margrethen. Eichmann justified himself, as we have seen, by claiming there was 'a lack of means of transport'. And he added sarcastically that it was now up to us and our friends abroad to pay over the ransom for these 318 first persons very quickly. Then would come the turn of the 1400 other members of the convoy while later on, other transfers might take place. Personally, he did not believe that the *Reichsführer* would get anything at all through us and these 'convoys', but he would see.

The first interview at Sankt Margrethen had greatly weakened our position, but we kept up our visits to the competent authorities. Kastner went to see Becher while I, as I had done for weeks, called at the Hotel Mirabel to visit Clages. It is true that Becher had promised to inform Himmler about Eichmann's behaviour, but he thought that, in view of Saly Mayer's meagre offers, it was much more important for us, at the moment, to get some positive results in Switzerland than to quibble about the number of passengers in the convoy and still less to mention the possibility of sending a second convoy

Clages, for his part, did not take into consideration our complaints about Eichmann, for in his opinion the Germans had already shown their good will by letting the 318 persons go. I pointed out to him that this number was far too small to make an impression abroad and to induce our foreign friends to take positive action. To my objection he replied that if we rapidly gave material proof in support of our promises, then Eichmann might allow those waiting at Bergen-Belsen to depart – then all the Jews who still remained in Hungary, and even other deportees detained in concentration camps.

I then asked him if it would not be possible to put Eichmann on one side or to remove him since he had deliberately disobeyed an order of the *Reichsführer*. This question elicited a very detailed answer. Despite the comparatively subordinate position occupied by Eichmann his transfer to another post would not be as easy as I imagined. Eichmann was the outstanding representative of a policy not only approved of by Hitler but considered by him as dogma. His replacement would provoke a great deal of comment and Hitler could not fail to hear about it. As our foreign friends had hitherto given no serious proof of their good will, the *Reichsführer* did not really see any valid reason for justifying such a measure. That Eichmann had sent off to Switzerland only 318 Jews instead of 500 was not a sufficiently grave shortcoming for one to be able to speak of 'ignoring an order' or even of 'refusal to obey an order'.

Clages finished by insisting once more that tangible results were urgently necessary, all the more since the interview between Becher and Mayer had produced nothing apt to satisfy the *Reichsführer*. Furthermore, such proofs were necessary to confirm that we, Kastner and I, were really delegated by the Jewish Agency (the International Jewish Congress) and the 'American Joint'. They alone could efface the memory of 'Joël Brand's defection'.

I then understood clearly what Clages meant and realized that I must not, at any price reveal what I knew of the little influence we had in Washington.

As a matter of fact we were not in the slightest degree the authorized agents of the American organizations as we had claimed; still less were we delegated by Roosevelt who was not at the time aware of our existence. A delegate of the American government would, moreover, never have been authorized, either through intermediaries or still less directly of course, to get into contact with important personages in the Third Reich.

I could not admit that our promises – the only and last recourse of a people condemned to death – had no guarantor outside our frontiers, nor could I reveal the fact that the great majority of our foreign friends frankly disapproved of our desperate attempt and of the contacts we had established with Himmler. Neither could I confess that the few telegrams we had received had been sent by individuals and with the sole intention of bluffing an adversary. Nor could I tell Clages that Becher, in his moderately worded report about his interview with Saly Mayer, had dressed up the truth about the real situation, which was that the Jews in the Allied countries refused categorically to make any deliveries to the Third Reich even if the Germans promised in exchange to put an end both to deportations and massacres.

This interview clearly had made me see that we must, at any cost, get some expression of opinion from our foreign friends. But I was also convinced that this first successful convoy would not suffice to stir up the western countries, nor to give us the symbolic or token help we needed to gain time. Several days had already passed since the arrival of the train. We did not yet know of the great sensation this event had caused in Switzerland, and especially in the USA, for no news had reached us on the subject.

That is why I drew up a second memorandum – addressed this time to Saly Mayer. We had learned then that a second interview between Becher and Mayer had been fixed for September 1, 1944, and that Kastner would again be present.

To make Mayer understand the conditions on which Himmler had consented to the formation of the first convoy I enclosed for his information a copy of my explanatory note dated July 22. While calling to his attention certain arguments or certain expressions in my explanatory note which were used in view of our enemies' mentality (and which should not be taken literally), I begged him earnestly to drop as soon as possible the uncompromising attitude he had adopted as a matter of principle. A few small advances would have practically no influence upon the course of the war, but would be sufficient to strengthen our position at Budapest, would give us the appearance of serious negotiators, and would at least allow the rest of the Bergen-Belsen convoy and the 18,000 persons of the Strasshof group to get abroad. I also proposed to Mayer that he should conclude a sort of contract with Becher, since this form of agreement was more suited to the mentality of our 'partners'. This would be a surer means of tying them down than verbal agreements, always liable to be called in question by Himmler or Eichmann.

Such a contract, specifying 'fixed deliveries' on both sides, could be drawn in such a way as to deal tactfully with Himmler's illusions. It would put an end to the massacres and would slowly get the 'affair' going without really costing millions since the end of the war could not be far off. Although the ransom collected by us in Hungary had been liberally over estimated (especially since my balance included considerable quantities of goods stated to be 'in process of being delivered'), I did not think that these comparatively modest sums would be enough to guarantee the passage abroad of the rest of the test-convoy and of the Strasshof group. But I hoped that the arrival in a neutral country of several thousand deportees would arouse general attention enough to allow us to continue our action until the end of the war.

On August 30 Kastner left Budapest. He took with him my memorandum which he was to hand to Saly Mayer. For security reasons I employed different codewords which seem to me today, more than twenty years afterwards, very transparent. In any case my prudence was unnecessary since the memorandum reached its addressee without hindrance.

My proposals to Saly Mayer were adopted as the basis of a projected contract with Himmler, but my requests for payments to be made remained, at first, without effect.

Several days later in Budapest we got some information which in part allayed my fears. The arrival in Switzerland of the first deportees' convoys aroused in the free world a considerable amount of notice, and this quasi-official liberation had made a deep impression.[1]

The President of the United States himself heard of the circumstances in which the Budapest Waada had induced Himmler to make this gesture, and we got from him later on moral support we greatly needed to achieve our aim – a stop to the extermination of the Jews.

It is now more than twenty years that Franklin Delano Roosevelt passed away and many of the acts of that man have been forgotten. I sincerely believe, however, that the assistance he, in his time, afforded us will not be forgotten for it was one of his noblest actions, though no one – and that is understandable enough – knew anything about it at the time. It is thanks to him in great measure, that finally success crowned the efforts to save what remained of the Jewish people condemned to death by an inhuman system.

The second meeting on the Swiss frontier took place on September 1, 1944, and it was even more of a failure than the first one. This time Saly Mayer was accompanied by a Swiss lawyer named Wyler. Becher had seen fit to be represented by his aide-de-camp Max Grüson and by Dr. Billitz while he himself remained at Bregenz. The Budapest Waada was represented by Dr. Kastner at this meeting. Naturally Saly Mayer came with empty hands and, what was worse, did not understand that in the circumstances one had to bluff that the fate of thousands of people depended on him and the attitude he took. To the great satisfaction of Saly Mayer, Dr. Wyler

1. The German ministry of foreign affairs, and probably Walter Schellenberg's counter-espionage organization, learned only then the real significance of our secret negotiations with Himmler's representatives.

allowed himself to condemn Nazi policy in general and especially the measures taken against the Jews. After that he said nothing more.

After having held up the conversations for two days in order to ask for fresh instructions, Saly Mayer came back to the frontier. His mission was 'not to say no'. As Kastner was anxious to know if we could, at last, hope for a definite answer, Dr. Wyler replied in the same Sybilline fashion. It was *Hauptsturmführer* Grüson – himself sincerely disappointed – who described to me later on the attitude of the Jewish negotiators who, covered by Swiss neutrality, did not understand what was happening on the other side of the Sankt Margrethen bridge. As I have already said, I had in the meantime, thoroughly won Grüson over to our cause. The fact that it was Becher's aide-de-camp who was doing all he could to extract a conditional 'yes' from Saly Mayer[1] shows how complex the situation was in which we were struggling. It would scarcely have been possible for the representative of the adverse party to have made his attitude plainer. He was alone and expressed himself without any ambiguity in the presence of four Jews, Saly Mayer, Dr. Wyler, Billitz and Kastner.

And yet Billitz, Kastner and he had to return empty-handed to Bregenz where Becher was waiting for them. Things being what they were, the latter judged it was useless to go back to the Swiss frontier and returned to Budapest where he awaited a definite reply from Saly Mayer.

If he got it, he declared he was ready for another meeting, but on condition that he got a Swiss entry visa, as he was not disposed to negotiate once again under such precarious conditions – walking up and down the Sankt Margrethen bridge.

1. While remarking to Saly Mayer that high authorities in New York and Washington would always have the possibility of refusing after the event, and that in the meanwhile 'many things could happen in the world'.

17. The Events of September 1944

In September 1944, while relations in Hungary became increasingly strained between the Lakatos government and the German authorities, and things were relatively quiet for the Jews,[1] there was drama in Slovakia. The approach of the Red Army had encouraged the population to revolt behind the German lines. To the intense fury of the Führer, the *Wehrmacht* command in Slovakia had to engage some of its precious divisions to crush the uprising. The information Hitler got about the events indicated that Jews had stirred up the population and that they were the main authors of attacks on German officers and their families.[2]

There was a certain amount of truth in these reports, since the insurgents had occupied some camps where several thousand Jews were incarcerated and these naturally joined their liberators in the struggle against the enemy. This news surprised Hitler who thought that Slovakia had been 'cleansed of its Jews' two years before. It was then obvious that Himmler could hide from his Führer a matter of such importance.

Hitler learned then that, at the request of the Slovak chief of State, Himmler had interrupted the deportations in 1942. The Slovak leader, Mgr. Tiso, was a Catholic priest and had been informed by the Vatican of what actually befell the Jews and their families deported eastwards, allegedly for forced labour. In virtue of an agreement concluded with the Germans at the beginning of the deportations, Mgr. Tiso had at once requested that Slovak inspectors should be allowed to visit the deportees. Obviously no satisfaction was given to this demand, since most of the deportees were already dead, but

1. Relatively calm since Himmler had stopped the deportations as from July and Eichmann had been recalled.
2. Vide Gerald Reitlinger *Die Endlösung* (The Final Solution), Munich, 1964, p. 35.

Himmler had, all the same, thought it advisable to hold up further deportations that had been prepared. The policy of the Third Reich was then to use Slovakia as a counter-balance to the Czech lands hostile to the Germans. Therefore the Slovaks had been allowed a certain appearance of sovereignty not possessed by the 'Protectorate of Bohemia and Moravia'.

In response to the uprising and as a measure of reprisal, Hitler himself, in the Autumn of 1944, gave orders that the remaining Slovak Jews – 30,000 to 35,000 persons – should be deported without delay, despite the possible protests of the Tiso government.

At Budapest we knew nothing about the real reasons for this drama, but we suddenly got alarming news from the spokesmen for Jewish Slovaks, Gizi Fleischmann and Dr. Neumann. The upshot of this was that new deportations were being prepared. On September 14 *Hauptsturmführer* Grüson, whom we had asked to get information, left with Kastner for Bratislava. The chief of the local Gestapo, SS Lieutenant Witezka, who depended on Eichmann's organization, said nothing to Grüson about what was afoot. With an exaggerated confidence in the ransom system the Slovakian Jews discussed with Grüson the establishment of a local service at Bratislava depending on the SS equipment section as a counterpoise to Eichmann's staff. Grüson and Kastner went back a little later to Bratislava, but they noted only that preparations for deportations were more and more evident. After the failure of the first two trips to the Swiss frontier, Becher had become very prudent. It is true he had not revealed to Himmler the real root of the matter, but he did not dare to submit new requests to the *Reichsführer* so long as the contacts in Switzerland did not bring about tangible results. Thus the plan for founding in Slovakia a local branch of Becher's office was given up, for on September 26 we got a telegram from Saly Mayer accepting conditionally the proposals in my memorandum.

But in the meantime another very alarming piece of news reached us from Slovakia. The liberty of movement of Jewish committee members had already been curtailed and we were urgently implored for help. Becher who, up till then, had tolerated, without protest, Grüson's trips with Kastner, thought it better not to take too many risks in regard to Eichmann. So he forbade Grüson to interfere in the Slovak affair. However, I managed to persuade Grüson to go with me secretly to Slovakia to do something on the spot to save the Slovakian Jews. With us in Hungary, deportations had stopped for the time being since at the end of August Himmler had recalled Eichmann and his staff. Grüson, for whom nothing seemed impossible, furnished me with false papers and we set off for Bratislava.

In the meantime SS *Obersturmführer* Brunner had been appointed there, in place of Lieutenant Witezka, to manage the Bureau of Jewish Affairs. As Gizi Fleischmann and Dr. Neumann had informed us, Brunner had obviously received orders to finish off the deportations. Grüson went to see Brunner and asked him for explanations – but without Becher's orders or authorization. Grüson pointed out that secret negotiations were taking place at Budapest, negotiations regarding the delivery of strategic material, and that the Jews of Slovakia could also play an important part in the exchange of men for goods . . . in saying this Grüson betrayed a 'state secret' about which he should have spoken to no one, not even to members of other departments ss. Brunner gave a flat refusal to Grüson's various requests for a mitigation of the restrictions imposed on the Jews, nor did he seem disposed to give any information. He pointed out that he took his orders from his chief Eichmann from the central Security Office of the Reich in Berlin and, in a curt tone, he refused to listen any longer to what SS Captain Grüson had to say.

From this interview Grüson came back very downcast. He proposed to Gizi Fleischmann to come with us to Budapest and advised the Slovakian Jews to hide. That was all he could now do for them. Gizi Fleischmann refused to put herself in safety and remained at her post. Before we left for Budapest she gave me a letter for Kastner in which she made him final offers of ransom to be proposed to the Germans. The letter began with these words 'By a miracle our friends Biss and

Max' (Max Grüson) 'arrived to see us today . . . ' This was our last meeting with Gizi Fleischmann, who was deported and murdered shortly afterwards, as were most of those she had tried to save at the cost of her own life.

We still did not know what was taking place behind the scenes. We had learned only that in those parts of Slovakia where the partisans had liberated several thousand Jews, cruel reprisals were being perpetrated.

The day after our return to Budapest, Grüson's driver turned up unexpectedly at our house in the early morning and informed me that 'they had come to fetch' his chief, to take him to the Gestapo HQ in Berlin. Grüson had been able to say a few words to his chauffeur and ask him to tell me at once what had happened. He asked me if I were questioned about him not to say anything about circumstances where he had too obviously favoured us. Brunner, after his interview with Grüson at Bratislava had immediately telephoned a report to the main office of the Reich Central Security. Hence Grüson's arrest only a few hours after we got back from Bratislava.

I then thought my own arrest was only hours away and began to wonder if the time had not come for me to go into hiding. However, together with Kastner I had by words and deeds so thoroughly entered into my role as official delegate of the great Jewish Power that my disappearance would cause the collapse of all the credit we had with the SS services opposed to Eichmann and therefore with Himmler himself.

During the afternoon I had a telephone call from the SS equipment section. Would I please go at once to see Becher? He received me alone. He was visibly ill at ease and more anxious than usual. But he did not say a word about our clandestine excursion to Bratislava. He just told me that Grüson had suddenly been appointed to another post; then he added he could not accept the programme he had before him – that which Grüson and I had drawn up together a few days previously. It contained an absolutely grotesque balance or estimation of the sum in valuables put at our disposal by the Waada to guarantee the departure of the 1700 members of

136

the test-convoy. These valuables came very largely from the 300 persons of the test-train who had been able voluntarily to pay sums, in certain cases quite considerable, to which were added my own more modest deliveries of goods. Grüson and I, it will be remembered, had estimated the value of this account with a generosity that would have appeared suspect to the least unwary.

Certainly Becher had no intention of accepting these figures, but I managed, without too much difficulty, to overcome the loss of Grüson and maintain my 'diplomatic immunity' as delegate of 'world Jewry'.

Grüson's tasks were assigned to *Obersturmführer* Grabau who looked after the coffers of the SS equipment section and was to take official charge of our account. Grabau evidently did not have the same attitude towards us as Grüson, especially as he knew the real reason for the disappearance of his predecessor, and was aware of his sympathies for our activities. It was impossible to find out what had happened to Grüson, though we had every reason to suppose, at the time, that the Gestapo had liquidated him 'in the greatest secrecy' which would hardly encourage his successor to follow his example.

If we had proceeded to make a new estimate – taking into account this time the real values – the total would not have amounted to more than 400,000 to 500,000 dollars in all, and would probably even have come to less than that. At best the sum would hardly have sufficed to secure the liberation of 500 persons. What I wanted to do most of all was to collect an amount sufficient to secure that the rest of test-convoy, still at Bergen-Belsen, should be sent abroad. We did not know then the great importance Himmler attached to payments in kind and we were not sure that political and personal motives alone dictated his conduct.

To get the Bergen-Belsen train abroad complete we had to produce a sum of $1,700,000 – on condition that Grabau accepted. I managed, however, not without some difficulty, to induce him to admit this assessment and then to get him to sign another protocol. The estimates Grüson and I had made gave at first a total sum of $3,500,000 which would have been enough to ransom 3500 persons. As Grabau had no initiative and did not seem inclined to take personal responsibility, I did not think I was mistaken in supposing that Becher had at least encouraged him to be conciliatory. It was important for him also that the train should reach its destination, since he hoped that there would thereby be a radical change in and a softening of the attitude of our foreign friends.

After these events we thought that our efforts to save the Slovakian Jews and to prevent a new wave of deportations from Slovakia had become almost hopeless. Kastner, however, continued to press Becher to intervene in favour of Gizi Fleischmann and her companions in distress though without any success for Becher was still not disposed to get mixed up in an affair which seemed to him very obscure indeed, and even to transcend Himmler's sphere of influence.

Clages also refused to do anything at all and added that if a definite reply was not received soon from Saly Mayer, the stoppage of the Hungarian deportations might be reconsidered.

We know that on September 1, 1944, Kastner and Grüson had decided in agreement with Wyler and Saly Mayer that the latter would telegraph his 'yes' as soon as he obtained the authorization of his principals. This telegram reached us on September 26, 1944. Kastner showed it the same day to Becher and I to Clages. It was a 'yes' on certain conditions that were not absolutely clear. It was, however, astonishing to see with what relief, with what joy, even, Clages and Becher welcomed this telegram. They promised to communicate its contents to Himmler immediately. Thereupon it was decided there should be a third meeting on the Swiss frontier. Forty-eight hours later Kastner left Budapest in company with Kettliz, a member of the SS equipment section. Although Kettliz belonged to the moderate group of the economists, we could hardly expect him to take risks for us or be ready to bluff with us. But the mere fact that this journey had been decided on so rapidly induced Kettliz to take his mission seriously.

On September 26, 1944, Clages had confidentially proposed

to me that I should go to the Swiss frontier in the place of Kastner. He was aware of the open disagreement between Kastner and Mayer, and that made him uneasy. According to Clages the reason for this mutual antipathy was that Kastner had not inspired enough confidence in Saly Mayer, who had not known how to handle him properly. It was clear that Clages was saddling Mayer with his own doubts. Naturally I refused the suggestion. It is easy to understand that I could say nothing about the real cause of the divergencies between Kastner and Mayer. However, I assured Clages that Kastner, the vice-chairman of the Hungarian Zionist Union, was a personality internationally known, and that for this reason, even if he behaved tactlessly with Saly Mayer, he would have more weight than myself – a Zionist of recent date. If I were to go to Switzerland instead of Kastner, and maybe against his will, Jewish communities would be prepared to think I was a docile tool of Himmler. Kastner, an elected representative, ran no risk of such suspicions. Clages accepted my arguments and Becher knew nothing of the proposal made to me. And I refrained from informing Kastner, since he was very jealous of the good relations I maintained with Clages, our most important link with Himmler.

The third meeting on the Swiss frontier revealed first of all a new and very clumsy manoeuvre on the part of our foreign friends to keep the negotiations dragging along. The peak of tactlessness was reached when Saly Mayer observed he would not yield an inch to blackmail. However, discussion then began on a subject which, as a matter of fact, had not much to do with the demand for trucks and goods originally put forward by Himmler. The proposition was as follows: the 'Joint' would pay first of all 20 million Swiss francs in cash of which 5 million was to be handed over immediately and the balance paid in three drafts at monthly intervals.

In exchange our adversaries would offer (a) the immediate cessation of deportations from Slovakia (b) the definite end to deportations from Hungary (the stoppage had been up to then only provisional) (c) authorization for the rest of the Bergen-Belsen convoy (about 1450 persons) to leave. This, at least, was how the proposals were drawn up by Kastner.[1]

Negotiations were then taking place on a purely commercial basis, even if there was no longer any question of trucks or war material, and although the sums to get operations started were considerably lower than those we had at first foreseen or promised. The point (a) was at once revealed as impossible even before negotiations got under way. In Slovakia deportations had started up on a new scale and a great number of the Jews referred to in point (a) were no longer alive. As we have seen it was Hitler himself who had ordered the sinister convoys to begin again. Eichmann and his henchmen had lost no time and the deportations were not delayed.

Gizi Fleischmann was arrested, put in chains, and carried off under special guard by the SS. She was then murdered at Auschwitz. Despite several pleas, backed by Becher, made to Eichmann's organization, she could not be saved. Eichmann justified Gizi Fleischmann's deportation on the pretence that she was the author of calumnious reports on the Third Reich, reports she had sent abroad by any means possible.

Kastner, during the third meeting at the frontier, received confirmation that the arrival of the first group in the test-convoy had made a great impression among many sections of the public in the West, especially in the United States, and that the definite telegram sent by Saly Mayer on September 26 could be considered as a first consequence of this event.[2]

I noted, furthermore, that the suggestions in my memorandum adopted later on quite clearly by him and Grüson – namely that it was necessary to make small sacrifices and big promises – had finally met with a favourable reception. Although he did not take positive engagements, Saly Mayer did hint at some new perspectives which the German negotiators welcomed with manifest satisfaction.

At this meeting we learned that a personal representative of the American President had certainly been sent to Switzerland. He was Mr. Roswell D. McClelland, one of the leaders of the

1. Vide, *Rapport Kastner*, p. 187.
2. The whole American press was full of reports on the event.

Quaker body in America. He had been appointed a special delegate of the War Refugee Board. He was to take part in our negotiations and use his government's influence, so it was said, to unfreeze the first slice amounting to 20 million Swiss francs. In the middle of a war an American charitable organization could obviously not promise such sums without the approval of Washington, even if the payments were to be fictitious and there was no intention of effecting real settlements.

Clages obviously thought this news extraordinarily important, as I was able to note during a conversation that took place on the morning of September 30. At first we ourselves thought that too much attention should not be paid to the allusion Saly Mayer had made to McClelland's mission. But this affair which had then appeared to us of minor importance was, nevertheless, to mark a decisive turning-point – and one providential for us – in the course of the negotiations.

As early as the evening of September 30, 1944, Clages informed me, in a second interview, that he had had a long telephone conversation with the *Reichsführer*. As soon as he had heard the verbal report on our preceding conversation, Himmler had told him that he would confirm that very day the order to interrupt the 'actions' in the camps. (The term *Vergasungen* – 'gassings', I remember precisely was not employed in the course of this conversation. Furthermore, Clages had never used it in my presence. The gas-chambers where millions of persons perished remained a 'State Secret' until the end of the war).

Clages advised me several times to forward Himmler's agreement to our Swiss and American friends at once. He laid particular stress upon the importance of this news, which I treated with a certain amount of scepticism, as did Kastner with whom I discussed the matter late that evening. Each day the situation in Hungary came closer and closer to a dramatic outcome and each one of us (I in my private thoughts) began to hope that a putsch, as had occurred in Rumania, would free the country from occupation and force the German lines back to the Austrian frontier. The Hungarian plan to leave the Axis camp was well known and seemed quite feasible, especially if the Rumanian precedent was taken into account and in view of the catastrophic crumbling of the fronts both to the west and the east.

In the following days, however, we went on discussing with Becher the arrangements for the Bergen-Belsen train. In a quite routine way we talked always about money and deliveries, and we cudgelled our heads as to how to get together the necessary means or how to boost the value of what we already had so that the rest of the Bergen-Belsen test-train could continue on its way to Switzerland before our liberation by the Russian troops. Becher exchanged telegrams with Himmler, who was playing tough and who, even with Becher, pretended to be first of all interested in the commercial aspect of the affair. I pressed Clages to ask Himmler to allow the second part of the train to leave Bergen-Belsen for Switzerland without any more taking into account the possible return of Joël Brand to Hungary.

Clages wanted to know if we had communicated to Switzerland the news about the interruptions of the 'actions' in the camps since September 30. I said 'yes' which was not true. Kastner, on whom depended our contacts abroad, was then very active with the Hungarian authorities, urging them as strongly as he could to leave the Axis camp. These efforts seemed to him much more important than sending to Switzerland an optimistic report about supposed measures of mitigation taken by Himmler.

To keep Clages in a friendly mood – he still had to do something to encourage the departure of the train – I told him we had received a message telling us that an American delegate, no doubt McClelland, would be present at the next meeting on the Swiss frontier. I had hit the bull's eye far more accurately than I had hoped. Two or three days later, on October 11 or 12, Clages informed me that Himmler had already given orders for the rest of the test-convoy to be sent to Switzerland at the time of the next meeting on the frontier, without taking into account either Brand's return or the first payments to come from Switzerland. These were the preliminary conditions of which Himmler – and especially Eichmann – had hitherto emphatically demanded fulfilment. All at once the valuables we had already handed over, after the successive estimations of Grüson and Grabau, seemed sufficient.

This decisive interview was the last I ever had with Clages.

18. Three 'Couriers' from Palestine

Here I should like to commemorate three heroes, two of whom gave their lives for our common cause. They were Perez Goldstein, Joël Nussbecher[1] and the Israeli national heroine, Hannah Szenes. By origin all three were Transylvanians. They had served with the British brigade in Palestine and in the spring of 1944 were parachuted by British planes into that part of Yugoslavia controlled by Tito's partisans. Their mission was to reach Hungary and there organize and direct the Jewish resistance, the Haganah.

As early as January 1944, a young lawyer of Ujvidék, our friend Dr. Moshe Schweiger, was appointed head of the Hungarian Haganah. Just before the war he had published an article in which he expressed regret that no one had been found to 'settle accounts' with Hitler. It seems probable that Schweiger, who was of a pacific nature and therefore by no means fitted for the task, owed his nomination as head of the Haganah mostly to this aggressive statement. Such a statement was, of course, regarded as a capital crime and the young lawyer's name was one of the first on the Gestapo's black list. When Hungary was occupied on March 19, 1944, Schweiger was immediately arrested and deported to the Mauthausen camp.

So it was that Hannah Szenes, Joël Nussbecher and Perez Goldstein had to take his place.

1. Nussbecher, the sole survivor, bears today the name of Joël Palgi and is a member of the Israeli diplomatic service.

Hannah Szenes, who had started off before the others, was arrested as she was crossing the Hungarian frontier. Her rucksack contained among other things a small transmitter and this left no doubt in the minds of the Hungarian counter-espionage agents that she was a British spy. We were unaware that she was shut up in the Budapest military prison. But although she was subjected to endless interrogations, she refused to give the names and addresses of those she was to have visited in Budapest – the Zionist leaders of the Waada. Perez Goldstein and Joël Nussbecher knew nothing of Hannah Szenes's arrest when, a little later, they in turn got to the frontier.

The guide who had also piloted Hannah Szenes was a Hungarian agent. Although the counter-espionage knew of their arrival, they were not arrested but kept under observation. In this way it was hoped to discover their correspondents. One trail led to a Budapest boarding-house which was one of Kastner's hiding-places and where he sometimes received visitors. The other trail led to the seat of the Budapest Jewish community where Goldstein and Nussbecher first made contact with the leaders of the Jewish organizations. A short time after that, Kastner learned that some persons, obviously members of the Hungarian police, had obtained information about him at the boarding-house. Furthermore, Goldstein and Nussbecher noticed they were being followed. Thereupon Kastner decided on a bold step: he introduced the two young men to Clages, in the German Security, where Mrs. Brand passed them off as our messengers arrived from abroad (from Istanbul in fact) who in the manner of diplomatic couriers were bringing us messages. I was not informed about all this since at the time – the beginning of my activity as liaison officer with Clages – I was still considered a 'young Zionist and it was not desirable to initiate me into the internal affairs of the Zionist movement. But Mrs. Brand was especially suitable for introducing the two 'couriers' to Clages, as he showed her a certain amount of respect since her arrest by the Hungarian police some time before. (See p. 58).

After the war Kastner was often blamed for this step but unjustifiably, since in Clages's eyes the Waada had no connection with the Jewish council set up on Eichmann's orders. For Clages the Waada was an important correspondent and one he dealt with on equal terms. Our behaviour then was such as suited our role. The fact that we possessed our own couriers could only impress Clages, just as he was impressed by all we told him about our contacts abroad with the international organizations whose delegates we pretended to be. Clages promised the two young men his entire support and assured them he would have them released should the Hungarian police arrest them. But Kastner made a miscalculation. He relied on the contacts he kept with the Hungarian counter-espionage to get it to call off the shadowing of Goldstein and Nussbecher. There is no doubt that Clages learned through his agents in the Hungarian counter-espionage that Goldstein and Nussbecher were wanted as British spies and that Kastner, in view of his approach to the Hungarians, was playing both sides at once.

Furthermore at that time Kastner himself knew nothing about Hannah Szenes's mission, since Goldstein and Nussbecher had received orders to speak to no one about their comrades' parallel activities so as not to endanger them. The two young men still believed that Hannah Szenes would sooner or later turn up at our Budapest address, looking for us. Kastner's efforts with the Hungarian counter-espionage were fruitless. Nussbecher was discovered by Hungarian agents although he had done his best to cover up his tracks. In June 1944 he was arrested. On June 28 we hid Goldstein in our Columbusgasse 'protected' camp where the passengers for the test-convoy were awaiting their departure. Among these were also his own parents who belonged to the Klausenburg group. Although he might have joined the convoy Goldstein stayed on in Budapest because his mission was so important. He hoped the Hungarian counter-espionage had finally lost trace of him.

In chapter XII I have told how Kastner, Mrs. Brand, my wife and I were arrested during the night following the departure of the test-train and how we were detained in the barracks of the Hungarian counter-espionage until the afternoon of the next day. When we were released (Kastner and Mrs. Brand had been separated from us and interrogated apart) Kastner still told me nothing about the two 'couriers'. As I was then entirely absorbed in my task – to induce Clages to let the test-train leave – I questioned Kastner no longer, since in view of his behaviour I was sure the matter was one of secondary importance. Much later, I learned that Goldstein had left the Columbusgasse camp soon after an interview with Kastner and that he had voluntarily surrendered himself to the Hungarian counter-espionage, so as not to endanger our rescue action, and firmly hoped that Kastner would get him out.

Before this incident I could not understand the efforts of my friends in entering into personal contact with couriers arriving from Palestine. This was evidently part of the party's policy, for after the departure of Brand, who was particularly active in this respect, my friends Kastner and Mrs. Brand always dealt personally with the couriers whom they treated with jealous care. I never had any desire to be let into these secrets, since I had no political ambitions in the Zionist movement. I considered my only duty was to obtain maximum results by exploiting the belief of our German adversaries in the existence of a world-wide Jewish power. In comparison with my task – the departure of the test-convoy abroad, the stoppage of the deportations, and as far as was possible, the rescue of the deportees still alive – the activities of the couriers seemed to me secondary, even if it had an importance from the Zionist point of view.

For Kastner the problem was a different one. Without compromising our rescue work, he was his aggressive temperament and his Zionist convictions urged him to support Goldstein and Nussbecher, who were to organize the armed resistance, the *Haganah*. He thus lost an immense amount of time and was led to incur grave risks himself. One needed to know personally the senseless hopes most of the Jews had cherished concerning a reversal of Hungarian policy toward the Axis, to understand the reasons why Kastner made the destiny of these two young men depend to such an extent upon Hungarian policy. He had known them at Klausenburg when they were members of the Jewish youth movement he ran – the Habonim. He acted then in all good faith and with the best intentions in the world – like a military chief who moves his troops into the positions he judges are most favourable. He was to be bitterly deceived as were all those who put their trust in Hungarians or Horthy

On Saturday October 14, 1944, he was still negotiating in the presence of the delegate of the C.I.C.R. (the International Red Cross Committee), Dr. Olah, the secretary of the Hungarian Minister of War and the chiefs of the Hungarian counter-espionage, Colonel Hatz and Lt. Colonel Garzoly. The following day not only the two young men but also Hannah Szenes were to be liberated – for Kastner had in the meantime heard of her presence in Budapest. But between these there was a memorable Sunday, October 15, when Horthy tried to follow the Rumanian example and through his own fault was unsuccessful. The Hungarians Kastner had been negotiating with the day before had known all about the imminent putsch and counted on its success. Kastner, who had sensed something in the air, was full of optimism, but the catastrophe that crashed down upon us all prevented the liberation of the three Palestinians.

Hannah Szenes was condemned to death and was executed by the Arrow Cross as soon as they seized power. She died heroically and will go down into Jewish history as a great legendary figure. The other two were deported. Perez Goldstein never came back; Joël Nussbecher managed to flee.

19. The Arrow Cross in Command

On October 15, 1944, at eleven o'clock in the morning, the radio broadcast Horthy's proclamation to the Hungarian people and to the world at large which announced that Hungary was ready to capitulate. Indeed, the Third Reich was not disposed to defend Hungary and would have used it as a battle-ground for the retreat of the German troops, condemning the country uselessly to destruction. Horthy had the impudence to add that the Hungarian nation had been forced by the Germans to persecute the Jews.

A wave of enthusiasm at once elated the Budapest Jews as well as the little group of our non-Jewish friends. Kastner and I exchanged perturbed looks. So optimistic of late, he had not expected such forthright language – it gave the impression of a measure dictated by despair. The situation seemed to us obscure and we feared the worst – which happened.

The illusion lasted just two hours. Over the same Hungarian radio came a quick disavowal of Horthy's discourse. The wireless station had in the meantime been occupied. A so-called proclamation of the chief of the army general staff was read ordering Hungarian troops fighting on the front (which was now not far from Budapest) to remain where they were and carry on the struggle. In the evening at eight o'clock we learned that the Arrow Cross Party under Ferenc Szálasi had seized power.

Who was this Ferenc Szálasi?

The new Hungarian chief of State was a former professional soldier, a captain who had left the service to found a Hungarian national-socialist party. He was a fanatical admirer of Hitler and his aim was to carry Hungary along with Germany to final victory. Those who knew him – and particularly his superiors – had always regarded Szálasi as crazy or at least weak-minded. His party was composed of riff-raff together with a few bourgeois opportunists.

In March 1944, when the German troops entered Hungary, Hitler had maintained the Regent Horthy though he did not seem reliable – there were some indications that he was doubtful about the final victory of the Germans. But Hitler had a certain respect for the old man. Former aide-de-camp of the Emperor Francis-Joseph, Horthy was one who was clever in employing all the resources of old-fashioned diplomacy in

148

order to win over those he needed and maintain himself in power. On the other hand the Nazis had nothing but contempt for the Arrow Cross party, despite its resemblance to their own. They had little use for Szálasi and his friends, who called themselves the 'Hungarian National Socialist Party'.

During all my meetings from May to October 1944, the German negotiators with whom I had business – including Eichmann – expressed nothing but contempt for this Arrow Cross party. What the Third Reich needed in Hungary was a partner able to carry on with the war and, from the administrative point of view, keep a firm grip on the government. The Germans feared the chaos which a Szalasi government must surely provoke as least as much as the many Hungarians hostile to National Socialism, whether of the German or the Hungarian brand.

After the October 15 declaration there was nevertheless for the German SS only one individual with whom they could deal – and that was Szálasi. Horthy, who by now was convinced of German defeat, had shown by his moving appeal that he wanted to rush to the victors' aid at the last minute. Hence his attempt to throw the responsibility for his past behaviour on to the crushing power of Germany.

To succeed in such a switch over in policy a minimum of personality, of honour, of courage and of fervour – qualities of which the regent was totally devoid – were necessary. He allowed himself to be arrested without offering any resistance and appeared relieved that events had taken a turn so comfortable for himself. His detention in a sumptuous German castle conferred upon him a martyr's crown in the eyes of a large section of the public. At the end of the war he was, for a short time, imprisoned by the Allies. He was then labelled an opponent to Hitler, and this screened him from any accusation as a war-criminal.

It was evident that information was lacking among Jewish circles about these matters. Thus, at the Eichmann trial, the prosecution several times defended Horthy, an attitude for which there is no justification. Today it has become a commonplace to say that Horthy was the 'saviour' of those Hungarian

149

Jews who escaped deportation. Even the Jewish representatives of the co-plaintiffs at the Krumey-Hunsche trial in Frankfurt (manifestly influenced by Joël Brand's allegations and those of some other former members of the Budapest Jewish Council) depicted Horthy as the supporter and the courageous saviour of the Jews. These Jewish councillors who were over-confident in Horthy, who for the most part abandoned their community at the moment of danger, and who hid or fled like Joël Brand, have deceived the world about the behaviour of Horthy the 'saviour'. It is also possible that this legend was due to a desire to belittle, as much as possible, the part played by those Jews who really did act in their place and obtained the stopping of deportations and the closing of the gas-chambers.

The SD laid a trap for Horthy and incited him to act pre-maturely. He should have seen that a concentration of Hungarian armoured units had gathered at Budapest before he read his proclamation. But instead it was the Germans who threw their armour around the capital. They had previously captured the regent's surest ally, General Bakay, perhaps the only man who would have been capable of carrying out the putsch. But a few hours before the time fixed for the putsch, the Germans had seized Horthy's son. It was an open secret at Budapest that young Nicholas Horthy was, on his father's orders, trying to get in contact with the social-democrats, the Communists, Tito's partisans and the Jews – in fact with all the enemies of the occupying Power – but going about it so clumsily that all Budapest knew what was afoot. On October 15, a little before the time fixed for the execution of the plan, Nicholas had been asked to have a inter-view with supposed messengers from Tito. At the meeting-place he found SS *Standartenführer* Skorzeny and the chief of the Budapest SD, *Hauptsturmführer* Clages. It was during this arrest that Clages got the bullet in the belly from which he died shortly afterwards.

I was to learn of his death two days later after I had tried in vain to get into touch with him during the chaotic condi-tions that reigned after the *coup d'état*. He was certainly not at his office and no one had been able to tell me what had happened to him.

Young Horthy's arrest was to have been, it is said, a means of putting pressure on his father to abdicate. In his Memoirs Horthy declares forthrightly that this was the reason why he ceded. If you read these Memoirs carefully you find an interminable series of self-justifications, for this man, devoid of willpower and strength of character, was never at a loss for a loop-hole.

In the afternoon of October 15 I decided we had to get some news and put an end to the state of uncertainty we had been in since the Horthy proclamation. I took my car and drove to Buda (Ofen), the district where the royal castle, Horthy's residence, was located. All the roads leading to it were barred by German armour and by Arrow Cross units. They seemed to have risen from the earth, although they had obviously been ready for several days. The men of one of these units arrested my chauffeur and me and led us into a house where an Arrow Cross man was examining the several hundred motorists who also had been arrested. As I learned later they immediately beat up and then executed all the Jews found among them. When my turn came I pretended not to understand one word of Hungarian. I shouted into the face of the Arrow Cross man that I belonged to the German police and I whispered to my driver to repeat it in Magyar. I had on me the photostat copy of an attestation belonging to a Jew of the compulsory labour service. On the orders of the Gestapo he had to work as servant and gardener in a German police unit at Schwabenberg. On the photostat was a large Gestapo seal with a striking swastika cross in the middle. Anyone who looked closely at this document could have seen that it belonged to a Jew of the labour service. But for the man who was dealing with me, my arrogant and decided tone of voice and a glance at the seal were enough. He clicked his heels and released both my chauffeur and me immediately. He knew no German. With every mark of respect an Arrow Cross man – who naturally did not speak German either – escorted me back to the car, and I was able to cross the barrage without difficulty. We were extremely depressed when we got back to our HQ in Semsey Andor utca, and reported the distressing news to our anxious friends. There was not the slightest trace of fighting. The situation was clearly in hand and Ferenc Szálasi in power.

In view of the new turn of events we had only the hope that our contacts with Himmler, and the illusions we had encouraged in him, would protect us from the Arrow Cross. A few days before, Clages had told me of Himmler's decision concerning the rest of the Bergen-Belsen convoy, whose departure for Switzerland was subject now to only one condition. Furthermore he had stated that, in accordance with our request, a definite order from Himmler had gone off to the concentration camps that the lives of the Jews there should be spared. On the same occasion he had strongly urged me to transmit this information to our friends in Switzerland. All this should serve as preparation for a series of more thorough-going interviews.

During the tense days that preceded the attempted putsch my friends had not attached too much importance to these statements by Clages, and I could not myself see very well how they were useful for the present. We feared that they were more vain promises.

All the hopes we had placed in Horthy's *volte-face* leading to the rapid liberation of Hungary had collapsed. Therefore we had to count on Clages and Becher, on our contacts with the Germans with whom lay our last chance of salvation. So Clages's sudden death was a dreadful blow for us.

When they assumed power, the 'Hungarists', as the Arrow Cross called themselves, set about copying the Nazis in many fields the Hungarians had somewhat neglected for some months. They had their own headquarters where the Jewish question in particular was 'dealt with'. Arrow Cross patrols now made the Budapest streets unsafe both by day and night. Rich or respected Jews; or those who, for some reason or another were on bad terms with their neighbours, were arrested or discovered in their hiding-places, then stripped and robbed and tortured in the 'Green Shirts' quarters. Then –

generally in the evening or at night – the victims were slaughtered and their bodies thrown into the Danube. But increasingly often there could be found in the mornings, even in the city's streets, the bodies of Jews killed on the spot. It was again considered a capital crime not to wear the yellow star (which many Jews no longer did, especially after October 15, 1944). During the hours that followed the seizure of power by the Arrow Cross, there was an armed uprising of Jews and socialists in some districts of the city. Tanks, artillery, and German troops soon crushed this attempted revolt that resulted in hundreds of more victims.

The Budapest Jewish Council could no longer carry on its work. The chairman, Samuel Stern, took refuge with an extremist Hungarian journalist who was looking for an alibi. This journalist wrote for an Arrow Cross paper and was, in this capacity, a man of the new regime; but he knew well enough that its power would be short-lived. The vice-chairman of the Jewish Council, Philipp von Freudiger, had taken refuge in Rumania as early as August 1944.

Jews could no longer leave their homes without risking arrest by a patrol. As the members of the Jewish Council also ran this risk, it was our committee, the only organized Jewish group, that had to take its place. Kastner, Komoly and Mrs. Brand had passes from the Bureau of Jewish Affairs which permitted them to go about without the yellow star. I had not received one at first and later on as I took more and more in hand the direction of affairs, I thought it incompatible with my position to ask for a pass from the German negotiators whom I treated on terms of equality. In my old papers dating from Bistritz nothing indicated my origins, but in most cases it was enough for me to shout at the Arrow Cross that I belonged to the German police, for them to move off sharply. But if that was not enough I pushed in their faces the photocopy of a German identity card which was not it was true in my name but which bore a huge swastika. The Arrow Cross people did not know a word of German and did not dare even to examine the *Ausweis*. However for the majority of our brethren the situation was tragic.

153

Forty-eight hours after the putsch, Eichmann had again turned up in Budapest. More than any preceding government, that of the Arrow Cross insisted on getting the surviving Hungarian Jews deported. Their numbers were not easy to estimate, but as the Jewish population had been calculated on March 19, 1944 to be between 800,000 and a million persons, and as since then about 450,000 Jews had been deported, there must have remained between 350,000 and 500,000 individuals left.

Eichmann was delighted with the new situation, but as the *Reichsführer*'s orders still held good he was unable to start up again with the deportations.

These orders, despite the anti-semitic attitude of the new regime, were not annulled. On the contrary, the fourth journey of Becher and Kastner to the Swiss frontier was being prepared, though this trip had been decided on before the latest happenings. It was in this connection that Becher showed he was really an upright man and ready if need be to show personal courage.

Kurt Becher has been mentioned several times, but I think more particulars should be given about this man who had a determining influence on our activities and who by intervening in our favour helped to save the lives of a great number of Jews.

When we managed to get him into our negotiations, Becher certainly did not imagine that, little by little, as our relations with him developed, he would assume an important humanitarian role. Becher was a soldier, sent to Budapest on an economic mission to acquire horses and equipment. At first, anyway, his ambition was confined to this task which he regarded as a military duty. Until he had been posted to Budapest, he had certainly managed to keep clear of the crimes committed by the SS, or in any case, to get himself entrusted with tasks which excluded all direct participation in criminal undertakings. In any case, up to this day, no one has succeeded in producing the slightest valid proof of his responsibility for any crime whatever.

The death of my friend Kastner was in a measure due to the

fact that, after the war, and at the Nuremberg trials, he made a statement – entirely in accordance with the truth – in favour of this high-ranking SS officer. When I also, during the Eichmann trial, gave evidence in Becher's favour, I was made the victim of a campaign concocted by fanatical, embittered and even interested parties who went so far as to threaten me with death. I always told Israeli journalists who questioned me on the subject (and also those who attacked me) that I maintained my statements in Becher's favour because they were true and that I would not go back on my depositions before I was furnished with irrefutable proof of culpable activities engaged in by Becher before the time of his activities in Budapest.

However, for a time, Becher was indeed the least easy negotiator for us to get on with among the three we had to deal with; Eichmann, Clages and Becher. Clages did make efforts not only to be polite and even considerate, while Eichmann himself – apart from occasional outbursts – used diplomatic tactics of a very slippery sort; but Becher's attitude was thoroughly military, that is to say stiff and unbending. Sometimes in fact he showed himself frankly hostile and disagreeable. This attitude became more pronounced when he thought we had got him in an inextricable trap (for he did not want to 'lose face' with Himmler), or when he tried to find some new trick in the business we proposed to him. But then he understood that, behind the 'trick' which related only to the purely economic aspect of the propositions he forwarded to Himmler, lay a unique humanitarian duty. It was to his credit that he then accepted a principal role in performing this duty and continued to play this part when he realized that the political results of our contacts abroad meant much more to Himmler than their economic aspects. Later, when Himmler dropped his projects and, on Hitler's orders, deprived him of his full powers, Becher remained, despite everything, on our side. Most probably he had learned on the eastern front a good deal about the cruel fate meted out to Jews and other inhabitants, especially if they were identified as adversaries or partisans. He always said, and repeats today, that he never took any part in these murders, which were, moreover, often regarded as a gauge of fidelity towards the Führer. Knowing him as I do after our long collaboration, I have no reason for not believing him.

When Kastner, Dr. Billitz and I mentioned before Becher the wholesale exterminations in the concentration camps' gas chambers, that is to say *murders committed behind the front*, he denied strongly that such things were possible, and added he did not believe in them. We, of course, did not at first think that he really did not know what was going on. The truth no doubt lies about halfway between Becher's denials and our knowledge. Just as many Germans would hear nothing about the atrocities when they were mentioned, or when they witnessed certain things (such as the numerous measures taken against the Jews), no doubt Becher, for a long time, just did not wish to know. In the ranks of the German army and even in those of the SS there were many men like him who, for their peace of mind and their personal comfort, shut their eyes on the 'State Secret' which they had the right to know nothing about, since they took no part directly in its execution. If only for this reason they did nothing to verify certain pieces of information or certain accounts.

20. Kastner Goes to Switzerland

In October 1944, during the troubles that followed on Horthy's abortive putsch, we had hoped the Russians would arrive in Budapest after a lightning thrust. Nothing of the sort happened.

For a time the Germans managed to establish and hold a front line before Budapest, and the Hungarian army was ordered by the Arrow Cross to carry on operations. We were henceforth very near the front but had to carry on with the struggle against our extermination.

On the programme was another trip for Kastner – the fourth. This time he was to go with Becher not to the frontier only but right into Swiss territory. Becher had insisted, as a preliminary condition, that we should get him a Swiss visa in good and due order. He did not wish to submit, once again, to the 'humiliating' necessity of conducting discussions on the frontier bridge of Sankt Margrethen. In 1944 it was no longer an easy matter to obtain an entry visa for an SS officer. The Swiss government which in the earlier part of the war was often accommodating for its all-powerful German neighbours, had plucked up courage when the victory of the Allies seemed near, and refused many German requests which would, a year or two before, have been granted without any great difficulty.

If one can believe information I got later, Becher's visa was allowed after steps taken by the American embassy at Berne. Anyway, for Becher and his chief Himmler, this visa was another proof of our far-reaching contacts and of the power of 'International Judaeocracy'.

On October 27 after we had been told the visa had been granted, Kastner and Dr. Billitz left for the Swiss border, while Becher and his assistant Kettlitz flew to Himmler for last minute instructions. While Becher was on his way to join Kastner in Switzerland I was to get a further telegram signed by another of our Zionist friends in Switzerland, but sent at the request of Kastner and Saly Mayer. This telegram is very revealing about the 'climate' in which our negotiations took place. Here is the text:

'Duly received Otto[1] of 30/10 stop inform Kurt his request assured for deliveries against corresponding counter-deliveries and ask Zir telegraphic prolongation return Wilhelm Rudolf expiring six stop Kurt awaited urgently with full powers greetings Reszo Zir Fleischhacker.'

In the meantime, Eichmann, who had received orders to that effect, was to send off from Bergen-Belsen to Switzerland

1. 'Otto' is Otto Komoly, 'Kurt', Kurt Becher, 'Zir' the German government, 'William' Dr. Wilhelm Billitz, and, 'Rudolf', Dr. Rezsö Kastner.

the rest of the test-convoy, that is to say from 1300 to 1400 persons. Furthermore Becher had assured us repeatedly that Himmler had, on several occasions, confirmed the order that Jews in the concentration camps should receive the same treatment as Allied prisoners of war. As a consequence, the wholesale exterminations in the gas chambers had ceased. Such were the principal signs of favourable dispositions on the German side. This also meant that Himmler was in no doubt about the defeat of Germany. Nevertheless, in order to avoid the appearance of a complete capitulation – and doubtless in accordance with the orders he had received – Becher did his best to maintain a firm attitude. In particular he must be uncompromising on matters of possible concessions which could not be granted even by Himmler himself.

The first question discussed was that of the Slovakian Jews. We did not yet know that these had been removed from Himmler's control and recently carried off to their deaths. Becher confirmed, in a few words that the measures adopted regarding the Jews of Slovakia had been necessitated 'solely by exigencies of a military nature' which as we knew were matters depending exclusively on Hitler himself.

Then came the question that was decisive for the fate of our people in Budapest – how could Eichmann be prevented from resuming the deportation of Hungarian Jews. The danger was all the greater since he could also invoke military reasons and thus remove the matter to a field where Himmler's influence was slight if not non-existent.

Since Budapest was near the front line, Eichmann put forward military considerations in demanding the evacuation of the Jews who, if liberated by the Russians, might well supply reinforcements to the enemy. The new Hungarian government, more than any other in the past, and especially the minister Kovarcz, demanded insistently that all the Jews still living in Hungary should be deported. Eichmann and Kovarcz maintained the same point of view. Both of them had recourse to arguments of a military nature in order to circumvent the order for stoppage of the deportations, which, indeed, Himmler had still not revoked. Eichmann's main argument was that in the Reich, as for instance at Vienna, the German population was itself mobilized for the construction of fortifications and defence works, since the approach of the Red Army no longer allowed for troops to be used for this purpose. Therefore good sense as well as Hitler's orders indicated that Jews also should be employed on these tasks. The situation, then, was such that it led us to ask Himmler to do something which might risk putting him into direct opposition to his Führer. But what else could we do? We undertook in Switzerland to put pressure on Becher to intervene with Himmler that the deportations from Budapest should cease, or at least that only those persons fitted for such work should be mobilized and evacuated. To tell the truth our demands far exceeded the concessions Becher was authorized to make. It was easier for him to approve of the departure of a few more convoys of deportees for Switzerland than to raise the question of Budapest in which Himmler himself would undoubtedly have risked his life.

As for the military situation no financial or material resources we might have furnished could have changed the fate of the Third Reich. Nevertheless, all liberations of deportees and all ameliorations of conditions in the camps at Budapest remained subordinated to 'deliveries' on our part. That our promises were in vain, events were to make it abundantly clear. For Becher and Himmler, however, the story of an exchange of strategic material for concessions constituted the necessary screen to cover their enterprise from certain circles in the Third Reich, including Hitler himself.

As regards our action the essential event was the conversation on November 5, 1944, at the Hotel Savoy-Baur-en-ville between the Quaker McClelland and *Obersturmbannführer* SS Becher. This interview had been prepared, very largely, by our friend Nathan Schwalb-Dror who was active in Swiss Zionist circles. He was also about the best supporter of Kastner in Switzerland.

More than a month previously I had announced this meeting to Clages and although at the time this statement had been more or less unwarranted, it secured me at once the success

I had counted on. And now we were to see realized what only a short time before had seemed nothing but a dream. This was a surprise which justified our renewed hopes. Although the Allies had agreed not to engage in negotiations with the Germans, except jointly and then solely with a view to unconditional surrender, Himmler would surely consider this meeting in itself as an important result – the most important hitherto achieved. We could at last offer him a 'result' which he must acknowledge according to the high value he attached to it.

Up to now the State Department has not made public the minutes of this interview nor the reports McClelland addressed to Roosevelt. The interview in question has not even been confirmed. The meeting however was held on purely humanitarian grounds and its sole object was to save the remaining European Jews in so far as they were still at Hitler's mercy.

From a strictly formal point of view the interview constituted, it is true, a violation of the Teheran agreement whereby the Allies had made an accord with Stalin that the Third Reich should be absolutely boycotted. For this reason no doubt the Americans up to this day will make no revelations about these contacts. However, there is no doubt that Roosevelt's courageous action made the saving of several hundreds of thousands of persons possible.

On November 5, then, McClelland, one of the leading Quakers in the United States, the manager in Switzerland of the War Refugee Board, and a man who had the reputation of being the confidant and the personal delegate of President Roosevelt, did meet *Obersturmbannführer* SS Karl Becher, Himmler's personal representative.

The importance of this meeting lay less in the subject of the conversations than in the interview itself. Becher did not present himself as the delegate of a conquered Power. He was the representative of the second personage in the Reich, the man who aimed at being Hitler's successor, and who, by the proofs he gave of his good will towards us, and despite his delegate's firm attitude, tacitly admitted that the war was lost.

McClelland, for his part, demanded what had always been the aim of our action, namely that those of our people still surviving in the territories controlled by the Third Reich, should be spared. In exchange for this he agreed to obtain the American government's permission for the transfer of the twenty million Swiss francs promised by the 'Joint', the American charity organization. Then it would be up to the Third Reich to find the goods in Switzerland and to pay for them.

These twenty million francs were promised as an advance against future payments. In reality neither McClelland nor anyone in the 'Joint' or among the Allies thought for an instant that this money would ever be used by the Germans for the purchase of arms or equipment. The war seemed to be approaching its end and it was at last admitted that promises could quite well be made since there would be no time left to keep them.

Although the minutes of the interview have been kept secret to this day, the McClelland-Becher meeting is well known to historians. We must hope that one day the archives will be at last opened so that light may be thrown on all the details of this incident.

After the war, we received from the representative of the War Refugee Board, Mr. Roswell D. McClelland, two attestations which show exactly how the Americans were informed about our activities and those of Becher.

An accord of a general character had been concluded. By it the Germans agreed to spare the lives of all civilians, and thus also of Jews; Becher, as Himmler's spokesman, could not, however, make any firm promises regarding matters beyond the control of the *Reichsführer* SS. On this point Becher had received very stringent instructions.

Regarding the situation at Budapest, it was stated that the German military command would not admit that Jews or Jewesses fit to bear arms or to work should be allowed to remain in the city when it was besieged or if it was abandoned. Such persons must certainly be sent away from the capital, not to the death-camps but at most to execute works of military importance, such as the construction of fortifications against the threat of the Russian advance. The rest of the Jewish population – children, aged persons and those seriously ill – could remain in Budapest and the agreement authorized that, in principle, representatives of the international Red Cross should come and inspect the conditions in which these people were living.

I must admit that after the Arrow Cross came to power, I went home, after a talk with Becher, prey to deep despair and a certain suspicion regarding Kastner, which could be explained perhaps on humane grounds. The interview in question took place at the end of October, before Becher left Budapest to join Kastner in Switzerland. The Bergen-Belsen convoy seemed to be on its way to the Swiss border and I was disappointed that Kastner should not keep the promise he had given us before he left.

No doubt, at this departure, we had all looked forward with some pessimism to our prospects of future activity in Budapest. Was it not on the arrival of this convoy (whose payment was to be effected in Switzerland so that the guarantee we had had to put up could be liberated and allow the departure of other Jews) was it not at this moment, at the latest, that it would become evident that no one in Switzerland dreamt of honouring our promises? Of course we had gained time by the suppression of the gas chambers and by the – at least temporary – stoppage of deportations from Budapest. But now the time seemed to have come for us to resign if we did not want the Germans to ask us for accounts. Therefore Kastner had promised to send me Swiss visas through Becher or any other person coming back to Budapest. He had also promised to ask Becher that the most active members of the Waada should get the necessary permissions to leave the country.

Now I found before me a very irritated Becher who, like ourselves, was beginning to fear for his own skin since our promises had not always been kept. He was literally a prey to panic and burst into a fit of rage when I mentioned our plans to emigrate. Kastner had not said a word to him about this.

From then on I began to fear that, after his family had arrived in Switzerland, Kastner would not come back to Budapest. So the day after I had seen Becher, I sent the following telegram to Saly Mayer:

Saly Mayer, Saint-Gall.
Kurt denied yesterday Rudolf's statement about permission our journey stop but demands immediately large amounts Kaspi and Sechora promised by Rudolf for yesterday stop affirms only agreed deliveries stop mills since August stop feel at least led into error and tired stop let Rudolf telegraph replacement representative at Kurtet-comp stop Biss.

As can be seen from this wire my nerves also were beginning to give way; I was seized with panic. I said to myself that those for whom we had by our energy and resources obtained a respite could well hold on alone for the few days or few weeks until the arrival of the Russians. I thought I had now the right to worry about my own life and that of my wife and nearest friends and all the more so since our activities up to now had specially exposed us.

The reader who has been good enough to follow me up to now, will surely understand what 'stop mills since August' meant. It was the stoppage of Eichmann's 'mills' – the gas chambers – especially at Auschwitz, following Himmler's instructions dated from August–September 1944. This was undoubtedly the most precious result we managed to obtain, even if, up to this day, it has not been fully recognized. Himmler considered himself justified in regarding all our previous payments as a settlement for the suppression of the gas chambers. In the above telegram, 'Rudolf' means Kastner, 'Kaspi' cash, and 'Sechora' goods.

In my troubled state of mind I had just announced my resignation with this telegram and asked for someone else to be entrusted with contacts with the SS, which I had baptized 'Kurtecomp'.

As soon as the wire had gone off I regretted sending it. For if Kastner, like Brand, had let us down, then the telegram would hardly have been any use. Saly Mayer did not answer but shortly afterwards, on November 8, Kastner turned up in Budapest. When we met we both burst out into loud laughter, though the position we were in was not at all funny. I felt profoundly confused and these gusts of laughter were no doubt a way of relieving our nerves. Kastner did not say a word about the telegram and I was careful not to mention it. Then it was that I was able really to appreciate the courage and bravery of the man. We were friends and colleagues for a long time but it was only then that I began to both understand and admire him.

Later on we were, more than once, of differing opinions. Maybe sometimes I saw clearer than he did; I must however recognize I could never have equalled him in devotion and spirit of sacrifice. Had he not quit the free country of Switzerland which his family and 1700 deportees were to reach (thanks in great part to his own efforts) and return to Budapest despite the circumstances and our hopeless situation? His trust in God, his courageous faith in the justice of our cause and his perseverance in our work, continued to inspire me until our action was happily crowned with success.

The fact was, as from November 4 when the Becher-McClelland meeting had already been arranged, Kastner had been informed by an enthusiastic Becher that Himmler had decided to send to Switzerland the remaining test-convoy from Bergen-Belsen. At once Kastner had telegraphed to us:

Gvoul awaits you all stop Bergbels settled stop greetings Rezso.

Gvoul is a Hebrew word that may mean 'frontier' or 'salvation'. The message announced that the members of the Waada who had remained at Budapest could now emigrate to Switzerland. As a matter of fact, nothing of the kind took place.

On November 8, 1944, Kastner and Becher returned to Budapest where they found a particularly complicated situation.

21. Budapest in November 1944

The situation in Budapest had changed. The town had become an inferno, especially for the Jewish population. Following the example of Eichmann's men, the Arrow Cross went about declaring that Horthy's 'faithlessness' had one sole cause. The Jews had got round him therefore the Jews only were responsible for Hungary's hesitating attitude. The time had come to stamp out the treason by which a great many Jews had been able to escape deportation, and it was high time to mend matters. But such demands came up against one obstacle – the famous order given by Himmler to cease the deportations. Another factor had also to be taken into account. Many Hungarians and also Germans were in search of alibis and judged rightly that the Arrow Cross's reign would not be a long one. Everything, in fact, led them to believe that shortly the Russians would sweep over Budapest – and the whole country. For the most part these alibi-seekers' courage did not lead them farther than words and tended to melt away when it was a question of acts.

Once again we had to leave our apartment, the HQ at Semsey Andor utca. We were now lodged at the Hotel Pannonia where the members of the Rumanian legation in Hungary were under surveillance. The Rumanians in fact had freed themselves from German occupation in August 1944 and if the Horthy putsch had only been successful they might have found themselves the allies of the Hungarians, for they were now enemies of the Arrow Cross and the Third Reich. The Rumanian diplomatic representatives were first deprived of their liberty of movement and then, as their premises had been requisitioned, they were put into an hotel under the supervision of the police.

For the Jews, however, to find themselves under police guard was not such a bad thing since it made them, relatively speaking, safe from the Arrow Cross and their patrols. In this same hotel I had already got rooms for Mrs. Brand, Komoly and several other Waada friends. My wife and I, since we were residents of Transylvania, a province now once more joined to Rumania, were counted as members of the Rumanian colony which had congregated around the members of the legation at the hotel.

MEETING WITH NUSSBECHER

One day a young Haloutz,[1] of whom I had caught a glimpse several times in our former apartment, visited me at the hotel. I learned his name only the day he called upon me. He was Joël Nussbecher. He had jumped out of a train and had thus escaped deportation (see pp. 143–7). This young man had, for the time being, only one ambition. He wanted to execute as soon as possible the military mission which had been the reason for his coming among us, that is to say to organize the Haganah[2] and to take command of it.

The possibilities for armed resistance now seemed somewhat more promising. While the Hungarian troops poured back from the front, the Jewish survivors of the compulsory labour service moved back with them. Their units finished by breaking up amid the general disorder and in part because their armed guards, who had supervised them, maltreated and often tortured them to death, had themselves deserted in a body. It was proposed that the units which had remained intact should be duly made up to strength, and sent across Hungary to be employed in Austria or even within the interior of the Reich. Here was a proof, in the eyes of supervisers of the compulsory labour service, that the war was undoubtedly lost – an additional reason for them to go to earth in their villages while awaiting the arrival of the Russians. The Jewish labourers tried to get away, in whole groups, from the forced labour. Among those from the provinces many were not to find their families, who had been deported in the meanwhile. Their

1. Haloutz, a pioneer in Palestine.
2. Haganah, in Hebrew, 'protection', 'defence' the name of the military organization of the Palestine Jewish Agency.

belongings had passed into the possession of some neighbour who would hasten to denounce them to the Arrow Cross. So such Jews, in their search for a hiding-place would make for Budapest and it was not unusual for whole units of the obligatory labour service to arrive in the capital without guards – surely a grotesque situation.

We did our best in Budapest to find them hiding-places when they applied to us or when the organizations of Jewish Youth managed to discover them. Thus it was that several hundreds of these deserters from the labour service turned up in the Columbusgasse where we had set up an encampment to collect and lodge those who, so we said, were to comprise the next convoys for Switzerland. When the first successful convoy left for Switzerland via Bergen-Belsen we had kept the identity papers of the emigrants. Thus we were able to furnish a great number of young deserters from the labour units, with authentic papers. These young people were to form the nucleus of the Haganah that Joël Nussbecher undertook energetically to organize and develop.[1] We agreed to separate the activities of the Haganah from those of our Hazzalah[2] which must not be compromised since it was devoted to the protection of the population unfit to bear arms. Nussbecher and I agreed to work on parallel lines and I promised him in the name of the 'Joint' to contribute to the financing of the Haganah. He told me what had happened to Hannah Szenes, Perez Goldstein and himself. But this was not the time for talking of the past. What we had to think about was the present and the future.

This conversation with Joël Nussbecher took place in my room at the hotel and while we were talking Mrs. Brand suddenly appeared. When she saw my visitor she was dumbfounded with astonishment and also with fear. Then she asked me to go out of the room with her for an instant. On the landing she asked, with great agitation if I knew with whom I was

1. French, British and other military allies who had escaped from the prisoners' and refugees' camps in Budapest also took part in this Resistance movement.
2. In Hebrew 'assistance'. *Waadat ha' hazzalah* 'Committee of Assistance'.

dealing – the most dangerous man for us in all Budapest. In the present circumstances he would definitely compromise us and ruin our work of assistance. This man, she said, caused our arrest on June 30, after the departure of the Bergen–Belsen convoy, and because of him the Hungarian counter-espionage had shut us up in the Hadik barracks. All this I knew. I had just heard it a few minutes before. I did my best then to calm this woman, whose nerves had obviously given way. Her reaction was, however, perfectly understandable. Mrs. Brand's first arrest by the Hungarians, during which she had suffered terrible tortures, had taken place only a few months before.

I made a sign to my wife to take Joël Nussbecher out of the room while I went back to Mrs. Brand and promised her to follow her prudent advice and to at once break off contact with Joël Nussbecher, who was waiting in the bathroom where my wife had put him. When Mrs. Brand had left we continued our conversation. Then he left me and taking with him a first contribution to his war chest, he went off to set up his first HQ at the Swiss legation. Here, thanks to the devotion of the consul, Karl Lutz, a huge camp had been prepared where several thousand persons had already found refuge.

Karl Lutz was entrusted with British interests and those of territories under British mandate, and was, of the non-Jews, among our most sincere and constant allies. Beyond the limits allowed by his diplomatic immunity and his functions, he fought against the barbarity that menaced and surrounded us on all sides.

He had, under his protection, those people who possessed certificates entitling them to enter Palestine, since they were considered, even before they left, as nationals of the mandatory Power, that is to say Great Britain. These at first numbered only a few hundreds, then they were seven thousand eight hundred, and finally there were tens of thousands of them owing to the almost unlimited distribution of 'protected subject' certificates. The Germans had recognized these and allowed the holders of these 'Palestinian certificates' to pass as subjects of the British mandate, only because I had assured the

German authorities that within the framework of our exchange operations, the beneficiaries of the Swiss action would also be 'settled' by the American 'Joint'. Eichmann had been informed of this guarantee and therefore had to tolerate the Swiss action, as well as, a little later on, that of the Swedes, together with enterprises of the same type, though on a smaller scale, undertaken by Spanish, Portuguese and Vatican representatives. As during the last months, Horthy and his gang endeavoured to prove to the diplomatists of neutral countries his good will towards the Jews, the possession of a Swiss or Swedish certificate of protection afforded a certain insurance against deportation or arrest. At least this was the position until the Arrow Cross seized power.

But even under the Arrow Cross these certificates were at first respected. Therefore they were still distributed. When the Swiss legation became more reserved, the Waada proceeded to print the certificates themselves. I myself had prepared no less than 30,000 of them at a printing-press that worked for the Swiss legation. Once these were stamped with the authentic seal of the consulate – which our friends had procured – the documents were distributed through us.

However, these documents soon lost much of their value. The Arrow Cross made less and less difference between 'protected subjects' and others. As there was no longer any protection against the patrols, either in the streets or in people's homes, thousands of people who possessed these 'protection documents' took refuge in the Swiss legation and in the two large camps attached to it over which the Swiss flag flew. A mass of terror-stricken persons crowded together in a quite insufficient space. The Jewish spokesman who dealt with the consul was Moshe Krausz, the representative of the Palestinian Office. Unlike Kastner, I was on good terms with him, and this fact was not without its importance for our work. It may be mentioned also that Dr. Karl Wilhelm, the only leader of the Council of Jews who was still in office (and with whom I was on terms of close friendship) also lodged at the Swiss legation.

Herr Lutz, the consul, hoped to be able to go on relying

upon the Hungarian government, and was encouraged in this by a favourable circumstance. Among the members of the Arrow Cross government, the minister of foreign affairs followed a more moderate line than that of the party, and in particular those of its most active members, at whose head was the minister Kovarcz. Szálasi had appointed as minister of foreign affairs a certain Baron Kemény, who aimed at getting the new government recognized by the neutral Powers. As such recognition was slow in coming, Kemény thought that some measures in favour of the 'protected subjects' might serve to encourage at least *de facto* recognition of the new regime. No one in Budapest was ignorant of the fact that there were not 7,800 but tens of thousands of 'protection certificates'. And the minister of foreign affairs so arranged matters that even the Arrow Cross government turned a blind eye on this state of things. But this 'generosity' was really of advantage to those only who were in neutral legations or in premises which depended on these legations. In the mounting chaos the Arrow Cross patrols were more and more brutal in their street attacks on the inhabitants, especially on the Jews, and little attention was paid to 'protection certificates'. No doubt some thousands or tens of thousands of persons might hope to escape the worst thanks to diplomatic protection, but the overwhelming majority of the Jews still in Budapest, that is to say between 200,000 and 300,000 people, were all the same exposed to the blackguards.

Obviously any aid was welcome, even if it helped only isolated individuals. But our first care was to save the great mass of those who hitherto had escaped deportation. This necessitated the intervention of appropriate authority, and this could henceforth come only from the SS. The paradoxical idea of putting the sheepfold under the protection of the wolf had already been exploited by Kastner and me and not without some good results. In spite of all their devotion, the efforts of neutral diplomatists would have been absolutely useless if they had not been tolerated by the Germans. And to benefit from this toleration, we had, as has been mentioned above, to take engagements in the name of the 'Joint'. I had already done this with Becher's staff in the matter of the action in Switzerland and now I had to do the same for Raoul Wallenberg's activities.

The personality of Wallenberg, his disappearance at the end of the war, and his probable death in the Soviet Union, have given rise to many legends. Both Lutz and Wallenberg have every right to the esteem of posterity, but – though this does not in any way lessen their merit – the actions of both could be successful only through our committee's 'intoxication' of the narrow minds of Himmler, Eichmann and their accomplices. It was an 'intoxication' we induced by maintaining and exaggerating the illusion that we were the spokesmen of the so-called 'International Judaeocracy'.

During all the month of November 1944 friction continued between those who, with Eichmann and the Hungarian minister Kovarcz, urged wholesale deportation, and those who behind our Waada, the neutral diplomatists and to some extent the Hungarian minister of foreign affairs who desired, as did Becher, that no new deportations should be undertaken.

Eichmann, it is true, no longer controlled the gas chambers, and therefore in principle had no longer the right to deport, but he did have the right to requisition valid Jews for work on defences and fortifications. These requisitions cost the lives of thousands of people since those who were rounded up for these purposes Eichmann forced to walk to the Austrian frontier, a distance of some 115 miles. Among the Hungarians the man who helped him most in this enterprise was Solymossy, the Arrow Cross police chief, who owed his job to the new government. But there was also Lt. Colonel Ferenczy, the head of the Hungarian gendarmerie, who had played a leading part in the first deportations under Baky and Endre and who did all he could to exterminate the remaining Jews in Hungary. Ferenczy had to get forgiven by the new regime – and by Eichmann – for having, at one time, recommended to Horthy that he abandon the Axis. He had also maintained personal contacts with Jews and the secret of this had not been entirely kept. Furthermore, it was particularly disagreeable to

Ferenczy that my friend Kastner (whom he had, in July, dragged off for interrogation, see p. 46) should know a good deal about these matters. So, his former goodwill towards Kastner changed to mortal hatred. Ferenczy had, indeed, made several attempts to suppress so embarrassing a witness.

Those condemned to the long march were rounded up, most brutally, into a tile works near Budapest. Some of them had been seized in the streets; others had been dragged out of their homes. Since valid men were rare among the Jews (for they had long since been requisitioned for compulsory labour), from 70 per cent to 80 per cent of the people at the tile works and on the march were women. Kastner kept on demanding that Becher should get Eichmann to spare the sick, the aged and the children – as had been agreed at the last meeting in Switzerland. But the Gestapo had no compunction in forcing women – even in an advanced state of pregnancy – to undertake the march. Becher had stormy discussions with Eichmann, but only a telephone message from Himmler had any, though very temporary, effect. After having received orders on the subject, Eichmann and his immediate subordinates, Hunsche and Dannecker, met Solymossy and Ferenczy the next day at the Hungarian ministry of the Interior. To their surprise the latter heard from Eichmann's mouth that Jewish children, old people and invalids no longer interested him. When it was asked what should be done with them, the reply was that the Third Reich was neither a kindergarten nor an alms-house.

The marches lasted about six weeks and caused about 5,000 deaths. No doubt this figure is monstrous; but it is small compared with the daily average of deaths in the gas chambers whose stoppage we had managed to obtain. Before the stoppage of the extermination operations as many people were assassinated in a few hours – in half a day. At the Eichmann trial no account was taken of this difference. It was not even mentioned. Quite the contrary. Previously it had been possible to undertake the extermination of all the members of a convoy without *any* witness surviving. However, in addition to the 5,000 victims of the forced marches, there were at least 35,000 to 40,000 persons who survived the ordeal and who could (and many of them can today) offer their evidence. At the Eichmann trial much ado was made about these forced marches which, in reality, amounted to a diminution of our daily losses to less than 2 per cent or 3 per cent of what had been normal before. So there was a change for the better. It is true that the forced marches went on making victims, but, thanks to our efforts, the wholesale exterminations had ceased. And this fact was neither stressed nor appreciated as it should have been during the trial. If we had not managed to get the gas chambers put out of action and the deportations stopped, everything would have gone according to Eichmann's plans, and in the lands occupied by the Third Reich – which included Hungary – not a Jew would have survived. Had it not been for the stoppage order, in six weeks – about forty days – Eichmann would have been easily able to murder 500,000 to 600,000 people more and it happens that this number corresponds to about that of those who survived.

Eichmann had finally found out that the number of persons possessing a certificate as a 'protected subject' was far greater than 7,800. In order to exercise his control, he insisted on their being isolated in so called 'Protected houses'. Most often these were buildings which were let and many of which had formerly belonged to Jews. Over these blocks the Swiss or Swedish colours had been hoisted. I was then running the clandestine 'Joint', and in most cases paid the rent. It would take a whole chapter to tell how I managed to collect the necessary funds. After having drawn on my own resources and having also exhausted all my personal credit, I drew vouchers in the name of the 'Joint' and payable after the end of hostilities. I was lucky enough to get M. Weyermann, the representative at Budapest of the International Red Cross, to put his endorsement on these vouchers.

Our camp in the Columbusgasse – which since the summer no longer had had its SS sentinels – received more and more people. Finally, more than 4,000 persons were collected there. Over the camp we hoisted the Red Cross flag to show that the place was under the protection of the International Red Cross.

But as it was not possible to obtain guards from Eichmann or the SS, it was not long before we had to suffer from Arrow Cross.

First of all the Green Shirts could be seen arresting in the streets and without any scruple increasing numbers of 'protected persons'. These, when they were not shot out of hand, were sent off to the tile works preparatory to being set off on the marches. Little by little there collected in this one spot almost all the 'protected subjects' who, according to the figures officially accepted, numbered the 7,800 Budapest was supposed to contain altogether. The Swiss consul Herr Lutz was then authorized to visit the tile works so that he might identify the owners of *authentic* documents. But all the documents were authentic in the sense that they all came from the same printer and all were stamped with the Swiss consular seal. The consul was faced with a terrible and tragic task. He had to label as false at least some documents, if he would not deprive his work of protection of its last remains of respect. But the consul managed to deal gently with those whose fate depended on his choice.

Shortly afterwards, the Arrow Cross took radical measures against some of the 'protected houses' – and all their inhabitants. The streets near the houses were cordoned off and all the people in the buildings were taken to the tile works or killed on the spot. At the beginning of December came the turn of the Columbusgasse camp.

This situation was characteristic of the total disruption of the Hungarian administration and its security services. All authority was abolished, all security had come to an end. Even the German security organization itself was crumbling and the possibility of their intervention was rapidly fading.

In this state of things our efforts to put a brake on if not to stop completely the forced marches suddenly received unexpected if only temporary help. On November 16, 1944, several high ranking SS officers left Vienna by car for Budapest. Becher had gone to Vienna there to fetch *Waffen-SS Obergruppenführer* Jüttner and his aide-de-camp Grässler. According to Kastner, the commandant of the Auschwitz camp and *Obersturmbannführer* SS Rudolf Höss, as well as Krumey, were also reported to be at Budapest at the same time.

When they got to Budapest they expressed the 'indignation' they had felt at the spectacle that had met their eyes. On the highway they had passed lamentable groups of marchers that Eichmann's myrmidons were leading to Vienna. Everywhere along the road lay the corpses of those who had not been able to keep up and had been shot down. These 'gentlemen' had just come from a conference with Himmler where they had been told that henceforth a 'wind of change' was going to blow. The Auschwitz gas chambers had already been closed for some weeks and, with increasing firmness, Himmler wanted to abolish the wholesale exterminations of the preceding period. The real reasons for this attitude were, no doubt, not wholly secret for those who had listened to it being expressed at this conference. Was not what they had just seen on the Budapest road in direct opposition to the instructions given by Himmler? True, up to then a much greater number of martyrs had been killed daily or even in a few hours, but the secret of these mass murders was so well kept that it was thought they could be denied in the face of the world. But the victims of the forced marches lay there sprawled on the road and visible to all comers. This spectacle was much more impressive and revelatory than the scanty rumours which, despite official orders of silence, filtered through about the fate of the deportees.

So the forced marches were stopped immediately – during Eichmann's absence for a few days. Better still, on November 17, 1944, about 700 marchers, who had just started off on the road the SS trio had taken, were sent back to Budapest.

A few days before, Becher had already, at our instigation, approached Himmler to get Eichmann's instructions, fixing at ten years the minimum age for the marchers, countermanded. Special directions followed from Himmler forbidding Eichmann to include in the operation any but adults.

22. New Trends

On November 18, 1944, the day after a stop had been put to the marches, Kettlitz, Becher's emissary in Switzerland, sent the following telegram:

> After several days negotiation residence assigned Saint-Gall – money not yet received – constantly new objections – am moreover persuaded absence intention or possibility settlement view lack total amount.

Furthermore Kettlitz reported that, for the first time, other Jewish organizations were negotiating with him about payment, in addition to the 'Joint' and Saly Mayer, obvious proof of divisions on the Jewish side.

These 'organizations' were in fact the Aguda group of orthodox religious tendency, composed mainly of Jews who had emigrated to the United States. As they were not in agreement with Saly Mayer nor satisfied with the results so far obtained, they wanted to act on a different plan that would compete with that of the 'Joint'. But this new plan led them also to contact Himmler. This lowered our credit and the squabble in Switzerland between the 'Joint' and the Aguda did much harm to our enterprise; for it was of a kind to depreciate us in Himmler's eyes.

Kettlitz's telegram surprised Becher who was preparing to leave for Himmler's HQ, there to report on the progress of the negotiations. So to make Becher's task more easy, on the day after he left we got Billitz to telephone this message:

> I am authorized to repeat that the 20 million francs are at disposal. Payment is held up by problems of a purely technical financial nature. Saly Mayer and the organizations on which he depends are working day and night to remove the final difficulties. Doubts about intention to effect the settlement are in no way founded.

176

To tell the truth this message – which Becher received at Himmler's HQ – was not founded either. Since Kastner had been back at Budapest we had had no word from Saly Mayer, and certainly no instructions to make such declarations as these. Nevertheless, Becher no longer had empty hands and could approach Himmler with a note concerning a 'telephone message just received'. Thus the negative effect of the telegram Kettlitz had sent from Switzerland the day before should be more or less counteracted.

So it was that from moment to moment we had to concoct – from nothing – some means of making an impression – even if unfounded – on Himmler. And this all the more since Becher's star was on the wane, for news from abroad made our results seem more and more meagre, while the *Reichsführer* suddenly caught a glimpse of hope on another side.

Schellenberg was the man responsible for the foreign information service of the *Reichssicherheitshauptamt* (RSHA, the Central Security service of the Reich) where he was head of the VIth section. As such he should have been fully informed about the contacts with us established by Clages and which Becher had now taken on. But Himmler had not let drop a word about the matter, even to Schellenberg, and the latter only now, in November 1944, began to grasp the general outlines of our enterprise. Even a man less intelligent than the head of the VIth section should have understood, by that date, that Himmler was much less concerned with obtaining arms, strategic materials or foreign exchange, than with Allied contacts. By August the first test-convoy had already reached Switzerland. The second train was now on its way; in the meantime Schellenberg's agents abroad had informed him of our negotiations. Then it was that Schellenberg made it his business to get a share for himself.

During his last trip to Switzerland, Becher had already told Kastner that in the Gestapo and at the *Reichssicherheitsamt* intrigues were going on against him with Himmler and against Himmler himself with the highest authority in the Reich. Becher had added that the chief of the *Reichssicherheitsamt*, Kaltenbrunner, disapproved of Himmler's attitude, while

Becher himself was made a target because he supported Himmler in this attitude. Becher even told Kastner that one of either Kaltenbrunner's or Schellenberg's informers, a Swiss named Trümpy, had addressed to Kaltenbrunner reports on the negotiations of Saly Mayer about which certain Jewish circles had evidently had information. Kaltenbrunner would thus have forwarded to Himmler very unfavourable statements concerning Becher.

Kaltenbrunner's reports declared that Becher was being hoodwinked by Saly Mayer, who would never hand over either money or merchandise, whereas the Aguda, on the contrary, both could and would offer more than the 'Joint'.

Schellenberg, then, aroused in Himmler doubts about Becher, as about us. He tried to squeeze Becher out so that he himself could carry on with the Aguda the negotiations begun with us who, after all, had to our credit a series of important results. The test-convoy had convinced foreign opinion that Himmler inclined towards accommodation. With the suppression of the gas chambers we had succeeded in securing the reduction of the massacres to a tiny percentage of what they had been in the preceding period. Hundreds of thousands of our people had gained time. In six months of secret and frantic negotiations since May 1944, by ruse and all the resources of bluff, we had won this. But the new team in Switzerland (and soon still others were to come on the scene) knew nothing of these results. They wanted at all costs to enter into competition with us and to start from scratch.

While Schellenberg and his foreign contacts were also anxious to get a test-convoy abroad, our main objective was no longer the departure of isolated convoys, convoys which could at the best save the lives of a few thousand more persons. In the ever increasing chaos of the Reich's collapse, the condition of the railway network in itself was enough to prevent the transfer abroad of the hundreds of thousands of survivors in the occupied lands of central Europe or in the concentration camps. Our preoccupation then was to find means to keep in force the instructions already obtained so that these masses of people should be spared and that their survival should be guaranteed until the last territories controlled by the Reich should fall into the hands of the Allies.

At their meeting on November 18 Becher handed Himmler a memorandum he had drawn up and urged the *Reichsführer* to confirm in writing the order closing the gas chambers. These instructions had, as a matter of fact, been in force for several weeks already, but they had been given as a verbal order which could neither be known or recognized abroad.

When he was told of McClelland's demands he flew into a rage and stated at first that the Americans wanted to stop things that had never existed. Then, yielding to Becher's prudent advice, he renewed his instructions, this time in writing. This order is mentioned by almost all the authors who have dealt with the subject. Here is the text according to the deposition made by Becher at the Nuremberg trials.

SECRET MATTER

To the chief of the central office of the Commissariat *Obergruppenführer* SS. Pohl.

To the chief of the central office of Reich security *Obergruppenführer* SS. Kaltenbrunner.

With immediate effect I forbid all extermination of Jews and I order, on the contrary, that care be taken of those weak or sick. I hold you personally responsible even in cases where this order may not be strictly carried out by subaltern authorities.

(signed) Heinrich Himmler

Later on, during his evidence at the Krumey-Hunsche trial, Becher declared that never before this occasion had Himmler admitted in his presence that gas had been used. Becher considered the above order to be Himmler's first avowal in the matter.

Becher, and we with him, seemed to have won a great victory. On this most taboo of all subjects Himmler had confirmed in writing his former verbal instructions. But this still remained linked with the – fictitious – idea that we on our side would furnish a tangible counterpart. First of all the twenty million Swiss francs, several times promised, must be paid into a German account opened in Switzerland. The time had not yet come for Himmler to let it appear that, beyond all other considerations, he was most anxious to maintain and develop the contacts established with McClelland. Eichmann also pestered Kastner and me to tell him the situation concerning the sums promised. Where and when would they be paid? Becher, also, who had taken the risks we have seen, hoped, in order to cover himself with the *Reichsführer* SS and with Kaltenbrunner's and Eichmann's Gestapo, to be able to point to the actual payment of the sums so often announced.

23. New Enterprises, New Difficulties

In Budapest we constantly had new worries. Eichmann, back on November 21, had at once taken measures to start up the marches again on a pretended order from Hitler himself.

He was, it was said, to concentrate 70,000 persons on the Austro-Hungarian frontier where they were wanted for building the south-eastern defence line that was to protect the Austrian border. In any case we managed in the time we had to suppress the most crying excesses. The new labour columns comprised only men – if these could be found – and women in a condition to march and work.

On their way the marchers were supplied by vehicles we sent along the columns. I was entrusted with the financing of these food vehicles and had taken into my apartment a young man named George Aczel together with his family and several of his friends. He was a Communist and was later a member of the Hungarian government. Surreptitiously Aczel conveyed to the tile works large quantities of foodstuffs and medical supplies. These were handed to the marchers before they set off.

Aczel also distributed supplies from vehicles on the way. He was very clever at organizing his work. He even managed to establish contacts with Lt. Colonel Ferenczy and Captain Lullay of the Hungarian gendarmerie in charge of the deportations. It was interesting to see such men beginning to 'swerve' before the prospect of the evacuation of Budapest and of the arrival of the Russians. By rendering small services to our committee of assistance they hoped to be sure of an alibi for the future. At the end of the war they were both brought before a People's Court and then hanged.

So as to provide a screen for our assistance activities we made an arrangement with the Budapest delegates of the International Red Cross, Friedrich Born and his assistant Hans Weyermann. By this agreement we were allowed to instal an office exclusively for help to Jewish civilians, under the name of 'International Red Cross, Department A', in Mérleg utca, 2–6. Our helpers wore Red Cross armlets and were supplied with credentials by the Red Cross. Otto Komoly ran the office. During the last weeks of the German occupation and after Komoly's death, I took over the management of this department.

As officials of the Red Cross our helpers could present them in a rather more official way and naturally they ignored the obligation to wear the yellow star.

We were in close touch with Raoul Wallenberg, a diplomatist, and representative of the Swedish Red Cross, and we had various other diplomatic contacts. Komoly thus met the Papal Nuncio and also the emissaries of the Hungarian Resistance whose members (not then very numerous) in Budapest secretly were preparing armed insurrection against the Germans. Joël Nussbecher was busy organizing his Haganah and I often met him in the Swiss legation where I had the opportunity of seeing my friend Dr. Karl Wilhelm and also Moshe Krausz as well as, from time to time, Karl Lutz the consul.

We had undertaken to launch a fantastic transaction which, however, was never to be realized. The project concerned an exchange of the remaining German minorities in Rumania for the Jews of Hungary, together with political militants detained by the Germans or the Arrow Cross – especially socialists, communists and members of various liberal parties. After the putsch organized by the young King Michael, the German units in Rumania must either surrender or beat a hasty retreat, leaving behind them hundreds of thousands of *Volksdeutsche* confronted with the prospect of deportation to Siberia. Did they not have good reason for thinking they were threatened with a fate resembling that which the criminal rulers of Germany had inflicted on their adversaries and particularly on the Jews? For Himmler, Hitler, and other Nazi bosses such conduct on the part of their victorious enemies must have seemed a matter of course.

But despite many trials they had to undergo the German minorities were, as it happened, far from having to suffer from the law of an eye for an eye and a tooth for a tooth, and although the German refugees from the east complained bitterly of a backlash of hatred, they never, thank God, had to undergo anything at all like the atrocities committed in their name against the Jews in the concentration camps and the extermination camps.

But in the atmosphere that prevailed then in Budapest and in the Third Reich, such perspectives seemed natural to the satraps with whom we were struggling to save what remained of our people. In these circumstances came an idea (in harmony with the air of importance we had given ourselves up to then) of suggesting an international agreement between Rumania on the one side and on the other Hungary and the occupation (SS) authorities in that country. Becher put up our proposal to Himmler. We asked that in exchange for the Germans of Rumania, the repatriation of Jews deported from northern Transylvania. Some of these, we imagined, although we were not quite sure, were no longer alive. We had asked Jewish leaders in Rumania to send us a telegram confirmation for this operation. I would mention here Dr. Ernö Marton, the former editor of the Jewish newspaper (in the Magyar language) *Uj Kelet*. Dr. Marton had also been one of the members of the Jewish minority in the Rumanian parliament. He and another

Jewish leader named Sissu conducted the parleys at Bucarest and we at Budapest. The International Red Cross (in the persons of its two representatives at Budapest, Friedrich Born and Hans Weyermann) also took part in the talks, as did the Swiss government through the consul Lutz. As Kastner had to go to Switzerland once again, it was arranged that I should go to the front with Eichmann, or one of his assistants, and a Hungarian with a flag of truce, and there meet Russian and Rumanian representatives, also with flags of truce, to see if this transaction could not be concluded.

It is hardly necessary to remark that these steps were just so many desperate efforts to keep ourselves going in the interval that still separated us from the capitulation of Budapest. What must be done was to arouse hopes in the Germans and so avoid the last-minute massacre of at least 150,000 Jews who, we reckoned, still remained in Budapest. Such massacres, which had been the rule in Poland and everywhere German troops had fallen back in retreat, were committed either by troops themselves or by the duly aroused local populations.

But what was the good of all this, when catastrophic news arrived from Switzerland, as witness this telegram sent by Kettlitz to Becher?

Impossible meet Saly Mayer last ten days. Stated on telephone to be away. Presence Switzerland useless. Ask for recall.

Clearly enough, Saly Mayer and the gentlemen around him thought the problems would solve themselves and the best thing for them to do would be to see no one.

Becher, who was himself in a delicate position, could not suppress so categorical a telegram. Eichmann did not hide his satisfaction at having been right when he had foreseen from the beginning that the Jews were only seeking to fool the *Reichsführer*. On this November 28, Eichmann was sure that in a few days he would be able to lay hands on the Jewish population of Budapest. He said, word for word, that if the Kettlitz business was not settled in forty-eight hours he would kill all 'the bunch of filthy Jews' in Budapest.

Estimates of the number of Jews still remaining in Budapest varied greatly. According to Eichmann's calculations they were about 250,000. We estimated at least 150,000. As a matter of fact, they were much more numerous, although not to as high a total as Eichmann stated. It is difficult to imagine the ingenuity, the imagination and the guile displayed by the Jews to hide their identities and pass themselves off as 'Aryans', but there were also all those who did not dare to leave off the yellow star and these amounted to between 120,000 and 150,000 persons.

But Eichmann was not alone. Though it was true that at this moment we felt Clages's loss as a tragedy, still we had in Becher a man on whom we could rely up to a point. At this time, although he was fully disposed to help us, Becher did not yet dare to advance without any backing. He could not manage to understand that the delegates of the 'Joint' in Switzerland would not play the game – that it was only a game, he had known for a long time.

We finally convinced him to submit a new proposal to Himmler, without taking account of Eichmann, whose formidable threats must remain a dead-letter without Himmler's consent. We must get permission for Kastner to go to Switzerland once more. We pointed out that neither Saly Mayer nor Kettlitz was diplomatic enough to accomplish the heavy task which had devolved upon them. In this proposal Becher also mentioned to Himmler the possible results of the negotiations that had just begun with the Rumanian government. In the state of panic that now had seized him, Himmler was clearly disposed to let himself be pushed in any direction provided he saw a chance, however small it might be, of getting into contact with the future victors. The upshot was that Becher got a free hand to send Kastner once again to Switzerland.

Let us recall here, once again, that our friends in Switzerland and ourselves (as also most of the Budapest population) were expecting the German troops to leave the capital any day. Each one of us did what he could, by improvising promises, to get through this short delay. This urgency, however, our Swiss friends did not share. They thought no doubt that the trouble was unnecessary. It is true that contact with the German authorities might lay those who participated in them from the Jewish side (however great the stake might be) open to the stupid and unjust accusation of being 'collaborators'. But if Saly Mayer and the others in Switzerland recoiled before the possibility of such charges, at Budapest it appeared to us absurd, and in a word, impossible not to grasp with both hands at any chance, wherever it might come from, to save hundreds of thousands of human lives. We did not care a fig for the puerile reproaches we might have to face later on.

What we did not know then was that Budapest would be defended and besieged and that we should not be liberated until the end of January 1945, that is to say almost two months later on.

On November 28, 1944, Kastner once more left Budapest with one of Becher's assistants, *Hauptsturmführer* SS Krell, and went first of all to the Swiss frontier. I was not to see him again until after the war.

24. The Last Four Weeks before the Investment of Budapest

Shortly after Kastner had left came the time of the hardest trials for us in Budapest. In the latter part of November a ghetto had been set up. The Germans declared that in no case would Budapest be surrendered, without fighting, to the Russians. In such conditions, the presence in the capital of at least 150,000 Jews – Eichmann said 250,000 – all hostile to the Third Reich – must seem, to say the least of it, to constitute a danger for the Germans. The creation of the ghetto had gone forward very rapidly without our being able to do anything to hinder it.

This measure at once aroused in us the memory of the horrible news we had received from the ghettos set up by the Germans in the occupied territories. The Polish refugees in Budapest, especially, and their leader Dr. Osterweil-Kotarba, refused to move into the ghetto. And although any Jew who stayed in the 'free' part of the city was threatened with summary execution, the number of those who preferred a clandestine existence to one in the ghetto was considerable. Almost every house in Budapest sheltered Jews with false papers. Since hundreds of thousands of people from the provinces had fled from the Russians into the capital, the disorder in the city increased all the time, and with false papers there was some chance of passing for an 'Aryan' if physical appearance did not betray Jewish origins.

Osterweil-Kotarba and his Polish compatriots were particularly concerned with Jewish orphans. These amounted to thousands, maybe tens of thousands. But the children were indeed not all orphans. Often their parents were still living but had been requisitioned and carried off very suddenly – often at a few hours notice – for forced labour, and had had to abandon their children.

In Poland many Jewish parents, before fleeing from the Germans or being deported, entrusted their children to 'Aryan' families generally in modest circumstances. In exchange for services rendered the adoptive parents often received everything refugees possessed. Many of these 'adopted' children were, nevertheless, to perish. Some were abandoned while others were handed over to their executioners. Nevertheless a certain percentage of them managed to survive the war.

The Polish refugees, then, attempted to save, in the same way, Hungarian Jewish children in Budapest. They were 'Aryanized' – confided to non-Jewish adoptive parents. For neighbours and other inquisitive people the new member of the family was passed off as the child of relations who were refugees from the east. For a sum of 5,000 to 10,000 pengoes (at that time $250 to $500) – and often more – the adoptive parents promised to keep the children as long as danger threatened, even if later on the adults who had handed over the children, were captured and killed.

Osterweil-Kotarba's scheme made heavy demands on my empty 'Joint' treasury. But even still larger sums were needed to supply the ghetto with a certain reserve of foodstuffs. The Jews had been ordered to congregate in the ghetto but nothing had been done to feed them. So I entrusted a former member of the Jewish Council, Ludwig Stöckler, with the task of buying on the black market everything he could find – lentils, beans, maize, flour and if possible oil, by the waggon-load. Stöckler was aided by Emil Bauer, Rudolf Weiss and Zoltan Weiner who knew all about the provision market. The task was, indeed, to feed from 80,000 to 100,000 persons for an indefinite period, maybe for months. The collection of funds necessary for these purchases was a problem in itself.

These food purchases were sharply criticized by Osterweil-Kotarba and his Polish compatriots. In their eyes, the concentration into a ghetto meant, as in all previous cases, the slaughter of the Jewish population. What I spent for the purchase of food was, according to these Poles, 'Money thrown out of the window.' Furthermore, I was reproached with treason since, as a responsible representative of the 'Joint', I approved and recommended entry into the ghetto. The young '*Haloutzim*' who, up to then had remained disciplined and who, after Kastner's departure, had followed the instructions of Komoly and myself, broke out into open rebellion. Osterweil-Kotarba demanded that I should devote to the 'Aryanization' plan all the money available or which could be collected. But I was certain that the whole of our resources would have been exhausted after the placing of, at the most, a few hundreds of parentless children, whose fate even then would have remained very uncertain. On the other hand I never tired of repeating that it would be the greatest of sins and the most monstrous of crimes not to stock provisions in the ghetto and thus to condemn its inmates to die of hunger in case Budapest was besieged. I persisted in the desperate and presumptuous idea that the Jews who remained in Budapest should not be deported – or only a very small number of them – and that by continuing negotiations with Himmler we could manage to preserve, in the ghetto, the greater number of them from extermination.

I had to face the most violent discussions but, with Komoly's help, we came finally to a decision – which was also accepted by the 'rebels'. About a third of my resources should be devoted to 'Aryanization' and the remainder to supplying the ghetto population. The importance of this decision became fully apparent later on. After the Russians had occupied Budapest, I saw Osterweil-Kotarba again and he congratulated me on the firmness I had shown in resisting him and his friends' obstinate and threatening attitude. Indeed, the stocks of food stored in the ghetto had prevented its inmates from dying of hunger. On the last day of the German occupation, the last sackfuls of beans and lentils were cooked and distributed. The stocks had lasted for more than five weeks. Of course, owing to the coarse and meagre diet, the death rate among feeble old people and the sick was much above the normal. But the great majority of the inmates of the Budapest ghetto managed to survive in spite of all the dangers to which they were exposed, and their case was unique.

After Kastner had left, the struggle to save Jewish lives went on in Budapest for a month longer between our committee and those we had won over to our cause among the National Socialists, on the one side, and Eichmann's Gestapo and the Arrow Cross, on the other.

Then the city was invaded by the Red Army.

During all this time Becher was on tenter-hooks in Budapest. He was supposed to risk his life every day for an undertaking he had long known was founded on fallacious promises. But he was entangled in the mesh and, for reasons as much humanitarian as practical, he thought his duty was go help us. Maybe he imagined that in this way he could dissociate himself from the crimes of the Nazi State. Perhaps also, he wanted, as far as he was able, to perform an 'act of reparation' on behalf of the German people.

On December 2, 1944, four days after Kastner left, Becher

received a telegram in Budapest from Krell stating that a first sum of five million Swiss francs was available and would be paid over almost at once. At the same time Krell mentioned that while the second test-convoy was still being held up by Eichmann, new difficulties were arising with the Allies. This telegram was also signed by Kettlitz. One must admire the skill with which Kastner had been able to extract such a message as this from the German delegates since clearly they had been given no such assurances in Switzerland.

While he was in Switzerland, Kastner was able to look deep down into the abyss of vanities, passions and resentments wherein the Jewish community had lost its way. Saly Mayer, as director of the 'Joint' had not only not sought the collaboration of the other Jewish organizations but had kept them firmly at arm's distance. When he arrived Kastner received formal instructions to confine his contacts to Saly Mayer, the director of the 'Joint', (who had provided us with the visas and was supported by our Budapest friends), and not to get into touch with any other Jewish organizations. These were, as a matter of fact, Zionist groups such as the Palestinian Office, under Dr. 'Haim Posner at Geneva and the delegation in Switzerland of the Jewish Agency headed by Richard Lichtheim. Furthermore there were also the delegates of the Jewish World Congress, Dr. Gerhard Rieger and Dr. Silberschein, as well as, for orthodox Judaism, the brothers Sternbuch of Montreux, who represented the Association of American orthodox rabbis and the Organization of Jewish Assistance, the *Hijefs*, also established in the United States. It is hardly necessary to say that Kastner did of course, have discussions with all these, for he always hoped he might find, during these meetings held as discreetly as possible, some help for our cause.

But he had to act with extreme prudence since the 'Joint' – which must not be indisposed – was not only the assistance organization which disposed of the most powerful resources, but in Himmler's eyes, as in Eichmann's and Becher's, it seemed to enjoy in the United States much more influence than it did in fact possess. Kastner must then not destroy the illusion that we were, first and foremost, the representatives of the 'Joint'.

There were real difficulties only with the brothers Sternbuch who, after the arrival in Switzerland of the first instalment of the Bergen-Belsen convoy, had secured the help of the Swiss senator Jean-Marie Musy who thanks to his good relations with the Third Reich could open, they thought, a way to Himmler himself. They also wanted to try to 'unfreeze', for their own account, to Switzerland a convoy of deportees from a concentration camp. They were so convinced of the excellence of their plan and of the advantages of such an undertaking that Kastner's efforts to dissuade them were in vain. It would, of course, have been much better to have joined forces so as to ensure that the great mass of Jews still living in the camps and in Hungary might survive where they were, rather than to transfer abroad – with quite insufficient technical means – a small part of these Jews while leaving the others to their fate. Kastner repeatedly said that our test-convoy's sole object was to show Jews abroad that Himmler really was prepared to establish contacts and make concessions. He explained also that once this object had been attained, what was now necessary was to employ all means to save the *totality* of the Jews who had managed to survive. But the brothers Sternbuch would not listen. They wanted at all costs to bring a convoy – their convoy – to Switzerland. And they demanded vehemently that Kastner should secure them Becher's aid in their enterprise.

Later on, when the war was ended, the Sternbuchs violently attacked Becher and Kastner because such help had not been forthcoming. In effect, what we were determined to do was to carry on with a task that was obviously less spectacular and more thankless (even easy to question as later events were to prove) but which nonetheless was to save from a last minute annihilation all the European Jews still surviving.

Finally, however, the Sternbuch-Musy operation did result in Himmler's liberating a convoy of a thousand persons to Switzerland. When, during the last months and weeks of the war, our channels appeared less and less promising to the

Reichsführer for his personal hopes, he showed interest in any possibility which presented itself for contacts with foreigners – if they seemed to him to offer advantages for later on. For these reasons, the Sternbuch plan was finally successful.

25. The Columbusgasse Camp

The day the telegram from Krell and Kettlitz reached Budapest, December 2, 1944, was the expiry date fixed by Eichmann after the first telegram from Kettlitz on November 27.

In the night December 2 to 3, Eichmann's team struck us a very painful direct blow. They had our Columbusgasse camp evacuated. The object of this measure, in the course of which several persons were shot, was either to send all the inmates off to Vienna or to execute them on the spot.

During the morning of December 3 some messengers from our youth organizations came with terrible news to my house. Units of the Arrow Cross and of the Hungarian police had invested the camp and shooting was going on. In the Columbusgasse neither could I find an officer responsible for the doings of the Hungarians, nor enter the camp. My first idea was to telephone the Bureau of Jewish Affairs. I was told Eichmann was away from Budapest and that nothing could be done. Then I decided to go to the SD which since Clages's death was under the orders of his successor *Hauptsturmführer* SS Neugeboren. He was a man without the slightest initiative and whose position in the ranks of the SS was so insignificant that after Clages's death the department had lost practically all interest for us. Neugeboren had no personal contact with Himmler. But although he was partially informed about the negotiations conducted with us by Clages on Himmler's orders, he was not the man – quite apart from his subordinate rank – to resume and carry on such an enterprise which, after all, constituted high treason against the Führer.

I already knew Neugeboren since I had met him several times during my visits to Clages. All the same, that day I asked Mrs. Brand to come with me, since she had been in touch with him at the time she was released by the Hungarians, and also afterwards. Moreover she knew how to handle him. It was still very early and there was not much chance of finding Neugeboren already in his office. We went, therefore, to his private address, which we had luckily been able to obtain.

Following tried tactics, we argued to the *Hauptsturmführer* that the nocturnal attack by the Arrow Cross and the Hungarian police was not only as a conspiracy against us Jews but also against the exchange operations organized by the Third Reich. The argument was logical enough in that theoretically the Columbusgasse camp was the assembly-point for the members of the 2nd, 3rd, and then the 4th convoys which would leave Budapest after the arrival in Switzerland of the first convoy and its payment. Of course I spoke to Neugeboren about the telegram that had arrived from Switzerland the day before.

The *Hauptsturmführer* was a prudent man and we had called upon him without notice. First of all he made enquiries by telephone. He rang Solymossy, the chief of the Hungarian police who said that armed resistance had broken out in the camp and that a 'cleaning up' operation was going on. He added that the operation had been undertaken at the instigation of the Bureau of Jewish Affairs. *Hauptsturmführer* Otto Hunsche and Theodor Dannecker had had the camp surrounded during the night and thoroughly searched. Neugeboren repeated aloud what Solymossy said so that we also heard it. Then he told us that in the circumstances the competent German authorities were fully informed and that he could do nothing at all. He advised me to apply directly to Hunsche and Dannecker.

So I set off for Schwabenberg while Mrs. Brand returned

to our lodging. I was filled with rage and despair. Judging from the outside it seemed to us that systematic extermination was going on inside the camp. This impression had been strengthened by several persons who from neighbouring houses had observed what was going on within the camp. Their accounts were horrible. Some people, on the Jewish side, hinted that none of this could have taken place if only Kastner (whom it was now my role to replace entirely) had been in Budapest. And I was convinced that if I really wanted to fulfil the functions fate had assigned to me, no daring and no effort would be too great.

It was in this state of mind that I got to Hunsche's and Dannecker's office. I was shown in at once and, without leaving them to ask the reason for my visit, I moved in to the attack. I protested strongly against the proceedings in our camp. I reminded them of the success attending Kastner's negotiations in Switzerland. I mentioned the telegram received the day before and I invoked Himmler's authority. Hunsche pretended to be astonished and said he knew nothing of the whole affair, that the operation concerned the Hungarian police only. Dannecker said nothing. Then I demanded to see Eichmann and was told that the *Obersturmbannführer* was absent from Hungary. I replied he must at once be sent a telegram informing him of the incidents and asking him to return. To make my demand more weighty I added that in case of refusal I would at once complain to Himmler, a perfectly gratuitous remark as I knew since Becher was away from Budapest and without him I could not make any such appeal. When I once again strongly called for the immediate stoppage of the operation against the camp, Hunsche left the room. He came back to tell me the Hungarians had found arms in the camp and because of this had executed a few hostages. He added all was now calm in the camp and that preparations were being made to evacuate the inmates to Vienna. Thereupon I was dismissed.

The next day, December 4, I went off once more to the Bureau of Jewish Affairs. I was more than ever decided to stake everything and not to allow myself to be shown the door.

Eichmann had meanwhile returned and he received me in the presence of Hunsche and Dannecker. For the first time since I had seen them, both the *Hauptsturmführer* were in full battle-dress with helmets on their heads and obviously ready to leave. The front then passed quite near the encircled city and only a little gap remained westwards with a road and a railway line still operated by the Germans, but often under fire.

I felt that perhaps only audacity could help us although the situation seemed almost desperate, so I resolved to be aggressive. For our Waada the Columbusgasse camp was – together with the test-convoy – the most important and evident symbol of success we had up to then obtained. Now I was no longer thinking of the train. Only the camp counted. Its collapse would entail mine, since I rightly held myself responsible for its fate.[1]

The man facing me, and his two assistants, were wholesale murderers but they were also exceedingly cowardly. They had become specialists in the art of sending unarmed and defenceless people to the slaughter-house. They 'served their country' by laying a monstrous responsibility on their fellow countrymen. But they themselves were too pusillanimous to fight in reality, to fight with weapons in their hands. They were accustomed to see other people meet them in fear and trembling. The firmness I displayed towards them first

1. Since the publication of the detailed article I wrote for the July 1960 number of the French review *Evidence*, on this subject, I have often been the butt of ironical or ill-natured comments from those who sabotaged our campaign of assistance – members of the Jewish Council who had fled Budapest, Jews who far from the front, lived through this period in neutral countries – and even some who were survivors from the Columbusgasse camp. They, as well as non-Jewish observers of the events of those days, cannot yet imagine that a Jew dared to confront Eichmann – that millionaire of murder – as I did. I threw away prudence and ruse. I was intoxicated with despair. It was neck or nothing. Immediately after the war – in June 1945, I repeated to Saly Mayer this conversation with Eichmann, but few people were informed of it. If I have now decided to inform a wider public about it, that is because of considerations touched on in the last chapter of this book.

surprised and then disquieted them. But for me and for those I had come to defend the result was – salvation.

Eichmann greeted me by saying 'I'm told you were very rough with my collaborators yesterday.' To which I answered 'Herr *Obersturmbannführer* I am obliged to speak in the same tone to you – if not even more roughly.'

He was, as often, slightly tipsy and I foresaw that he might well pull out his pistol. But he did not. I went on in a still firmer voice 'I think your *Reichsführer* will be obliged to you when he sees your staff break the liaison we had established with him. It is you who are responsible and you will have to account to him.'

At that time I did not know, neither do I know today, how far Eichmann was aware of our influence on Himmler. But I was certain that a conciliatory attitude would get nowhere with him, whereas he might be imposed upon by self-assurance and firmness. His reply showed this clear enough.

'But anyway, M. Biss, you must understand that we are within our rights. In this camp have been found arms used to fire on Hungarian policeman. According to the laws of war I am justified in having the whole camp annihilated.'

Then followed a sort of pleading for Hunsche and Dannecker. In front of me a Jew, Eichmann declared that in this affair both had acted in a proper manner. He admitted that it was at their instigation the Hungarian police had acted against the camp. The execution of the hostages would have been ordered by himself had he been in Budapest. Hunsche, who the day before had at first denied knowing anything about the affair, kept obstinately silent.

After this Eichmann pointed out to me that the people in the camp had been very lucky to get off so lightly. As punishment for the harbouring of arms, it had finally been decided to shoot only a few hostages. But I must understand that the inmates of the camp, a large percentage made up of men capable of bearing arms, must not remain in a city the Germans (Eichmann said 'we') have decided to defend and which might have to support a siege. He was therefore going to send the whole lot to Bergen–Belsen. If our operation with the first convoy was successful, nothing would prevent us, after it was settled, from sending these people from Bergen-Belsen to Switzerland.

Then I protested especially against the evacuation of women, children, the sick and the aged, recalling Himmler's instructions in this respect. I also objected strongly to the others marching to Vienna. Eichmann promised that, as an exception, he would assign waggons for this convoy. Clearly he expected thanks for such an act of generosity. But the comment escaped me 'Yes, I know all about that; you will pack them so tightly that three-quarters of them will be dead when they arrive at Bergen-Belsen.'

Upon that he first assumed a really offended air and then said indignantly:

'It seems to me, M. Biss that you also indulge in propaganda about the supposed German atrocities.'

'Herr *Obersturmbannführer*', I answered, 'what is the use of you and me telling tall stories? You know what I am referring to and I know very well what you do.'

He did not reply at once. But later on during the interview he finally consented to except the young people not old enough to bear arms, children, the sick and the aged, but insisted that both men and women in a fit state to work must leave the camp and be evacuated. He reiterated his promise to allocate two trains, one for the men and the other for the women, and 'guaranteed' that in no case would more than 70 or 80 persons be put in one waggon. The convoys would be sent directly to Bergen-Belsen and to the 'privileged camp' for a 'provisional stay' while awaiting their further journey to Switzerland.

As a matter of fact the two trains did leave Budapest shortly afterwards while the remainder of the inmates of the camp were led into the ghetto. The man's convoy did indeed reach Bergen-Belsen, but the women's was held up a little distance from Budapest since in the meantime the Russians had bombed and destroyed the railway line. The women had to get out and march as far as the Austrian frontier. They were set to work on constructing fortifications. After the Russian troops arrived the women were able to go back at once to Hungary.

The men's convoy suffered many losses since it was bombed on the way and machine-gunned by Allied aircraft. The survivors did reach Bergen-Belsen from which they were not liberated until April, 1945. Some, as a result of the treatment they had suffered in the camp, died before this date.

In our Columbusgasse camp there were indeed several hundred men of combatant age, deserters from the obligatory labour service who had come there to hide. Arms had also been camouflaged, it is true, in a neighbouring building whose garden was separated only by a fence from our land. This building sheltered an organization of the Hungarian Youth, the *Levente* which corresponded to the *Hitlerjugend* as far as its conception and constitution were concerned.

Now the front was nearing them and in view of the obvious defeat of the Germans, these young people found they were democrats at heart, and in agreement with the Jewish deserters from the compulsory labour service who were hidden in our camps, had planned an uprising against the German intruders.

No member of the *Levente* was executed but Moscovics, the commandant of our camp, as well as the medical officer, Raphael and his son aged sixteen, were shot on the spot. Also we had to mourn some victims among those who had put up a resistance.

26. Various Actions

As the Jewish population was obviously disinclined to go into the ghetto, the Arrow Cross leaders decided to use energetic measures to get them in. Whole blocks of buildings were surrounded and thoroughly searched. Jews, men or women, fit for labour and fighting, were immediately evacuated; the others were led into the ghetto. During these operations summary executions were numerous but those responsible could never be identified, so it was impossible later on to bring them to book.

The normal procedure was as follows: in the evening before the search a block of buildings would be surrounded by the Hungarian police. Immediately, and with great daring, our young *'Haloutzim* would set out on a field-day. They put on SS officers' cloaks (the Gestapo officers wore green leather cloaks) in company with two real German SS men we knew and who in exchange for money or a bottle of brandy (though often for nothing at all) agreed to join in the escapade. In this way our young men would get into houses invested by the Hungarian police and where to their knowledge friends were living; deserters from the labour battalions (and therefore especially threatened) or militant Zionists who must at all costs be freed. The Hungarian police had the greatest respect for a German uniform and therefore no one dared to bar the way to young Gestapo officers, accompanied by German soldiers, who had come to proceed to an 'arrest'. Generally they were able to leave unmolested with their 'prisoner'.

Ordinarily the porter was informed that the Gestapo had come to arrest so-and-so or a certain family and take them off to a camp. But more than once disagreeable incidents occurred, such as for instance when a man who had just been 'arrested' received the visit of the supposed Gestapo men with joy and in the porter's presence wanted to fling his arms around their necks. With great presence of mind the 'SS officer' bawled out 'God damned Jew have you gone crazy?' and before the porter could recover from his amazement, the 'officer' hurried off with his prisoner. On occasion, I myself took part in these expeditions and 'arrested' some friends and acquaintances.

One of our fellow workers by the name of Vicki Fischer several times visited a temporary camp at the Teleki Tér where arrested Jews were collected, awaiting deportation, among them many of Fischer's *'Haloutzim* friends. He gave the inmates news and managed to get a few out of the camp. But, during one of his visits he was searched, questioned and exposed. He was then interned himself in the camp but other friends succeeded, after a short time, in liberating him by similar stratagems. One afternoon they brought him to me at our Red Cross office in Mérleg street. Fischer of course no longer had any identity papers, and the first thing for me to do was to find him a lodging for the night, since it was not possible, before the next day, to provide him with new papers. I generally passed off as a German and had a photocopy of a card from the obligatory labour service stamped with a huge swastika, as we have already seen. I went out with my wife and Fischer and found a car at the nearest taxi-rank. At that time civilians were no longer allowed to use taxis without a special pass. I opened the door of the car, showed my 'pass' and called out, as I usually did, *Deutsche Polizei*. The driver seemed to understand scarcely any German, but the word *Polizei* was enough and he let us get in. I sat next to him while my wife and Fischer took the back seats. First of all we drove to a bunker where we sheltered Slovak refugees. A little before we got there, I noticed one of our men at the corner of a street. When he saw the taxi slowing down he made a sign for me to go on without stopping. Obviously there was danger in the air and the bunker was threatened. So we went on towards another bunker at the other end of the city, not far from where I lived.

A 'bunker' was generally a large apartment where, owing to the understanding attitude of the owner of the building or the resident itself, a fairly large number of endangered people could be hidden.

In order to get to this second bunker we had to cross the little wood in the middle of the city. At such a late hour, and because of the prevailing insecurity, this was usually a deserted spot. But after a turning, at the place where the road was cut by a level crossing, we found the way barred. Before the barricade was a so-called 'mixed patrol' – two Arrow Cross, two policemen and a gendarme. When the latter approached the car, I lowered the window and shouted I belonged to the German police. But in the confusion of the moment I did not manage to find at once my 'pass'. The gendarme then opened the door, checked my wife's (also false) papers, and then asked Fischer for his. This young man, only sixteen or seventeen years of age, might quite well be a deserter from the Hungarian army who had slipped away from the crumbling units during the retreat. It was the duty of these patrols to arrest such deserters as well as Jews.

When Fischer answered briefly 'I haven't any', the gendarme stared straight at him and said 'You're not a Jew, eh? Why aren't you wearing the yellow star? Just then I found my 'pass' and pushed it under the gendarme's nose while I bawled out 'German police, I'm taking him off as you can see.' Obviously the gendarme and his colleagues knew no German and he gazed, in perplexity at the swastika stamp. 'You've heard what's been said' Fischer abruptly remarked in Magyar 'I'm being taken off by the German police.' The gendarme nodded his head with a knowing look, slammed the door and saluted. The barrier opened and our car set off again. As I turned round I saw my wife's face was wax-like.

Once more we had been lucky, for generally the police handed over arrested Jews to the Arrow Cross who led them without delay to the Danube's banks, where they were shot.

At the Margitkörut military prison in Buda there were several hundred '*Haloutzim*' who had been rounded up either as deserters or because they were suspected of spying. We learned that, every night, Arrow Cross patrols shot a group of these men, without any pretence of a trial, on the banks of the Danube. It was certain that in a short time all these Jewish prisoners would be liquidated. Among them was one of our best and bravest '*Haloutzim*' leaders, Zvi Goldfarb, and his wife Neska. One day Joël Nussbecher (Palgi) came to tell me that the Haganah had the idea of getting these prisoners out of jail. A patrol was to be composed of Jews from the obligatory labour service in Hungarian uniform, together with a few 'real' Hungarian soldiers (paid for the part they were to play). These, under the leadership of a worker from the labour service, who played the part of an officer, were to march up to the prison's entrance. There the patrol would present false orders to appear before the military tribunal which sat at the Hadik barracks – and would take delivery of the prisoners.

The operation would cost money since the Hungarian soldiers must be suitably paid and the summons to appear – drawn up on authentic official forms – must be bought. Without any hesitation I gave the money – a relatively large sum – and a few days later was delighted to hear that Zvi and Neska Goldfarb, as well as their comrades had been delivered and were already in hiding, either in the Swiss legation or other shelters. They had been 'called for' in the twilight and the procession of prisoners and their armed 'guards' had broken up in a dark and deserted street. Then each of the liberated men made off for the shelter assigned to him beforehand.

Immediately afterwards a similar operation was carried out at the Föutca prison, and if my memory serves me, these sudden raids alone resulted in the freeing of some 240 persons.

Another complicated problem was that of introducing into the ghetto the stocks of food bought on the black market.

Arrow Cross patrols kept constant guard at the ghetto's entrances and examined very carefully everything that arrived. They confiscated anything that took their fancy without there being any question of the police interfering.

One day our purchasers succeeded in procuring a considerable quantity of sunflower seed oil and of fats, but the trucks carrying the precious loads were seized. Ludwig Stöckler, who was responsible for the purchases, came to see me. He was in a great state since this oil was the most valuable of all the supplies he had been able to obtain – and the one also we lacked the most.

Jews were forbidden to purchase fats, butter and oil. The ration cards distributed to them up to then, had no coupons permitting the buying any of these food-stuffs.

I was in a difficult situation. It was true that I had on several occasions, either through Becher or even Eichmann's office, managed to get confiscated food-stuffs restored to us. This time, however, we were up against two infringements of Hungarian regulations. Not only was it punishable to make use of the black market, but we had tried to introduce into the ghetto supplies forbidden to Jews. I neither would nor could submit this problem to Becher, and thus add to our already long list of claims, for we were, just then, through Becher, endeavouring to get from Himmler an assurance that the ghetto would be preserved. And this assurance we would then have to make the most of with the Hungarians. This was our main preoccupation. Furthermore, my position was a particularly delicate one, since I had no good news from Switzerland I could give Becher and nothing tangible to offer Himmler. So I decided to go to Eichmann's office.

There Hunsche understood at once what the matter was, and informed Eichmann who, of course, refused categorically to 'contravene Hungarian regulations' or to support 'illegal operations'.

'What can be done, the Jews have no right to oil and fats' he said 'with regret'. But I was insistent and then suddenly he made me a counter-proposition. Christmas was coming on and I could give him something for his men's festivities. I accepted and the business was concluded. I handed a hundred and fifty thousand pengoes to a certain Röder, an SS commandant and Eichmann with a few telephone calls did what was necessary for the Hungarians to return our trucks, which were still at the entry to the ghetto.

Thanks to this exchange of 'good proceedings' it became possible to prolong decisively the physical resistance of the population confined in the ghetto.

27. The Test-Convoy Finally Arrives in Switzerland

On December 8, 1944, I got a telegram from Kastner telling me that the train from Bergen-Belsen had crossed the Swiss frontier.

At the same time Becher received a wire from Krell and Kettlitz, his two representatives, confirming that 5,000,000 Swiss francs had been paid over and ear-marked for the purchase of Swiss products. They added that the payment of the other 15,000,000 was going forward, but that on the Jewish side it was hoped that Billitz would be sent to the Swiss frontier and that Kastner – who was already there – should be authorized to leave Reich territory and enter Switzerland. Furthermore, Krell and Kettlitz said, they were asked about the position of the Jewish population in Budapest as well as about the measures taken for its protection.

It was up to Becher to decide whether Kastner should or should not be permitted to go into Switzerland. Now that Kastner's family was outside the Reich, such a decision implied a much increased responsibility. I urged Becher to take this on himself and pointed out that all the members of the Waada could be regarded as hostages for guaranteeing Kastner's return. But Billitz could not go to the Swiss frontier. The Manfred Weiss factories, though still working, were being partially evacuated and Billitz as managing director had to supervise these operations himself. The Third Reich had naturally taken care to remove plant of military importance from seizure by the Russian troops.

The owners of the Weiss works, of which Becher was in theory the controller, assured me, after the war, that they entirely approved the measures taken by him. If the plant had remained at Budapest, under the communist economic system, it would have been expropriated without any indemnity, as was done with all the real estate and industrial properties which had had to remain in Hungary. It goes without saying that the point of view of the Hungarian Communist historians – who accuse Becher of having pillaged their country – and that of the legitimate owners – who later approved of Becher's decisions – were entirely different.

In his reply to the telegram of Krell and Kellitz, Becher strongly demanded the payment of the remaining 15,000,000 francs (which in his telegram he called *Ackersegen* ('rural prosperity'). As far as the situation of the Jews at Budapest was concerned he had nothing new to mention – and especially nothing favourable.

We were to learn only after the war the difficulties Kastner encountered at the Swiss frontier to get the Bergen-Belsen train into Switzerland. Kettlitz especially wanted to hold up the train because the 20,000,000 Swiss francs had not been paid over as arranged. Furthermore Kastner had all the trouble in the world to persuade our Swiss friends that if the convoy was stuck at the German frontier because our promises had not been kept, it would have incalculable consequences not only for the passengers but also for the Jews still in Budapest.

Finally 5,000,000 francs were indeed paid, but were secretly blocked. The Swiss Bank got orders not to obey the instructions of the SS concerning this sum and if necessary, to let things drag until the end of the war. The SS of course knew nothing of these arrangements made by the person who had put up the money. As a matter of fact the credit remained in the bank until the end of the war when it was returned to the backer who had provided the funds.

Strictly speaking, the passengers in the Bergen-Belsen convoy had been entirely 'paid for' by the valuables collected in Hungary and whose worth had been estimated by me, first with Grüson and then with Grabau. Nevertheless Himmler went on demanding the complete payment of the 20,000,000 francs on account for further 'deliveries' of Jews and, above all, for the keeping alive of the Jews still in Budapest and in the camps.

Eichmann, in his irritation at Joël Brand's defection, kept Brand's mother and three sisters at Bergen-Belsen. He did not even permit them to leave with the second train. Certain other persons who had left Budapest as part of the convoy were also retained at Bergen-Belsen – for having broken some rule of 'camp discipline'. They were the victims of an inhuman system. Like Mrs. Brand, Drs. Andreas Kassowitz and Eugene Kertesz and his wife as well as Alexandre Weiss, all lawyers from Cluj, died at Bergen-Belsen before the liberation of the camp. Shortly after they had arrived at Bergen-Belsen these latter learned that their daughters, who had not been allowed to leave Cluj with them, had also been sent with other convoys into the Reich, to Bergen-Belsen, but to a different block. Inmates of one block were not allowed to communicate with other blocks nor even to find out what prisoners were in them. The parents had broken the rules in this matter and had furthermore betrayed themselves by a request to the camp commandant in which they asked that their daughters should be transferred to be with them in the 'privileged' persons camp. As a punishment for this infraction they were excluded from the Swiss convoy. They had to remain at Bergen-Belsen where they met with miserable ends.

28. The Ghetto

Krell got back to Budapest on December 8, 1944, and informed Becher of his mission's poor results. Kastner had told me confidentially that he had had to scrape together everything he could lay hands on in order to collect the 5,000,000 francs and it was quite useless to expect 15,000,000 more. Naturally Becher knew nothing about all that. Indeed, how could he have imagined that our 'Joint' – an organization thought to dispose of several hundreds of millions of dollars – could not dispose of the advance agreed upon Becher no longer dared to forward the requests I addressed to him, all of which were intended to get from Himmler instructions or interventions in our favour, for we, and Becher with us had more or less given the impression that the business of the 20,000,000 francs had been long since settled and the payment effected.

It is true that now 'competitors' to our line of action had appeared who had now become less demanding, and that they negotiated with Himmler, not by proposing payments or goods, but making the same requests as ours without offering an exchange. But all these steps, without exception, were taken only at the end of 1944, or even later, at the beginning of 1945. That is to say they occurred long after our action and were based solely on the success we had already won.[1]

Although our information was vague, we had learned that other Jewish 'feelers' had also been put out for discussions with Himmler, but for the present, without proposing any counterpart. In consequence we modified the terms of our preceding offers and proposed that future payments should be exclusively utilized for the benefit of German prisoners in the hands of the Allies. Becher sent this suggestion to Himmler who replied favourably. Hence my telegram of December 10 addressed to Switzerland. These were its terms:

Saly Mayer, Saint-Gall.

Regarding telegram, NIKI Kurt must again decide if this method suitable stop regarding fifteen remaining. Wilhelm thinks has new propositions that can be amply suitable also view utilization type purely humanitarian stop for prestige Kurt desirable effect payment as facilitating his positive attitude concerning new propositions Wilhelm. Biss.[2]

But these new dispositions were envisaged without prejudice to the preceding agreements, and for the future, that is to say after payment by the 'Joint' of the first twenty millions – and Himmler on the faith of Becher's reports thought this had already been done.

So Becher was completely nonplussed when Krell confirmed that only 5,000,000 francs had been paid. Himmler had

1. The description of these different activities does not come within the scope of this book and I would refer the reader to Walter Schellenberg's 'Memoirs' for information concerning them. It should, however, be noted that the very considerable difference in date between our action and Himmler's later contacts, has up to now hardly been mentioned by historians.

2. As the first phrase has no importance for our theme, it will be enough for us to say that in this telegram the reference is obviously to the 15 million Swiss francs already mentioned on several occasions. Kurt means Becher, Wilhelm Dr. Billitz, and Stephan is the code-word for the American government.

expressly ordered that the despatch of the convoy into Switzerland should be made to depend on the payment of the 20,000,000. Now the train was already in foreign territory Becher did not dare to admit to Himmler that his instructions had not been obeyed by his men and himself. In spite of everything, even Krumey, Eichmann's representative at the frontier had allowed himself to be outwitted by Kastner and had, in flagrant opposition to the orders Eichmann had given him, allowed the train to pass. So Becher at Budapest had not only to face an Eichmann furious at the turn events had taken but our continued urging that he see Himmler and ask him for assurances that the Budapest ghetto would be spared.

On December 1, 1944, Becher telegraphed to Kastner:

Situation Budapest explosive please inform me without delay regarding 15 rural prosperities.

On the same day I sent this wire to Switzerland:

Saly Mayer, Saint-Gall.
Goods stored separately and on Kurt's side assurances given stop seen side Hagar certain threats. Kurt also intervened there stop demands in return loyal continuation payment fifteen remaining stop inform Rudolf contingent 30 ordered by Steger also promised and delivery already ordered. Biss.[1]

I have said that we were pressing Becher to act for the preservation of the ghetto. We had good reasons for this. Reasons that had also induced me to send the above telegram. Two days earlier I had been called to a secret meeting at the Swiss legation. There I found gathered together my friend Dr. Wilhelm, Samuel Stern, chairman of the Jewish Council that had practically ceased to exist, and other notable Jews.

Stern had been able to hide in the house of a Hungarian

1. The 'goods stored separately' meant that in the interval the ghetto had been formed and isolated. Kurt is Becher, Hagar is the Arrow Cross Hungarian government. The fifteen remaining were the millions of Swiss francs still due. The contingent of 30 designated the Siovak trucks. Rudolf was Kastner.

journalist, a member of the Arrow Cross and even the editor of one of the Party organs, but who, by concealing in his home the leader of the Jewish Council hoped to provide himself with an alibi for later on. Stern told us the journalist had learned from an absolutely sure source that, at a recent meeting of the Arrow Cross cabinet, it had been decided to wipe out the ghetto as soon as it had been finally established and isolated. It should be noted that Szálasi, the head of the government had taken position against this project but had not been followed by the majority of the cabinet, influenced by the extremist minister, Emil Kovarcz. The argument of the 'ultra' gang was that since Budapest looked like being shortly occupied by the advanced troops of the Red Army, therefore every Jew who remained alive would be a witness against an Arrow Cross partisan or any other anti-semitic Hungarian. If matters were looked at in this way, then these witnesses must be done away with if it was desired to avoid trouble later on.

Our improvised conference then agreed unanimously that there was no chance of being able to act efficaciously against this project with the Hungarian government itself. So all present, beginning with Samuel Stern, turned to me to save the some 150,000 Jews who, according to our calculations, still remained in Budapest. There was no other possibility than that of getting the Germans to put pressure on the Hungarian government. So, after so many hopes and so many discussions with Hungarian representatives, finally the only resource for the Budapest Jews lay in contacts with the Germans. Of course neither my friends of the Waada nor myself meant with Eichmann or his Gestapo.

The task I assumed was no easy one. I had to persuade Becher to ask Himmler for precise orders as well as for an undertaking guaranteeing the lives of the ghetto's inmates. However, for the reasons I have already mentioned, Becher no longer dared to appear before Himmler – and then of course there were Eichmann's intrigues. He, indeed, knew as well as we did that only a quarter of the 20,000,000 francs demanded by Himmler had as yet been paid and not the whole amount as the *Reichsführer* believed. For my own account, I could not admit to Becher that the three-quarters left unpaid just did not exist, and that their payment must not be counted on.

In the meantime American policy had stiffened. Stettinius, who had succeeded Cordell Hull as Secretary of State, had repudiated the agreement on fundamentals his predecessor had accepted at the beginning of the secret negotiations in Switzerland. The Western Allies had every reason to fear that contacts might be established between the Russians and the Germans, with a view to the conclusion of a separate peace. Hitler's minister of foreign affairs was making approaches simultaneously both in the West and the East, whereas, on their side, the Russians had learned that their Western Allies were getting ready to grant the Germans 'a ransom for the Jews' in the shape of material which if massed on the eastern front might modify the situation to the disadvantage of the Soviet Union. This sort of argument easily impressed the Russians who were already suspicious and were always in fear – not entirely wrongly – that Churchill might hold up the advance on the western front just to inflict more blood-letting on the Communist forces during the delay.

It was for these reasons, no doubt, that we no longer enjoyed any material assistance in Switzerland, and that there was not even any further inclination to make use of bluff in our favour. All the same I sent a telegram to announce that I had promised the 15,000,000 Swiss francs, for Becher's department, as well as the Gestapo and the SD, had access to the German censorship records. Furthermore, as an advance for Becher's economic department, I gave an order for thirty lorries to a Slovak dealer called Steger. He was in the import-export business but was still more active in black market affairs and had already on several occasions supplied us with goods.

As a deposit for the lorries I made over to Steger all the resources I then had and which I had obtained with the greatest difficulty. It was agreed that Steger should get the balance, in Swiss francs, after the war.

Here is the text of a telegram we received. It was dated December 6, 1944:

Received letter 17, XI and wrote yesterday Szalia detailed letter stop Affair Harbel going well. Greetings also from Rezsko. Schwalb.[1]

In our eyes this telegram confirmed our authority to buy on credit goods to be paid for in Swiss francs after the war.

The most curious thing about this transaction was the origin of the lorries we had ordered. These vehicles were not at all foreign, but were German. The Third Reich had concluded an arrangement with the Slovak State (a country detached from Bohemia) and had kept this economic arrangement, despite the Germans' own economic and financial difficulties. While the other 'occupied countries' were subjected to the extortion of supplies of economic importance – and often without any form of payment – the Reich paid the Slovaks with other goods for their exports to Germany. Indeed, for the Third Reich, Slovakia constituted a sort of counterweight at the back of the protectorate of Bohemia, where opinion was anti-German. It was desired then to leave the Slovaks a certain measure of sovereignty and to respect as far as possible, the contracts concluded with them.

So, I was led to buy back trucks Germany had delivered to Slovakia and which were to allow me to preserve from destruction the Jews of the Budapest ghetto.

As a matter of fact, we were to learn after the war that these vehicles were not handed over to the SS. These thirty trucks represented less than 1 per cent of the 300,000,000 francs we had, in our despair, been led to offer in exchange for the lives of the Budapest Jews. Even for this purchase there were no credits available in Switzerland.

Kastner informed me confidentially by diplomatic courier from Switzerland that I had not been authorized to buy or order the trucks. The reply, this time from both Komoly and myself, ran as follows:

1. 'Szalia' means Saly Mayer; Harbel, cash; Rezsko, Rezsö Kastner. Schwalb, was our friend Nathan Schwalb-Dror, the Zionist delegate in Switzerland whom we have mentioned several times.

'Saly Mayer, Saint-Gall, received Rudolf 10 xii stop order vehicles irrevocable stop ask extended powers Weyermann from Intercroix Geneva stop his activity without hindrance indispensable for Kamole stop we await most urgently Kessef Harbe stop best wishes Komoly – Biss.

Komoly wrote the draft of this telegram by hand and I still possess this proof of our collaboration and of his complete agreement with me.

We asked for fuller powers for the assistant delegate of the International Red Cross, Hans Weyermann, his help being precious to us. Contact with the principal delegate was then difficult, for he lived at Buda on the right bank of the Danube. Moreover, in those days when our lives were constantly in peril, his attitude, though unquestionably displaying good-will, did not show the same devoted daring as did Weyermann's. The expression *Kesef Harbe* means in Hebrew 'cash' and was intended to inform the addressees of this telegram that our financial resources were completely exhausted. 'Kamole' was Komoly, in other words the Waada.

Here is the text of the reply we received:

Fifteen assured discussions satisfactory stop Alois arranged stop. I arrive end week stop greetings Rudolf Kastner.[1]

Then there happened something that at times in our hours of distress we had no longer dared to hope for. Before even the payment of the 15,000,000 francs was confirmed, Becher once more decided to apply to Himmler and to convey to him our hope of getting an undertaking in favour of the ghetto and an intervention on the subject with the authorities of the Arrow Cross. Our request was rather exorbitant inasmuch as it presumed Himmler would allow his Hungarian allies to glimpse through his game and that he would forbid the destruction of the ghetto, 'for reasons relating to Germany's economic interests'.

But the improbable happened. Himmler accepted.

A few days later, a high officer of the police and the SS,

1. 'Fifteen' here again meant the 15,000,000 Swiss francs. 'Alois arranged' signified that agreement had been given for the order of thirty trucks from Alois Steger.

General Winkelmann, senior officer in the German Budapest garrison, received orders to inform the Hungarian authorities concerned that, 'in the interests of German economy', the ghetto must not be touched. Winkelmann got these instructions by telephone.

He summoned the Hungarian minister Emil Kovarcz and told him of Himmler's wishes. Owing to this meeting the ghetto was miraculously saved. The Hungarian police even received instructions to make use of their arms against any possible excesses of the Arrow Cross. In the event, though the siege of the city lasted nearly two months (a time sufficient to allow of the total annihilation of the ghetto) this operation, that elsewhere demanded only a few days or a few hours, did not take place at Budapest. The Hungarian police stationed inside the ghetto got strict orders to see that it was protected. In their repression of Arrow Cross excesses the police showed a remarkable keenness. Not the least of their motives for this was, no doubt, the hope that they would in this way provide themselves with an alibi when the Russians arrived. But the inmates also paid large bribes to the police. After the war, I met more than one Jew responsible for a group in the ghetto and persuaded he had 'saved' it because of the sums he had given to the Hungarian police.

Of course, during the siege, the misery in the ghetto was great. The food was bad and consisted mainly of the beans, peas and lentils we had been able to buy in time. As we have already indicated, with such rations the mortality rate, especially among the old people, was above the normal. And to this insufficient food was added the winter cold for there was nothing to use as fuel. But happily, deaths due to violence were rather few. In all, out of 84,000 inmates, more or less, between 200 and 300 persons were assassinated – mostly by the Arrow Cross. For instance, one night during an air-raid warning, several Arrow Cross patrols broke into the cellars of a building where the occupants of the house were jammed together. The Arrow Cross asserted that some of the skylights had not been blacked out and that from the roofs of the house signals had been made to Russian planes. The Jews charged with maintaining order in the building could themselves obviously do nothing against the Arrow Cross. But though they ought to have alarmed the nearest post of the Hungarian ghetto police, they did not dare to leave the house and venture into the street. The Arrow Cross made more and more uproar and finally machine-gunned the compact mass of people in the cellar. It was a horrible massacre and cost more than a hundred lives.

Tens of thousands of Jews, despite all the decrees and orders, had not gone into the ghetto and lived, with false papers, in the 'free' part of the city. Their fate was more harsh. At the time we estimated the number of these Jews at about 35,000. At the end of the war we found there were two or three times as many of them. Among them were many Jews from Slovakia, Yugoslavia, Poland and even Germany who had sought refuge in Hungary.

According to Hungarian regulations these could be shot on sight since Himmler's protection extended only to the ghetto. Any Jew found outside the ghetto was considered a spy and might be executed on the spot. I think the numbers who thus met their deaths during the siege of the city was about 10,000. Among them was Otto Komoly, my friend and unforgettable companion in our struggle.

The members of the Waada who decided to carry on their work in favour of our cause lived in the 'free' city after the ghetto had been hermetically sealed off. They had, however, no papers which might have protected them had they been arrested by the Arrow Cross.

29. In Budapest Besieged

Eichmann left Budapest on December 17 or 18 – after all his staff had already gone. Two days earlier I had tried in vain to get an interview with him. I was told he was away. On December 22, Becher and all his men, together with Dr. Billitz, went to Vienna. In Becher we lost a real friend. Shortly afterwards the Russians threw a ring right round the city. We hoped to be freed in a few days' time and thought we should be able to get along without Becher's assistance for a short time. However, still harsher trials awaited us. Budapest, in fact, was conquered house by house, street by street, between January 16 and February 13, 1945. The population suffered cruelly – especially the Jews shut up in the ghetto, not to speak of those who were hiding in the city.

Despite all pessimistic fears, it soon appeared that the Budapest Jews were safer inside the ghetto than outside. The Arrow Cross did not confine themselves to checking the identity of passers-by in the streets but also entered houses and demanded the identity papers of the inhabitants.[1] Every suspect was examined to see if he was circumcised. But sometimes non-Jews are circumcised. Thus, several 'Aryans' fell victims to these investigations. Once even an SS officer in civilian clothes was accosted in the middle of the street and hustled off under a porch and there taken for a Jew. Under a rain of blows he was dragged off to the nearest Arrow Cross post. No one there spoke German and the officer knew no Magyar, so without more ado he was shut up in the cellars with several Jews who, according to custom, would be taken after nightfall to the Danube's banks and there shot. The German managed, through an air-hole, to throw a piece of paper into the street. He had scribbled a message asking the person who found the message immediately to give the alarm to his unit. He was freed shortly afterwards. The SS applied bloody reprisals. All the Arrow Cross at the post were lined up against a wall and shot.

Soon no one dared to venture out into the streets. The Russian planes controlled the air and strafed anything that

1. The Arrow Cross in green shirts, were, after Szalasi's rise to power, the masters of the city and the police did not dare to oppose their exactions.

moved. And then there were the bombardments. The population had to spend most of its time in the cellars.

Komoly, however, a few of our friends, and myself, were outside all the time to maintain contacts and to be of use whenever possible. My friends and I as well as Mrs. Brand were still living at the Hotel Pannonia. But as they left the Germans seized the leading members of the Rumanian legation who had been interned there. Those who remained formed with other Rumanians who lived there a sizeable colony. There were frequent police raids on the hotel and several times Jews with false papers were carried off.

After the arrival of the Russian troops it was seen that nearly one half of the guests were Jews cleverly camouflaged. One of them, for instance, had passed himself off as the chief editor of a newspaper belonging to the Arrow Cross party. He was never tired of announcing, in all circumstances, the final victory of the Third Reich and the Arrow Cross. His 'character' was by far the best of any achieved by any of the guests who lived in the hotel cellars. One Arrow Cross who boasted all the time of the successful arrests he took part in and showed us the jewellery and valuables he had stolen was, however, a true-blue Nazi. He was hanged the day after Budapest was liberated.

During the partial evacuation of the city, the Germans blew up the Danube bridges and the Red Cross representation was cut in two. Hans Weyermann, representing the Red Cross delegate, was at Pest and we were also on the eastern bank of the river, while the principal delegate, Friedrich Born, had sought refuge at Buda on the western bank. We did not see him again until after the end of the war. Hans Weyermann was lavish with whatever help he could give. In the besieged city the Red Cross still enjoyed a good deal of authority – sometimes even with the Arrow Cross. Shortly after the Germans left, Weyermann suggested to Komoly, myself and our friends that we should leave the Hotel Pannonia and go to stay at the Hotel Ritz where he himself lived. In the Ritz, the best and most luxurious hotel in the city, we could continue to keep our 'Bureau A of the International Red Cross' functioning even during the siege of the city. The owner of the Ritz was, in fact, ready to put a whole floor at our disposal.

But we preferred to stay on at the Pannonia where we were relatively safe. The Hungarian police, posted at the hotel in order to exercise surveillance over the Rumanian colony, did their best to protect us from the Arrow Cross. Although they pretended ignorance, they did know that a great number of the hotel's clients were Jews. Just like us they waited from day to day to see the Russians arrive. As they belonged to the Arrow Cross government police force, they could not hope for much pleasant treatment after the city's liberation. So they were obviously counting on their devotion to us to furnish them with an alibi in the days to come.

In view of the situation, however, I did urge Komoly to come with his wife and live with us at the Pannonia, and I had a room reserved for them. But Komoly chose rather to accept Weyermann's invitation. He was sure he could work better at the Ritz. This complete devotion to a cause for which he sacrificed himself was to bring him calamity. On January 1 an Arrow Cross commando arrived at his hotel to carry him off – despite the Red Cross and every sort of identity paper. Weyermann tried in vain to accompany Komoly but he was promised that the prisoner would be brought back after a short interrogation.

When, after a few hours, she had no news Mrs. Komoly set off under the bombs and came to see me at the Pannonia. As quickly as possible I rounded up my informers to try and get in touch with the Arrow Cross organization. Then I went to see Dr. Vajda, Komoly's secretary, in his refuge. He said he was sure he could do something with money. Soon after I got back to the hotel, he joined me. He had learned that Komoly would at once be liberated on the payment of several thousand pengoes. I got together the sum as soon as possible and gave it to Dr. Duban, one of Vajda's colleagues.

During the following days several dates fixed by Vajda passed by and there were no signs of Komoly nor did we get any news of him. Then his secretary Duban came to see me and to say that Komoly had been taken off to the ghetto. In the company of a Hungarian 'interpreter' I went there. Once again I passed myself off as a member of the German police. At the main entrance to the ghetto I explained I was in search of a 'Jew named Otto Komoly' whom I wished to question. The officer on duty was called but no one could give me any news of my friend. While I was talking to the sentinel I was puzzled by the tactics of a group of civilians. They were keeping in the background – and the lapels of their coats were adorned with Arrow Cross badges.

The officer on duty had just told me he could do nothing to help me when I saw one of the men in civilian clothes point in my direction or at least in that of our little group. I took leave rapidly of the officer and disappeared with my 'interpreter' down the next side street.

We were never to see Otto Komoly again. After being questioned he had at once been shot and his body thrown into the Danube. We were to learn this only later. On the same day a group from the Arrow Cross organization had also surrounded a house in Vadász street (which was under the protection of the Swiss legation) and had carried off the spokesmen of the Jews there in hiding, Arthur Weiss, the owner of the building, and Simcha Hunwald, leaders of the Shomer Zionist group in Budapest. Both were executed at the same time as Komoly.

The Arrow Cross had also put a price on my head as well as on that of Offenbach. After the liberation of our group of friends from the military prison, active search had been made for the backers of that operation – and of others as well. It was presumably the interrogation of some of the prisoners that allowed our names to be known. It was in the same manner presumably that the hiding-places of Komoly, Weiss and Hunwald were discovered.

It is then easy to understand what danger I was in at the ghetto entrance, as a 'German officer', and why I had beat a hasty retreat.

Even before she had learned of her husband's fate Mrs. Komoly came to live with us at the Pannonia. We did all we could to make her painful waiting less distressing. But as the days passed by Komoly's death seemed more and more certain. It was admirable to see how his wife, her husband's courageous and faithful helper during the preceding months, accepted the idea of his death. At present Mrs. Komoly lives in Israel with her only daughter who was able, with the Bergen-Belsen convoy, to reach Switzerland. I do not know what happened later to Drs. Vajda and Duban.

At this time Offenbach took up his quarters in a refuge on the west bank of the Danube at Buda. The rest of us stayed on in Pest at the Hotel Pannonia and divided up the work among us. One very painful problem demanded our attention during the last few weeks of the SS occupation. In various buildings – placed theoretically under the protection of the International Red Cross – we had installed orphanages for Jewish children. There were several thousands of them who were either orphans or whose parents had been deported or who had just disappeared. The very numerous staff of these homes – doctors, nurses and teachers – had received passes from the Red Cross. These people were almost all Jews and Jewesses who had not wanted to go into the ghetto. The existence of these orphanages outside the limits of the ghetto had received the approval of the authorities and an agreement had been made with the Arrow Cross government which guaranteed the inviolability of the orphanages.

However, the agreement was not respected. In the city there was no longer any police force capable of effectively opposing isolated acts of the Arrow Cross patrols. More and more often the orphanages were invaded by armed patrols who very soon, after a few intimate examinations, found out whom they had to deal with. Then a whole series of executions took place. Panic seized the staffs and there were numerous desertions. Several thousand orphans were thus left to themselves in dirty dormitories and without food or care. Among these children were a great number of babies and the very young.

Our women went secretly to these homes and did all they could. I will never forget the battles I had to fight (even with some members of the Waada) to get the food necessary for these orphans, whose prior claims in those days of famine were more and more contested. Money had always to be found and one had to take action here, there and everywhere.

Even the black market was drying up and although we did all we could we could not prevent hundreds of these wretched children from dying lamentably from cold and hunger.

The entire management of our Hazzalah activities since Otto Komoly's disappearance had devolved upon me, since his successor, Rezsö Kastner, had not been able to come and join us. A young man called Weisskopf, however, gave me very effective help. We owed the success of a great many operations to his courage and devotion. Furnished with false papers in the name of Horak, he undertook dangerous tasks day after day. He succeeded in enterprises often thought impossible.

During the Eichmann trial I had the pleasure of meeting Weisskopf at Tel-Aviv where he now runs a research office.

Our days and nights in January and February 1945 were filled with an ever more severe struggle against hunger and cold, with help for the orphans and the people shut up in the ghetto, with the saving of prisoners and with individual operations for Jews in hiding. Budapest had become a ghost town. Under a thick layer of snow, the streets were empty. There were corpses everywhere, those of anonymous victims of the Arrow Cross patrols or of the low level machine-gunning of the Russian air force that harrassed the city without respite. From time to time from afar off could be heard the gunfire from the anti-aircraft units of both Hungarian and German defences, set up in batteries at crossroads, on the roofs of public buildings and on a great number of houses.

When the Russians took Budapest we were to see another face to war's horrors. On February 13 we thought we had come to the end of our miseries. The Red Army held Budapest.

30. After the Liberation

After the liberation of Budapest and the fall of the Arrow Cross regime, an appalling famine afflicted the Hungarian capital which the Russians apparently could not deal with. Help was urgently needed, especially for our orphans. So, in March 1945 I took one of the first trains for Bucharest. After a journey of several days, some of which were spent in a truck, on March 15 I got to the Rumanian capital from where, at that time, there was provisional telegraphic communication with Switzerland. As soon as Budapest was liberated I had sent by courier to Bucarest a telegram addressed to Saly Mayer and to Rezsö Kastner who were in Switzerland, since from Budapest there was not yet any telegraph communication with western countries:

Saly Mayer, Saint-Gall   From Bucarest February 1945
    Komoly arrested by Nyilas[1] 1st January stop Weiss Arthur and Hunwald Simcha and several others also stop Offenbach disappeared but said to be working as interpreter with our friends stop Zwi Neska about 132 friends liberated from prison stop Gardo Josef with us stop Hansi children we all good health stop liberated from ghetto 68,000 international missions 12,000 Swiss 4,000 total 84,000 persons stop congratulations especially you and Rezsö stop about 20,000 others saved with papers stop for needs feeding completely starving population we have put out up to now drafts payable Zurich value 120,000 Swiss francs signed Monsieur Weyermann and self Biss.

On April 13, 1945, I got a reply. In his telegram to Bucarest Saly Mayer asked me to go on provisionally running the current business of the Budapest 'Joint' with my two friends Dr. Karl Wilhelm and Offenbach.

    The Rumanian section of the 'Joint', whose financial situation was incomparably better than ours in a city starving and

---

    1. Nyilas is the Magyar for 'Arrow Cross'.

drained of its substance, had already received instructions to give us as much help as possible until we were once more in a position to get into direct contact with the western countries. At the end of April I got back to Budapest – again by a roundabout route.

During my absence, Dr. Ernö Marton, a member of the Bucarest 'Joint', had visited Budapest. Thanks to our Bergen-Belsen convoy, his family had been able to get to Switzerland. He himself had managed in May 1944 to escape from Klausenburg into Rumania. Our paths had, so to speak, crossed though we did not meet. When he got to Budapest, Marton on his own responsibility appointed a representative of the 'Joint' entrusted with the task of carrying on the work I had begun in secret under the German occupation. I did not know this Dr. Frederick Görög, for he had stayed hidden for the last few months and had taken no part in our activities; but I did know his daughter Vera Görög who, first under Komoly's direction and then under mine, had worked at section A of the International Red Cross in Mérleg street. At first Görög refused to recognize the nomination in Switzerland of our Committee of Three. He had no intention of giving up his brand new job. Ernö Marton had handed over to him both funds and food that had been brought to Budapest. In a city where people were ready to exchange a gold watch for a crust of bread, the absolute disposal of these considerable resources represented great influence. Thanks to Hans Weyermann, the delegate of the International Red Cross, it was possible to get Görög to recognize our Committee of Three and also, at first, to be satisfied with the role of financial director. Generally speaking, our activities were not paid; however, Görög, who for the time was without means, asked me to fix a salary for him. As he would not otherwise be able to support his family, I allowed him $100 a month. It was a huge sum if one remembers that in the Budapest of those days the dollar was by far the strongest currency. It was worth more than gold.

Things in Budapest got better only very slowly. The Allied troops had already linked up near Linz in March 1945, but the crossing of the Danube near that town was extremely difficult and the passage through Russian occupied territory most perilous. What happened to Raoul Wallenberg illustrates this. A short time after the occupation of Budapest, this young Swede left for the Soviet HQ, there to protest against the exactions of the Russian army. He never got back and has never been found to this day. The confidence he had in his position as a Swedish diplomat proved illusory, just as did the confidence of Danielson, the Swedish envoy at Budapest who, it may be mentioned, had charge during the war of the Soviet Union's interests with the Horthy government. But the buildings of the Swedish legation were, during the street fighting, completely pillaged by the conquerors. The people who were living there, including members of Danielson's family, had to undergo some rough treatment. Many Jewish families had deposited their valuables in the legation. But even the safes in legations were forced and emptied of their contents. The cars in the courtyard disappeared of course first of all. This affected me personally since my chauffeur had there garaged my new American car. Out of thanks for this accommodation and in return for the protection I counted on, I had taken to the legation a certain amount of petrol, a very precious commodity at the time. After the war Danielson let me know he had informed his government of the incidents that had taken place, and that it was engaged in discussions about compensation with the Soviet authorities. I never heard any more about the matter.

The funds from Rumania were soon exhausted. The situation of the 'Joint' became more and more precarious, so that, practically speaking, we were prevented from any useful activity. Thus, on the decision of our Committee of Three I was sent to Switzerland. Bauvé, the Vienna delegate of the Red Cross, came with me. Görög also agreed to the proposal and, indeed, urged me to undertake the journey as soon as possible. Before this I had applied for material help to the Russian general commanding the garrison. But the Russians were themselves in want and were, practically speaking, in no position to aid us. All the same, they were quite prepared to leave us entire freedom of action, though this it is true was not very useful since our financial resources were exhausted. It was then absolutely necessary for me to go to Switzerland where I was to get into contact, through Saly Mayer and American organizations, with committees of assistance.

A few days before the date fixed for my departure, I was arrested by the NKVD (the Russian security police) in Budapest. Almost all the persons who had had the slightest contact with the German forces of occupation were also arrested; for instance, the Swedish minister and several other neutral diplomatists who, on official business, had been in touch with the Germans. I informed the NKVD officer who interrogated me about our activities and mentioned, incidentally, that we had worked with, among others, an officer of the British secret service. This information interested the NKVD man very much. Finally I named Joël Nussbecher-Palgi and said where he could be found – at the Jewish camp within the Swiss legation.

The next day I was again interrogated. This time the officer was accompanied by Joël Nussbecher-Palgi. It was evident that vodka had brought the two men together, and I also had to drink a 'little glass' – although I do not like alcohol at all. After I had promised the Russian I would help him to find 'Gitler' (Hitler) I was set free. I remained true to my principles – to confine my 'political' activity to helping those of my own people who had escaped. So, later on, I refrained from collaborating with any secret service. Nor did I keep my promise to the NKVD functionary. However, several of my friends and fellow workers of the time did help to unmask and hand over to justice a certain number of Arrow Cross and Nazis in hiding, who had committed crimes for which there was abundant proof.

While I was crossing the Soviet occupation zone on my way to Switzerland, I stayed two days in Vienna where I prepared a report for Saly Mayer. Then we started off for Linz. We had, as identity papers, typewritten 'travel documents' in Russian and English which I had drawn up on paper bearing the heading of the American Join Distribution Committee of Budapest. These documents, for Bauvé and me, bore the signatures of

Dr. Karl Wilhelm and myself, and proved more useful even than a passport or any sort of certificate from the International Red Cross.

A little before the Linz bridge we got alongside a car stopped by the edge of the road. Its owner, Gábor Péter, chief of the Hungarian Communist police, hailed us. I had met him during the Russian occupation of Budapest, as I had several matters concerning the 'Joint' to settle with him. Peter told us he was on his way to Dachau to look for young Dálnoky. He was the son of the Hungarian prime minister and had been interned by the Germans at the time the Hungarian government in exile had been constituted. He had just been liberated by the Americans. Although he showed his Hungarian diplomatic passport, Gábor Péter had not been able to get into the American occupation zone. For the Americans, Hungary was at war with the United States and Washington had not yet recognized the new Hungarian government. According to Gábor Péter's predictions a similar misfortune awaited us. But after having bid him a hasty good-bye we went on our way. When the American sentinel made out on the papers I showed him the words 'American Joint Distribution Committee' he shouted to his neighbour 'Americans' and passed us through at once. A few hours later we met Gábor Péter again, this time wearing Soviet uniform. As a Communist *émigré* he had been a colonel in the Red Army, so the Soviet command in Linz furnished him with a Russian uniform and papers testifying that he was in charge of the repatriation of Russian war prisoners from the American zone. So Péter had managed to get to Linz, though after us. He said laughingly to me:

'If I had known, I would have dispensed with a Hungarian diplomatic passport. I would have done better to have asked you for a certificate from the American "Joint".'

My arrival in Switzerland caused something of a sensation. I was the first traveller to arrive from Budapest since the siege and the liberation of the city. After having lived through them myself I was going to be able to describe the events of the last few months culminating in the entry of the Russian troops into the capital. Professor Max Huber, chairman of the international committee of the Red Cross received me officially at an extraordinary meeting of his committee. I presented a report and then had to answer innumerable questions. However, my greatest joy was of course to see my mother and my friend Kastner as well as some other members of the Bergen-Belsen convoy.

I had many interviews with Saly Mayer and had the opportunity of submitting my accounts to him. Several times I asked him to make arrangements for my return and urged him also to ask from the Swiss National Bank for a permit to take with me the funds in dollars necessary for the work of the 'Joint' in Budapest. At the time the dollar bill was quoted in Switzerland at from 1·70 to 1·80 Swiss francs, whereas in Hungary it had a purchasing power five or six times greater than the Swiss franc.

A group of several hundred people who had been members of the test-convoy wanted to go back with me to Budapest, and part of the group wished to return to Klausenburg. There was also another group getting ready to emigrate to Israel. I had numerous conversations about the repatriation. I promised the people concerned I would do all I could for them, but I did not hide from them that the situation in Hungary had changed entirely and in Transylvania, a province that had been restored to Rumania. Things no longer bore the slightest resemblance to the pleasing picture that lingered with those repatriated.

A few weeks later, on the eve of my departure, Saly Mayer told me he could put at our disposal credits only in Swiss francs since the Swiss National Bank would not give permission for the exportation of dollars. During our interview I learned that the bank had been consulted the day before – and then by telephone – and that it had given a first and unfavourable opinion.

My great nervousness – due to our desperate efforts against the Nazis but also to the thoughts that haunted me of the orphans dying of inanition at Budapest – made me feel as little pacific as possible. Faced with Saly Mayer's negligence and indifference, I could no longer control myself but let out in some very harsh words. I even went so far as to hold Saly Mayer responsible personally for the deaths that would occur among the children deprived of food and care. The old man felt deeply hurt, and I suddenly realized he did not understand. All his life had been passed in peaceful Switzerland and as he had no experience of such horrors, he could not have the remotest idea of what an inferno Budapest had become. The next day I left, full of bitterness and convinced that I had not done all that ought to have been done. I carried an authorization with me. Each month I could negotiate in Budapest bonds amounting to two million Swiss francs, payable in Switzerland. The Jewish population in Budapest lacked everything and was to all intents and purposes destitute. Everyone depended on charitable organizations and this sum was far from being sufficient to meet even the most urgent needs. If Mayer had busied himself in time about the export licences and if he had handed to me the equivalent of this sum in cash, that is to say in dollars, we should have been able to alleviate four times as much misery in Hungary.

To understand my sentiments when I was about to return to Hungary one must have seen at close quarters the victims of the concentration camps, seen them dead in the trains taking them home, seen the people unable to stand and who must be carried when the train arrived, one must have shared the daily misery of hundreds of children deprived of food and all care, and have received regular reports of the numerous deaths each day in the orphanages. And I was going back with absurdly insufficient funds when a greater sense of responsibility and a little more efficiency would have sufficed to multiply these funds many times. Later on I made it up with Saly Mayer. I had to recognize that the reproaches I had heaped upon him before I left Switzerland must have seemed incomprehensible to him. His attitude was less due to lack of good will than to the impossibility of his imagining things almost inconceivable to a man in his position.

Several hundred persons from the Bergen-Belsen convoy left Switzerland with me. I was to accompany them to Budapest.

On Austrian territory, various Jewish organizations with their headquarters in Switzerland entrusted to me sums of money for their branches in Budapest, for no postal or banking communication with Hungary had yet been established. I had absolutely refused to receive these sums in Switzerland since I did not want to make myself responsible for any illegal activity of any sort, especially in view of the delicate nature of my mission. On the other hand it was not forbidden to possess foreign currency in the French occupation zone of Austria and it was possible to obtain a permit for its exportation into Hungary. With this in view I wanted to make a short stop at Bregenz.

We arrived without let or hindrance and I went at once to an hotel. During the night following I was arrested in my bed. I was led off, my hands above my head and with several revolvers pointed at my back. It was only afterwards I learned that several members of the Hungarian Gestapo working with French Intelligence, had, to save their own skins, denounced me as an agent of the Gestapo. Several of these men had noticed me from time to time at the Budapest HQ of the German secret service and the Gestapo. After Kastner, Komoly and Mrs. Brand had been freed from the clutches of the Hungarian secret police some of its members, especially in the lower ranks, were persuaded the Waada was a sort of Jewish secret police. They could not otherwise explain our contacts with the German Gestapo.

The 'Joint' could have quite easily had me set free the next day, since an American army colonel, M. Reznik, a member of this organization to which I belonged, was questioned about me by the French. However, he refused to guarantee me. As for Saly Mayer, he was indignant to learn I had taken charge of large sums for Hungary, and for the account of organizations that were 'rivals' of the 'Joint'. Immediately there was presumption of fraudulent exchange dealings and I was left to my fate. I remained a prisoner of the French for two months in the company of all sorts of criminals and Nazis.

In the meantime Görög had taken my place in Budapest.

had now at his disposal a monthly budget of 2,000,000 Swiss francs to supply food to the Jewish population in Budapest and also to assist Jews returned from the concentration camps. The 'Joint' had allocated this sum on the strength of my reports. It may be remarked here that during the twelve months of our activity to save the Jews who had stayed in Budapest and those who had survived in the concentration camps, the 'Joint' had expended a sum smaller than that earmarked in the new budget, each month, solely for food.

Görög then became increasingly an important personage in the eyes of the Hungarian government. After the war the 'Joint' was for a time the main supplier to Hungary of foreign exchange. By utilizing the sums thus made available, the Hungarian National Bank created a new currency. The new Hungarian government and president of the republic gave numerous receptions in honour of the 'Joint' delegates who came to Budapest.

As for me, thanks very largely to whom the activities of the 'Joint' in Hungary were still possible, I remained in prison at Innsbruck, where I had been transferred. Finally the World Jewish Congress sent a Swiss lawyer to defend me at Innsbruck. During this time the 'Joint' continued to ignore my case.

Then I was quickly set free by the French authorities. All the valuable assets which had been seized on me were returned – with formal apologies.

31. Conspiracy of Silence

During my two months in prison I had lost about thirty pounds in weight. I had a heart condition – contracted it is true at Budapest – and it had developed dangerously. I often asked myself if my return to Budapest was really desirable. Now the funds I had helped to get available were arriving regularly.

I should not, for a considerable time, be in a fit state to work. I was treated for a number of years in Switzerland where I had managed, after numberless difficulties, to return. My wife joined me a few months afterwards. Our little circle of friends in Budapest, who had been drawn close together by our common struggles and sufferings, broke up little by little. Those who escaped with their lives – such as Kastner and Nussbecher – had moved off in various directions. A great number were dead. The people who were now at work were those whose names we hardly knew. It was common knowledge that I had been improperly imprisoned and that I had been completely rehabilitated. Still, the old saying was true in my case . . . 'some mud always sticks'. It was obviously much simpler to attribute my arrest to 'currency frauds' and to 'shady dealings with the Gestapo' than to admit the truth. I had been left for several months to my fate, so that my job – now perfectly simple – could the more easily be occupied. In view of my illness, the slightest emotion might be fatal, so I preferred to keep silent for a long time. My conscience was easy. I had not spared myself and I had sacrificed all my possessions in a noble cause. The great task fate had laid upon me was now accomplished.

My relations with Kastner, who was also living in Switzerland, and who had drawn up for the 1949 Zionist congress a report on our activities, were clouded by differences of a personal nature. His attitude regarding me was rather feeble. But this was understandable in view of the campaign of abuse to which I had been subjected. Had he taken up an energetic attitude he would have been exposed to similar attacks since we had collaborated until the end.

Kastner had also made it up with Joël Brand. From the time of my arrival in Switzerland he had tried to persuade me that if Brand had not come back from Istanbul, it was not because of cowardice but for reasons beyond his control. Later on, I learned that in speaking thus Kastner was going against his own convictions, although he thought he had valid motives for so doing. In the end I let myself be convinced of Brand's innocence, since I knew what it was to be the victim of false accusations. At the time, under Kastner's influence, I even took up the cudgels on behalf of Brand.

Later on, Kastner went to Israel where he became an influential member of the Mapai government party. When fate struck him in his turn, he was chief press officer for Ben Gurion, then prime minister of Israel. During the parliamentary election campaign, he was violently attacked by his political adversaries who taunted him about his former contacts with the Gestapo and also about our activities, of which he had made but incomplete mention in his report. He won a defamation action he brought against his enemies who were fined £1,000,000 for having calumniated Kastner by accusing him of financial irregularities but the comments that accompanied the court's verdict were not at all flattering to him. It was stated that he 'had sold his soul to the devil' to assist 'a few hundred persons', among whom were members of his own family.

I am still convinced today that the result of the case – before it went to appeal – would have been very different had I been asked to give my evidence. I was the only person who was completely informed about all the circumstances and I could have helped in bringing out the facts. Instead of 'a few hundred' it was most certainly several hundreds of thousands, probably more than half a million people who escaped. But Kastner was very ill-advised and thought he could dispense with my evidence. He had not taken into account the almost total defection of his 'good friends' in Israel, many of whom owed their lives to him. On March 3, 1957 some young fanatics shot him down in the middle of a Jerusalem street before his case had come up before the appeal court. He died nine days later. His posthumous rehabilitation, though not absolutely satisfactory, was pronounced by the appeal court. Shortly before his death he had asked me to go and give evidence at the second hearing. This I promised to do in a reply from Paris where I was then living. After his death my evidence was no longer thought worthwhile.

At the elections the Mapai lost several seats and so its overall majority in the parliament. This result was attributed mainly to the violent nationalistic campaign of the opposition parties, which had concentrated their fire on Kastner. Ben Gurion, leader of the Mapai, gave instructions that the affair should not be raked up after Kastner's death, and his rehabilitation had been to all intents and purposes pronounced.

Eichmann's capture and trial occurred a few years later. I thought that at last the truth about our activities would be fully exposed in all their details to the whole world. I hoped it would be clearly established that we had snatched from Eichmann several hundred thousand of his last victims and that in acting as we did, we were the artisans of the sole victory obtained over him. I sent Ben Gurion a telegram in which I expressed the hope our activities would at last be revealed in the full light of day.

My hopes were not to be fulfilled.

Aharon Karie, charged by the public prosecutor's department to conduct investigations in Europe concerning Eichmann, assured me that I was the best informed witness about Eichmann of all those whose existence he knew of. He was convinced I would be a capital witness for the prosecution at the trial and he begged me not to wait for an official invitation before going to Jerusalem. Therefore I left for Israel on April 9, 1961.

At the Eichmann trial 102 witnesses for the prosecution were heard. At least ninety of them had not only never met Eichmann, but until the end of the war had never even heard his name. I myself had seen the prisoner a greater number of times than all the other witnesses together. No one knew him as closely as I did.[1]

The date of my appearing before the court was fixed, yet finally I was not heard officially. The public prosecutor, Gideon Hausner, had asked me to omit from my evidence any mention of our action in Budapest, and especially to pass over in silence what was then in Israel called the 'Kastner affair'. Furthermore I should not speak of Becher's activities

[1]. Kastner was no longer alive, but as a matter of fact he had met Eichmann more often still.

in favour of the Jews. Hausner absolutely refused to believe in these. I told him I could not give evidence unless I was free to tell the whole truth. Hausner finally preferred to dispense with me as a witness.

I was able to see this trial transformed. What had started by being just and objective became an act of collective accusation against the whole German people. In an atmosphere over-heated by general excitement, the prisoner himself – guilty several million times over of murder – no longer counted, nor did the Gestapo and the SD suffice. I was exasperated at seeing that the prosecution also intended to accuse, at any price, the only SS officer who, with Grüson, who had helped us and who in so doing risked his life several times. The prosecutor, the judges and the witnesses at this trial – and to these must be added the deserters who had betrayed our Waada and now in their false evidence enlarged in self-satisfied fashion on their misfortunes – none of these had done as much for the Jewish people as Kastner who had been mur-dered, and Becher whom it was desired to put in the dock. I could not tolerate this attitude of the bench and did not fail to manifest publicly on every occasion what my sentiments were. So I did not escape plenty of attacks. Thus in several newspaper articles (whose main instigator proved to be Joël Brand) I was abundantly abused and threatened with the same fate as Kastner.

I tried, also, to get to the bottom of the 'Brand case'. I soon realized that neither Brand's own statements nor Kastner's soothing words about him represented the truth. Brand had well and truly been prevented from going back to Budapest but that was after he had, with no justification, gone to Syria at the expiration of the fifteen days fixed for his return to Budapest. Of his own accord he had gone to throw himself in the arms of the British, although he had been warned, and had known he would be at once arrested. Brand could never have been in any doubt as to the consequences of his act. Eich-mann himself had clearly intimated to him, before he left, what would happen if he did not return on the agreed date. Thus it was Brand who bore the responsibility for the unnecessary death of at least 400,000 Hungarian Jews who would certainly have been saved had he come back in time. Kastner had tried to stifle this affair, because of his apparent reconciliation with Brand, and so as not to harm our position by internal quarrels, but his efforts recoiled on his own head. During the Kastner case Brand joined the accusation and during his evidence heaped abuse on Kastner.

During the whole of the Eichmann trial, Brand endeavoured, with some success, to minimize the influence of our work – work he had himself betrayed. According to his evidence all we had been able to do was to get the test-convoy to Switzerland and with fewer than 2000 people out of a million. He did not think it necessary to describe our efforts to delay the deportations, nor our false promises and bluffs, thanks to which we secured the suppression of the gas-chambers. Yet all this did result in the saving of at least 500,000 persons – that is to say more than the half of the million Jews Brand had abandoned.

Joël Brand declared to the court that in the month of May 1944, when the German troops entered Budapest, he was under 'preventive arrest', when, as a matter of fact, he was hiding in the apartment of a dancing-girl and had abandoned his family.

Joël Brand, who had seen Becher only once before he left Hungary, and had not spoken a word to him, called Becher 'a war criminal of the worst sort', but this statement did not prevent his going to see Becher after the war and asking him for a certificate to use in an indemnity case then being heard in the Federal Republic. Becher, however, refused in view of the inexactitude of the facts advanced by Brand. More or less the same thing happened with the witness Philipp von Freudiger, a former member of the Jewish Council and of the Bureau of the orthodox Jewish community, who had fled from Budapest. He had had occasion to complain to me of Becher, whom he had asked to sign an accommodation certificate which Becher flatly refused to do. Freudiger, also, though he had not known Becher at Budapest, thought himself obliged to give evidence against him.

I applied to the Israeli minister of justice and even to the prime minister to demand Joël Brand's prosecution for perjury after I had discovered seven false declarations in his evidence. I also asked that the public prosecutor, Hausner, should be withdrawn from his part in the trial. Neither of my requests was granted.

The former prime minister, Moshe Sharett, was in a painful position. He it was who, at the time, had invited Brand to go from Istanbul to visit him in Israel, since he could not himself get an exit visa from the British. Brand had accepted the invitation although he was perfectly aware what results his defection – and possibly arrest – would have in Budapest. After the war Brand accused Moshe Sharett of having betrayed him and, by enticing him into Palestine, of having sold him to the British. When faced with the commotion caused by this accusation, Moshe Sharett, the Mapai, and especially Gideon Hausner, covered up for Brand, who was appeased in this way.

My friends in Israel were disconcerted by the attitude I took up. They could not understand how I dared to brave the public opinion of a whole country; most of these friends owed their lives to our efforts, but they did not know how much these efforts had demanded in determination and desperate courage from Kastner, Komoly, and all my Budapest friends. These friends in Israel could not understand that our past obliged me to serve justice and truth even in Israel.

But I have not yet referred to another aspect of things, an aspect I did not suspect then and which I realized only in 1965.

Through the secretary of state attached to the prime minister, one Theodor Kolleck, I asked for an audience of Ben Gurion. I could not obtain it. Ben Gurion at that date was getting ready to leave for the United States. We have learned since that he there met Adenauer, the German chancellor. Under the formidable moral pressure excited by the revelation of the crimes denounced at the Eichmann trial, the chancellor gave the green light for the delivery of German arms to Israel. At the time this decision was to be of capital importance for Israel. For the Federal Republic, legal successor of a Germany twice vanquished in world wars and rightly discredited for its armament industry, this was certainly a decision hard to take and one that must have cost a considerable effort.

The Eichmann trial, advocating the collective guilt of all the German people, could not at that moment tolerate any exception that might present the German people in a better light, even if truth had to be sacrificed. It was quite unimaginable to present an SS officer as a human figure, as one who had even acted with heroism in order to help the last survivors of the Jewish people. A Jewish victory over Eichmann, a victory that allowed several hundreds of thousands of people being saved from death, had no place in the official version of the Jewish martyrology, that is to say the *total* extermination of Jewry in central Europe.

My dead friends and myself were then sacrificed to the *raison d'état*.

32. The Freeing of the Camps

I did not myself live through the events described in this chapter. They happened in Germany at the time when Budapest was already occupied by the Russians. If I deal with these matters it is because in a great many publications on contemporary history, both those written by historians and those by authors who did not witness the liberation of the German camps, we may read that the credit for having saved in time the inmates still alive in the concentration camps (in the spring of 1945) belongs exclusively to the American, British, French and Russian troops. Practically no one up to now has noted that, in a certain number of cases, it was thanks to the courageous action of two men that this work of life saving could take place.

Furthermore, I think it my duty to correct certain errors. The two men I am referring to, Rezsö Kastner and Kurt

Becher, deserve that the truth should at last be known about their activities in favour of the Jewish people, but also in favour of tens of thousands of non-Jewish prisoners.

When at the end of December 1944 Kastner decided to go to Germany, Budapest was already surrounded by Russian troops. He had returned from Switzerland and was now to expose himself voluntarily to all sorts of dangers in an area where, in view of the imminent collapse of Hitlerian Germany, he risked death at every instant. But he knew that Becher still enjoyed wide powers which could be used in favour of prisoners in the concentration camps and he determined to do all he could to induce Becher to intervene in time.[1] In his 'report' Kastner describes his activities in detail, first at Vienna and then at Bratislava where he managed to organize a convoy for Switzerland composed of Slovakian Jews who had succeeded in escaping from the last deportation orders emanating from Hitler himself. They had lived in hiding and conditions in their shelters had become intolerable.

In Bratislava Kastner nearly paid with his life for his daring. By chance, he ran across Lt. Colonel Ferenczy, an awkward witness, who had attempted to rid himself of Kastner in Hungary, and he denounced him to the Gestapo. He was arrested. However, the Gestapo official who conducted the interrogation was, it happened, informed of our contacts with Himmler and by playing this card Kastner managed to get himself set at liberty before Becher had been warned or had been able to intervene.

After that, he continued urging Becher to act more and more vigorously by using his authority and the relations he still maintained with Himmler. Becher was soon, at the peril of his life, engaging in activities in favour of the concentration camp prisoners. And this was at a time when he, like so many others, might have 'disappeared' until the end of the war. After all,

1. In this connection Becher, later on, during an interrogation, was to declare: 'Dr. Kastner came to see me on 31st December 1944 and said these words: 'I have come so that you may not enter the New Year with the thought I might no longer come.' He said also that 'he felt completely on my side out of gratefulness for the constant help I had brought him.'

what he had already done for the Jews up to then assured him a personal and perfectly unquestionable alibi.

In the meantime Eichmann had been transferred by Himmler to another sector, to a great extent because of the steps we had taken. This last minute change had no doubt a favourable influence on the fate of a great many prisoners who were doomed to die, since it was certain the Gestapo would do everything possible to suppress the greatest possible number of witnesses to their evil deeds. Already in some camps mass extermination had begun again. Becher applied to Himmler – in the name of the German people's future – and asked him to veto this new wave of murders in the camps. Himmler realized that his own fate was also in the balance. He repeated his instructions, that is to say he confirmed his decrees of September 1944, by which he laid down that the Jews must be left alive. He also gave orders to hand over, without any fighting, the concentration camps to the victorious Allies. However, some of his Gestapo subordinates, with Kaltenbrunner at their head, took no further notice of these ordinances.

Kastner relates, in this connection, how Becher finally induced Himmler to publish military instructions that the Bergen-Belsen camp should be unconditionally surrendered. Thus, at least, the prisoners in this camp who had not succumbed to hunger and sickness were able to survive, thanks to the rapid liberation of the camp by the British. The same was true of the Neuengamme, Oranienburg, Ravensbruck and Buchenwald camps. In his book *Bergen-Belsen* Eberhard Kolb writes on this subject:[1]

'On 8th April Kersten got a letter from Dr. Brandt, Himmler's private secretary, informing him that a new commissary had been appointed in the B.-B. camp. Indeed, on April 8, 1945, *Standartenführer* Kurt Becher had been appointed "Extraordinary Reich Commissary" for all matters concerning the Jewish and political prisoners. Becher showed Dr. Kastner this document signed by Himmler and addressed to *Standartenführer* SS Kurt Becher:

1. Vide Eberhard Kolb *Bergen-Belsen. Geschichte des 'Aufenthaltslager'* 1943–1945, Hanover, 1962, pp. 159 et seq. *H.*

'In view of the urgent problems relating to organization and sanitary matters, I appoint you Extraordinary Reich Commissary for all the K.L. – i.e. *Konzentrationslager*, concentration camps'. Becher decided at once to undertake a tour of inspection of all the K.L. so as to be able to take necessary measures on the spot. The first trip he decided on was to the B.-B. camp. He and Dr. Kramer left Berlin on April 10, 1945, and got to Belsen at 17·30 (5.30 p.m.). Becher retired to confer with Dr. Kramer and an hour later Dr. Kastner was allowed to join them. Kramer then gave his hearers an account of the dreadful conditions prevailing within the camp. 1000 prisoners were suffering from exanthematic fever. No bread had been distributed for two weeks. There remained only a week's supply of turnips and potatoes with a small quantity of meat and fats. The number of deaths daily was estimated at from 500 to 600. After he had heard this report Becher was appalled. Kastner suggested that the only possible solution was to hand over the camp at once and unconditionally to the Allies. Becher agreed and decided to act at once. Without having really inspected the camp, Becher and Dr. Kastner left B.-B. at 19·30 (7.30 p.m.) for Hamburg.'

On April 11, 1945, Becher went to the H.Q. of the Hamburg S.D. and telephoned to Himmler a report on the situation at Bergen-Belsen. In reply, Himmler gave Becher authority to see that without delay all the Belsen region should surrender to the British forces. At 14.00 hours (2 p.m.) Becher went back to Belsen to take measures in accordance with Himmler's orders. This time Kramer accompanied his visitors through part of the camp. It was a shocking spectacle that presented itself to Dr. Kastner's eyes. 'In their thousands the prisoners in their jail-clothes, were crouched on the ground around the hutments. They were just living corpses. We were not shown any bodies or the crematorium, but the food-stores were still stuffed with Red Cross parcels.'

Following this visit Becher got into touch with the officers at the military encampment near the KL. As regards his conversations there, there are two versions which differ on several points. The first report, based on the evidence of Hans Schmidt, a Panzer colonel, stresses the personal initiative of some army officers from which originated the Belsen zone neutralization. On the other hand Dr. Kastner's report, which is founded on Becher's declarations, insists on the fact that the unconditional surrender of the camp had been ordered by Himmler and was affected by Becher against opposition from the officers. This seems to agree rather better with the facts than Colonel Schmidt's version. According to Kastner's report, Becher, as soon as he got back to Hamburg from his visit to the camp in the afternoon of April 11, 1945, had an interview with Colonel Harries, who represented the commandant of the Belsen instruction camp, and with four other officers he met in the building of the army HQ. The *Wehrmacht* officers were opposed to an immediate capitulation, since, as Colonel Harries expressed it, the time did not yet seem 'ripe'. For the moment the British were keeping quiet and in the case of a British attack, Bergen-Belsen could be defended for several days. Becher, on the other hand, demanded capitulation. As no agreement could be reached, Colonel Harries, his aide-de-camp and *Standartenführer* Becher went off to the HQ of the northern group of armies situated at about fifteen miles north of Bergen-Belsen. According to Dr. Kastner, Becher managed during a discussion, to get his point of view adopted. Colonel Schmidt was ordered to transmit at once an offer of capitulation to the British. It was understood the Germans proposed that with the exception of a small number left to maintain order, the whole staff should withdraw from B.-B. two hours before the camp was handed over. The small group under the camp medical officer, should be allowed to retire freely after the surrender. The conference ended at 19·30 hours (7.30 p.m.) after these proposals had been set out clearly, the group went back to Belsen and very early the next day, the German with a flag of truce crossed the front lines.

Contrary to Dr. Kastner's version of the facts, the report based on Colonel Schmidt's declarations specifies that on April 11, 1945, before Becher arrived and independently of him, a certain number of officers had gone to the general-staff and there asked for full powers to engage in negotiations with the British.

However, during the interview with Becher that followed, no precise agreement could be reached as to the persons whose responsibilities were engaged. It was for this reason that Colonel Schmidt and Lieut. Bohnekamp, with the tacit agreement of Colonel Grosan, in charge of the area of future military operations, would then on their own responsibility have made the offer of surrender to the enemy. This version does not seem very probable inasmuch as one of the officers of the military camp had insisted, later on, that he had obeyed only after having received a written order for capitulation from the hands of Colonel Harries' aide-de-camp, an order establishing without any doubt that the commandant of the military camp was authorized to conclude a cease-fire agreement.

About noon a telephone message from Hamburg informed Becher that a British staff officer had arrived at the German HQ to discuss the details of the handing over of the camp. Becher wanted to go there at once, but, nevertheless, telephoned to Himmler first, who told him, 'Becher, that's not your business, let the Army negotiate the capitulation.'

We must entirely share the opinion of Sington who declared in his evidence that the conclusion of a cease-fire agreement was a great blessing for the inmates of the camp. In view of the physical condition of most of the prisoners, an evacuation would scarcely have been possible. The SS would have been able to carry off only a very small proportion of the inmates and would doubtless have proceeded to wholesale slaughter of the rest. It is certain that many of the prisoners would have died had the SS defended the sector where the camp was situated. The cease-fire arrangement spared these human lives though, all the same, a considerable number of 'last minute victims' must be deplored. The days preceding the surrender and those which immediately followed it, were among the most dreadful and heart-rending in all the history of the camp.

Kolb writes further:

However, an important commission made its appearance on 18th or 19th March 1945. It consisted of Pohl (chief of WVHA), Höss (chief of section D.I.) and Lolling (chief of section DIII).

It must not be supposed they came to organize the fight against epidemics or even to take any measures in favour of the inhabitants of the camp. These men came solely to convey to the camp commandant Himmler's orders. No Jew must be put to death for any reason whatsoever, all possible means must be taken to limit, by all possible means, the mortality among the prisoners. Pohl who accompanied Glücks to Himmler to receive this order, noted 'He (Himmler) seemed to attach so much importance to it that he rejected my objection when I pointed out to him that, in view of the serious situation in which we found ourselves – we were in the month of March 1945 – I thought I had a more important part to play in Berlin than that of a postman.'

The same author writes further on:

'Thus as early as the end of September and the beginning of October, 1944, Himmler had signed an ordinance recommending that Jews' lives should be spared and that executions should cease. This ordinance further recommended that measures should be taken in favour of the sick and people who were feeble. These orders of Himmler's were given personally by *Standartenführer* Becher to the chiefs of sections, Pohl and Kaltenbrunner. That this same Himmler, it is true could give at about the same time, orders to evacuate the prison camps – at the cost of tens of thousands of Jewish lives – must be attributed to the *Reichsführer*'s paradoxical mind.

This attitude hardly indicates that the new ordinance in favour of the Jews was very sincere. It is, however, interesting in order to judge of the mentality of those officials at work in the camps, that they could in no case, invoke any order from Himmler ordering 'the destruction of the camps by their evacuation and abandonment.' It is, on the other hand, significant to note that Himmler's precise instructions for everything to be done at to combat the epidemic of exanthematic fever in the B.B. camp, were totally ignored.'

Himmler was counting on exploiting all this through his doctor and masseur, the Finn Felix Kersten, thanks to whom he hoped to establish contacts abroad.

Eberhard Kolb, who cites Kersten several times, omits to stress in his book that without Himmler's instructions for moderation in the months of September–October 1944 (which were obtained thanks to our efforts) two months would have been enough for the destruction of all remaining Jews by the end of 1944. Kersten's attempts in the spring of 1945, to establish new contacts would have been quite useless, since no Jew would have then been alive. When Kolb says that Himmler's instructions, prescribing a fight against epidemics, were not respected, he does not point out that, at the time, the collapse had already begun and that in the chaos which preceded the end, even Hitler's own orders were only partially executed. Himmler's instructions for moderation given in September, 1944 (and which Kolb does not analyse in detail) were certainly followed at least in their main lines.

In fact, if the average of 10,000 executions a day (still the figure in August 1944) had been kept up, certainly no

Jew would have been alive in the spring of 1945 or perhaps even not after the end of 1944.

In his book Kolb writes:

'When Karsten, Himmler's personal physician, came to speak on 10th March 1945 of the epidemic of exanthematic fever at Belsen, he mentioned that Himmler had not yet been informed of it. He at once ordered that 'all medical means necessary to combat the epidemic should be employed ... there can be no question of cheese-paring either with doctors or medical supplies. The prisoners are placed under my personal protection.' This order was sent to Pohl, to Glücks, to Dr. Grawitz (SS and police doctor) and to Dr. Kaltenbrunner (chief of the Sipo and the SD). And here it is worth while mentioning a significant fact. This clear and precise order from Himmler had no effect. No doctors or medical supplies were sent to B.B. It is out of the question that 'all medical means necessary to combat the epidemic' were adopted. It seems (and this is confirmed in other circumstances) that the officials in the camps showed themselves much more zealous in executing extermination orders signed by Himmler than in obeying his orders for moderation even if these were dictated by opportunism and tactical reasons. These officials were certainly rather inclined to destroy.'

Eberhard Kolb does not take into account the two distinct dates of these ordinances. The order for moderation was signed in the autumn of 1944 when Himmler still enjoyed all his authority. The order for medical attention was signed in the spring of 1945 in the chaotic conditions of the war's end.

By taking the military decision to hand over, without resistance, the concentration camps to the Allies, Himmler, no doubt, exceeded his authority and trespassed on a domain Hitler reserved to himself. In this connection Kaltenbrunner declared at the Nuremberg trial of war criminals:

'With regard to Becher I must go back a little. Himmler to accomplish the worst acts that will be mentioned here, had recourse to Becher. Through Becher and the 'Joint' Committee in Hungary and in Switzerland, he negotiated the release of a certain number of Jews against war material at first, then raw materials and finally foreign exchange. My informers had kept me aware of these negotiations and I then at once expressed my disapproval – not to Himmler, that would have been useless, but to Hitler.

Himmler, at that time, lost all his personal credit with Hitler, and indeed this enterprise could only cause considerable prejudice to the Reich's prestige abroad.[1]

Kaltenbrunner, no doubt ignorant that 'material' and 'foreign exchange' were most often nothing but vain promises, thought it his duty to denounce Himmler and Becher to Hitler. Both of them, with the help of Kastner and myself in Hungary and that of Saly Mayer in Switzerland, were indeed 'setting the Jews at liberty' and were thus committing the 'most heinous crimes'.

After Kaltenbrunner's denunciation, Hitler also got other proofs of Himmler's treason. In his fury at the attitude adopted by the 'faithful Heinrich' Hitler took vengeance on his brother-in-law, the SS officer Fegelein who was a member of the General Staff and was also liaison officer with Himmler. It was he who had to pay in the place of the *Reichsführer*. Fegelein, after having disguised himself in civilian clothes, was arrested as he was preparing to flee from the Führer's bunker, and executed.

Hitler, under the influence of radio reports describing the condition of the camps when Allied troops arrived, and also of stories broadcast by liberated prisoners, sent a telegram to Himmler on April 15, 1945, ordering him not in future to allow any camp to be surrendered with the inmates alive. Himmler had the good sense not to obey his Führer's instructions to go to Berlin. However, he definitely accepted Hitler's judgement about Becher's work of rescue.

On April 4, Himmler had received Becher at his urgent request and instructed him once more, in writing, that the camps still existing should be unconditionally handed over to the Allies. These camps were in particular Mauthausen, Theresienstadt and Dachau. When he got Hitler's telegram Himmler summoned Becher once again and despite his pro-

1. *Vide: Prozess Hauptkriegsverbrecher, Militärgriechtshof*, Nürnberg, 1947–1949, Vol. XI, p. 371.

tests, took back from him the written orders and authorizations Becher possessed.

What followed I learned from Becher's own mouth and I have no reason to doubt the truth of what he told me – and I would like to insist on this point. Henceforth the *Standartenführer* SS Becher behaved much in the same manner as Kastner and myself had ever since the month of May 1944. He took his decision not only from day to day but almost from hour to hour, constantly improvising and concerned not to fall from the tight-rope on which he was balanced.

A few days before, about April 20, 1945, the almost complete encirclement of the Reich territory had resulted in the Gestapo organization being cut in two. Kaltenbrunner, installed at Salzburg, had taken command of the southern sector, while Himmler commanded in the north.

After interminable parleying, Becher finally obtained agreement for the camp commandant of Mauthausen to hold up for 48 hours execution of the instructions he had received for destruction. Becher promised that during that delay he would get Kaltenbrunner's agreement, since the head of the Gestapo could not be got on the telephone. Without paying any attention to the warnings of friends he happened to meet, he therefore set off for the HQ of his sworn enemy, Kaltenbrunner.

Once more he presented all the arguments which had, earlier on, struck Himmler so forcibly. These last massacres, more than any others would have disastrous consequences for the whole German nation. Even those not directly implicated in these murders would be called to account. He adjured Kaltenbrunner to weigh well the consequences of his decision. Finally he threatened him. Then the unhoped for happened. Instead of having his visitor at once arrested and shot, Kaltenbrunner tried to get Hitler on the telephone. But in vain, the lines were cut. Then he confirmed the instructions Becher had given at Mauthausen. Becher went back to that camp with written orders from Kaltenbrunner in his pocket. A few days later Mauthausen was unconditionally surrendered to the Allies.

It is the historians' task to marshal the facts related here.

However, I feel obliged to throw light upon the efforts of two courageous men who risked their lives. The one undertook to save from massacre the last remnants of his people. The other wanted to snatch several tens of thousands of those condemned, from death and thus to atone, in part, for the crimes that had been committed in the name of all his fellow-countrymen.

After the war some embittered victims of Nazi persecution, on the one hand, and on the other, a certain number of political opponents, abandoned these men to the reprobation of ill-informed and misled 'public opinion'. They were treated as collaborators, as opportunists, as war criminals, etc. Kastner's political enemies, by reproaching him with having given evidence in favour of an SS officer before the Nuremberg tribunal, managed to make him the butt of the direct and indirect attacks which finally caused his death. But Kastner had said nothing but the whole truth about the part played by Becher in our common struggle.

The *Standartenführer*, for his part, had trod a long path before, deciding in the spring of 1945 to burn his bridges behind him, to rely on himself, and to attempt the impossible.

Exactly a year before he had allowed 40 members of a prosperous Jewish family to leave Hungary for a neutral country and thus save their lives. He had yielded to the entreaties of the chief of this family of industrialists, Dr. Franz Chorin, and accepted, in exchange, the provisional management of the majority of the shares in the trust. The price paid by the Weiss family was very high, the equivalent of several million dollars. What, however, is the main thing is that Becher agreed to their request and allowed this family to leave the country and save their lives. In any case the Weiss fortune would, according to current practice in national-socialist regimes, have been confiscated without any compensation at all.

Becher, by 'inflating' the valuation of belongings used to calculate the sums to be paid by another group of Jews, also enabled them to leave. Becher again obtained permission from Himmler that a convoy of 1,700 deportees should be sent to Switzerland. It was mainly thanks to Becher that Himmler in September, 1944, stopped the gas chamber executions and gave orders to hold up deportations. Thanks to Becher's help the Budapest ghetto escaped destruction by the Arrow Cross and the 84,000 inmates were saved.

The future will tell if it is suitable to label a man as opportunist just because he wore the uniform of an SS *Standartenführer*, a man who braved death, knowing quite well what he was doing, in the service of a just cause.

In the Book of Moses the story is told of King Bin Nun and the woman Rachaw Roshana. It shows us that the feeling of gratitude existed among the Jews in those ancient times. I do not want to believe that the high ethical duty to show gratitude has, in spite of everything that may have happened throughout the centuries, disappeared from among the Jewish people of today.

33. Epilogue

Everything in this book may appear absurd to the reader who is unprepared for the facts. I myself was long in doubt as to whether I could, one day, offer this report to the public. Probably I would be accused of having displayed a great deal of imagination. Yet every word is based on fact. Moreover, without the help of imagination, would our enterprise have had any chance of success? I could also be asked what proofs I could produce for the truth of what I advance – namely that it was indeed our activities that induced Himmler to take the decisions he did.

First of all I should like to make it clear that contrary to the sensational declarations of Joël Brand and of other persons who have maintained that with the exception of the passengers in the test-convoy, all the Hungarian Jews perished, at least half a million to 600,000 persons escaped extermination in Hungary itself and in the concentration camps. Of course these people do not know of the circumstances which delayed their massacre and allowed their preservation. The extermination programme was one of the best-kept of the Third Reich's secrets. Few documents are available concerning it. It is not then astonishing that written proofs relating to the stoppage of these massacres should be still less numerous, since the measures to suppress this wholesale murder constituted not only an act of insubordination of Himmler towards Hitler but were also the starting point of a plot against the Führer. I must, however, go back a little and deal with the declaration made before his death by Dieter Wisliceny, one of Eichmann's principal associates.[1]

'The efforts made, from the spring of 1944 onwards, by the representatives of the Joint Distribution Committee led Himmler to sign in October, 1944, the order annulling the

---

1. Vide, Poliakov-Wulf *Das Dritte Reich und die Juden*, Berlin, 1955.

"final solution". Wisliceny mentioned no names. It was by no means in his interest to recall all this affair. But as Eichmann's assistant he knew more than enough about it. Up to the beginning of our action he had, in fact, extorted funds from Jews. But he never kept his promises or offered the slightest thing in exchange for the money he received, quite in accordance with the common practice of Eichmann and his men. However, Wisliceny had to cease his exactions when we began our campaign with the supreme head of the SS, for he now had a rival in the person of his own *Reichsführer*, Heinrich Himmler. He, at least, did offer something in exchange to the American 'Joint' and tried to keep his engagements even when the payments of the promised Jewish funds ceased entirely. No one was better placed than Wisliceny to know just who was able to give orders to annul the 'final solution' – and who did precisely that. The historian Josef Wulf, himself a former prisoner at Auschwitz, has informed me that the gas chamber executions ceased in September–October 1944. He attributed this stoppage, it is true, to the fact that Soviet troops, at the time, had occupied the extermination camp at Treblinka and had shot out of hand all the German wardens as well as the commandant and the 'doctors' of the camp. In Wulf's opinion this event had deeply impressed the Gestapo.

In regard to this I must however specify that what happened at Treblinka provoked an entirely different response. The Gestapo, in full force under the orders of Kaltenbrunner (and especially of Eichmann), concluded that the time had now come to immediately finish off the last prisoners in the camps and the remaining Jews, thus eliminating all witnesses to the atrocities committed. The time the Gestapo had at its disposal before the liberation of the camps was quite sufficient for the extermination of all those remaining there.

When on our entreaties Himmler opposed the continuation of the massacres, the extremist wing of the Gestapo did all they could, by sabotage, to nullify the instructions given, but they could not prevent the definite stoppage of executions in the gas chambers. Since, the perfectly adjusted murder-machine (which had up to then, permitted the discreet 'suppression' of several million persons) was no longer available, the Kaltenbrunner gang of the Gestapo did not succeed in massacring most of the Jews still alive. In the confusion of the war's last phase it is true that several tens of thousands of Jews were killed, but at least five hundred thousand Jewish lives were saved. Without Himmler's instructions all these would have been murdered before the end of the year 1944 several months before the Allies arrived.

Here is the text of a letter addressed by Himmler to his former masseur, the Finn Felix Karsten:

The *Reichsführer* of the SS

> Berlin SW, 11, 21st March 1945
> Prinz-Albrechtstrasse, 8,
> Feld-Kommandostelle

Dear Herr Karsten,

Let me first of all thank you for your visit. As usual I was very glad to see you and to take advantage, in all friendship, of your great medical experience.

During the years of our friendship we have discussed a great number of problems. Your point of view has always been that of the doctor far removed from politics and concerned with the welfare of the individual and of mankind.

It will interest you to learn that during the last three months I have put into execution a plan about which we once spoke. Two convoys with, in all, 2,700 Jewish men, women and children, have been sent to Switzerland. This measure is quite in accordance with the line of policy closely followed by my collaborators and myself until the beginning of the war. But the madness then aroused by it in the world put an end to this policy's continuation. You know well that in the years 1936, 37, 38, 39 and 40 I arranged with several Jewish organizations in America, a very effective scheme for emigration. The departure of these two trains for Switzerland continues, despite all the obstacles that have to be overcome, a procedure that has already proved its worth.

Recently, a report from Bergen-Belsen stated that a relatively serious epidemic of typhus seems to have broken out in a prisoners' camp. I immediately sent there, Dr. Mrugrowski, an SS physician and a specialist in questions of hygiene, together with some of his assistants. It is a question of cases of exanthematic typhus unfortunately fairly common in camps where there are people from the countries of eastern Europe. Thanks to the application of modern medical treatment the epidemic can now be considered as checked.

I am sure that despite all demagogy and setting on one side secondary problems, wisdom and logic will triumph in spite of opposition and the bloody wounds suffered on all sides.

Of course, whenever possible, I would consider with the greatest attention any human problems you may care to bring to my attention. Every time that I may be able I will endeavour to find a satisfactory solution, just as in the past few years, whether in happy or less happy days.

With my respectful greetings to your dear wife, I am with great friendship to you and your children,

H. Himmler

The date of this letter is of capital importance. March 21, 1945, was nearly five months after the stoppage of the executions in the Auschwitz gas-chambers, and a few weeks only before the end of the war. Himmler wrote to his old crony to tell him about events apparently as yet unknown to Karsten – that is to say the despatch of a convoy of deportees to Switzerland at the end of 1944 – and thanks to the steps taken by us. This letter proves that the unwarranted publicity built up around Karsten's supposed activity in saving lives, is devoid of any foundation. Neither the stoppage of the executions in the gas chambers, nor the despatch of test-convoys to Switzerland was in any way the work of Karsten. There stand, however, to his credit a certain number of alleviations he had earlier obtained from Himmler. These concerned various persons of Scandinavian origin – among them several Jews.

While he was a masseur in Himmler's service, Karsten had put aside a certain amount of money and he meant to keep it. So, when he saw the end of the war approaching he left Himmler and had no longer been with him for several months when he got the above letter in which the *Reichsführer* quite obviously claimed the merit for events that had been due to our efforts. He addressed himself to Karsten, a man with foreign contacts, and more or less invited him in a capacity of mediator with the conquerors, to make Himmler new proposals.

At this point in the war the *Reichsführer* had lost touch not only with McClelland and Saly Mayer but also with ourselves who were in a Budapest freed by the Russians. Himmler, like a drowning man who clutches at a straw, was trying by all means to get into contact with foreigners. Kersten was one of the numerous persons living abroad with whom he got in touch either verbally or in writing, as the above letter clearly shows.

Before I refer to a series of other manoeuvres – all more or less the same – I would like to call attention to one strange aspect of this matter. The reader who knows little about Himmler's mentality may well be disconcerted by this attempt to elude responsibility for the dreadful events of the preceding years and by his wish to persuade his correspondent (and through him the Allies abroad) that he had, on the contrary, done everything to attenuate if not to prevent these atrocities. Perhaps he was trying to fool himself through these fables. There is no doubt that Himmler really did imagine that he could by pleading the concessions he had accorded us, gain the indulgence of the Allies. I think, furthermore, that he, like certain psychopathic criminals, ended up by persuading himself that only Hitler, Heydrich, Kaltenbrunner, Eichmann and company were responsible for the massacres, and that he was guiltless. This way of thinking provides the key to all I have recounted in this book and furnishes an explanation for our influence on him – an influence exercised, one might say, by remote control.

Before the end of the war there appeared around Himmler – who had by this time lost practically all power – a number of individuals whom he sought, as far as possible, to convince that he had undertaken a number of steps in favour of the Jews and that he was full of good intentions for the future. These persons included the Swiss councillor of State, Musy (whom I have already mentioned), Count Bernadotte, Mazur, the delegate of the Jewish World Congress at Stockholm, Hillel Storch, a notable citizen of the Swedish capital, and General Schellenberg, the chief of Himmler's secret service. The upshot of these people's approaches to Himmler (which were much commented on in the international press) was that they obtained practically nothing. But one point, however, has not been specified – the date at which these contacts with Himmler took place.

In Schellenberg's *Memoirien* (Cologne, 1956) we can read a letter dated June 17, 1945, addressed to M. Hillel Storch at Stockholm:

Becher negotiated with Saly Mayer the liberation of the Jews. If my memory serves me right, two SS officers, Becher's permanent representatives, took part in the discussions. Becher confined himself strictly to the financial questions, that is to say he demanded a certain amount of money, in foreign exchange, for each Jew liberated. In the place of foreign currency, tractors and trucks were still also demanded. In October 1944 the former president Musy got in contact with Himmler and it seemed then that the organization of the 'Joint' (Saly Mayer) collaborated with Becher.

In the following pages of Schellenberg's book there is given the beginning of a diary which opens as follows:

On 23rd January 1945, General Schellenberg ordered me to free a certain number of Jews from various concentration camps in Germany and to hand these people over, at the Swiss frontier to the former president, Musy. On this occasion Schellenberg informed me that he had been in contact with M. Musy since October 1944 and had already accompanied him to Himmler in order to obtain the authorization for the liberation of the Jews. At that time Himmler had already allowed the freeing of some Jewish families.

In this *Diary* we can read a little farther on:

about this same date General Schellenberg told me he had, in agreement with Musy, conceived a plan for the liberation of all the Jews in the German concentration camps and to arrange for them a number of trains to Switzerland. Musy himself was already in touch with the executive committee of the Union of American Rabbis that was represented in Switzerland by Dr. Isaak Sternbuch.

It appears clearly from these extracts that Schellenberg got in touch with Musy only in the month of October 1944 and then solely in order to intervene in favour of a certain number of families. It was later on, in January 1945, that he took the decision to set free all the Jews still living.

It is worthwhile now to draw attention to some dates. Our first steps were taken six days after Joël Brand's departure, that is to say on May 22–23, 1944, when the first interview occurred between Kastner and Eichmann, while I went to see Clages and Hunsche on May 30 or 31 after the arrest of my friends by the Hungarian secret police. At the end of June Clages had to intervene with Himmler regarding the departure of the test-convoy, which indeed left Budapest on June 30. Before that, between June 20 and 30, Kastner and I had contacted Becher and had managed to get him interested in the affair.

Despite unfavourable circumstances, due especially to Brand's defection and notwithstanding the strong opposition of Eichmann and all his staff to our projects, it was possible, thanks to my memorandum of July 23, 1944, to get Himmler to allow the departure, even before the final valuation of the objects furnished in exchange. Furthermore, on our insisting, Himmler agreed to Horthy's request for a temporary halt to the deportations in Hungary.

My opinion is that it was indeed at this date that Schellenberg, thanks to the new counter-espionage set up of the SS, was informed of our contacts with his chief and also of our activities, camouflaged as in the past as 'financial transactions'. The order for the departure of all the other passengers in the test-convoy for Switzerland, as well as the instructions (verbal and strictly confidential it is true) to cease the deportations, were given in the month of October, 1944.

A cunning fellow such as Schellenberg could scarcely any longer remain blind to the real state of things. Only men who were quite obtuse, fanatical and narrow minded, as were Eichmann and his closest assistants (some of who however were beginning to be less firm in their convictions), could still believe in the 'financial' nature of our activities. Schellenberg's intervention came only at this point. It was in this manner he found himself in 'competition' with Saly Mayer, and thus also with Becher. Schellenberg in his turn wanted to arrange a test-convoy and to get Becher relieved from his duties. Hence his approach to Himmler suggesting that the *Reichsführer* should rely on his own diplomatic skill rather than get involved in Saly Mayer's 'dirty tricks'.

(It was very regrettable for us that Saly Mayer, by preventing them from taking part in the negotiations, attempted to push aside all the other Jewish organizations working in Switzerland.)

We, on our side, thanks to our test-convoy, had in the meantime ensured that a leading member of the American Quaker community, Mr. Boswell McClelland, should, as the personal delegate of President Roosevelt, take part in the negotiations. This was a good deal more than we had hinted to Himmler: the presence of Messrs. Schwartz and Dobkin, though these were, it is true delegated by McClelland.

All these other enterprises, therefore, came much later and happened when the first convoy from Bergen-Belsen had already long since arrived in Switzerland. On the other hand, when the order came for the departure of the second convoy, the executions in the gas chambers had long ceased and there were no more deportations from Hungary.

At this period we did our best to get these last two measures applied to all prisoners. Musy, and much later on Bernadotte, Mazur and Hillel Storch negotiated the formation of test-convoys to be sent abroad but these could benefit only a tiny minority of the surviving deportees. As a matter of fact the Germans no longer possessed means of transport for evacuating such a great number of people to a foreign country.

Here is another document. It proves the importance Himmler attached to his 'conversations' with McClelland. It bears annotations in Himmler's own handwriting and constitutes a sort of report on the negotiations with Musy.

To be put in my files

MEMORANDUM

On Monday 15th January, 1945, I met at Wildbad Dr. Jean Marie Musy. He was apparently entrusted with a mission by the Americans. He asked me if it would not be possible to find a generous solution to the Jewish question. He himself wanted to do everything to achieve this. He was very surprised to learn that a Jew named Sally Meier (*sic*) had been entrusted by the Jioint (*sic*) with the duty of getting into contact with one of my representative, *Obersturmbannführer* of the SS Becher and an American called McClelland.

After a long interview, we agreed on the following points:

(1) He would get information as to Sally Meier's exact mission and find out exactly who it is who is dealing with the American government. Is it a rabbinical Jew or indeed the Joint?

(2) I explained once more my point of view. The Jews are used by us for certain sorts of work. There are, of course, some forms of labour that are arduous such as road or canal construction, and mining. Therefore the death rate among those so employed is high. Since, however, conversations began for the amelioration of the Jews' condition, they have been employed in normal labour[1] but as all Germans they also must work in the armament factories.

Our point of view about the Jewish question is as follows: we are not at all interested in learning what is the attitude towards Jews in the United States and Great Britain. One thing is certain, we do not want any of them in Germany and German territories. We learned our lesson during the years after the First World War. On this point we are uncompromising. If America wishes to receive Jews, we willingly take note of this. The possibility of being transferred to Palestine must not be allowed to the Jews we let go to Switzerland. Guarantees must be given on this point. We know that as far as the Jews are concerned, the Arabs also . . .

Himmler regarded the interviews, and the negotiations of Becher with the 'Jew of the Jioint' (*sic*), 'Sally Meier', and especially with McClelland, as of the highest importance. He was then all the more disappointed to discover that his new

---

1. The reference is to our discussions which had been going on since May 1944.

interlocutor, Musy, was entirely ignorant of these conversations. Himmler had apparently not understood that Mayer and McClelland regarded all these negotiations as compromising for them and that they did all they could to keep them secret, since these conversations had one single object, to confirm Himmler in his illusions and to strengthen our position at Budapest.

Other objections may concern the interpretation I give of the direct contacts which existed between Himmler and Otto Clages, an SS officer of comparatively low grade. One might, for instance, question what I say about the considerable influence this SS *Hauptsturmführer* had on the *Reichsführer* of the SS. But in order to have no further doubts on this point, it is enough to read Skorzeny's 'Memoirs', to take note of Reitlinger's and Shirer's evidence about Himmler, to open the monograph on Himmler written by Josef Wulf, or again the researches of Wolfgang Scheffler.

With all we know about Himmler, one thing is undeniable. He followed very closely all the details of the activities, the development and the composition of the SS machine which he controlled. He acted, indeed, in a rather astonishingly patriarchal manner and went as far as to interfere in the private life of his subordinates. When he chose one of his men for a particularly secret task, the first order the man received was to communicate nothing to his direct superior. When the importance of the matter justified it, he was to refer solely to Himmler in person. There can be no doubt that the most secret and important enterprise was, in Himmler's eyes, the preparations for leaving Hitler's ship before it sank. It is not then astonishing that the head of the Gestapo secret service, Schellenberg himself, was not let into the secret of Himmler's dealings with SS *Hauptsturmführer* Clages and with SS officer Becher, also of a rank considerably inferior to that of an SS general. We may also mention that Clages belonged to the SD, that is to section III (Interior) of the Gestapo, while Schellenberg was chief of section VI (Foreign). The lines of communication of all the SD sections led to Himmler. Clages, who **was** at first charged with keeping an eye on affairs in which Eichmann was involved, had come on the scene only later when he had learned the details about the contacts established abroad by Canaris's staff with the help of the Waada. It was quite in Himmler's manner to follow a new line in the greatest secrecy and without informing Schellenberg, the chief of section VI.

Mussolini's celebrated 'liberator' Skorzeny was also only at the beginning of his career when he was chosen for his first important mission. Although he was only a *Hauptsturmführer*, he was entrusted with 'State Secrets'. He was given a free hand to act as he saw fit and forbidden to mention his mission to his immediate superiors. Skorzeny's task in Budapest – to carry off young Horthy – was also kept secret and his superiors learned about it when the deed was done.

We manoeuvred Himmler 'by remote control', that is first with the help of Clages and then with that of Becher, and the *Reichsführer* was for us the only possible resource for achieving our aims. At that time (i.e. from May to December 1944) Himmler still enjoyed a considerable amount of power. After this period Hungary, and the Jews who were there, had already been liberated, as was Auschwitz in January 1945. It is enough to know that in March and April, 1945, during the last weeks of the collapse, Himmler was hardly able to have his foreign visitors, Count Bernadotte, Mazur etc escorted, in order to realize that nothing more could be expected of him except empty boasts about his supposed great deeds in favour of the Jews.

All those who have dealt with this subject (especially at the time of the Eichmann trial) have also omitted to make an important distinction between, on the one hand, the attempts made at Budapest by neutral consulates (with the assistance of the Hungarian ministry of foreign affairs and even with the tacit agreement of Ribbentrop's staff in the Reich ministry of foreign affairs), and on the other hand the activities of the all powerful Himmler, who at our suggestion acted in a perfectly independent manner. In doing this the *Reichsführer* felt competed with by the Hungarian authorities, as well as by Ribbentrop, and for that reason opposed their efforts. If the Jews under the protection of the neutral consulates were saved, after everything, that was owing entirely to measures in favour of all Jews we managed to obtain from Himmler.

On October 9, 1946, Joe Schwartz, director of the American Joint Distribution Committee in Europe, wrote to me about the work we had accomplished in Budapest:

We thank you for the services which you have rendered and realize that there very few men at that time who were in a position or were willing to undertake the work which it was so necessary to have done.

The Jewish World Congress wrote in its annual report for 1948:

The possibilities offered by the ransom avenue of rescue can be dealt with here with the utmost brevity only. Suffice it to say that the Economic Warfare argument and Jewish hyper-patriotism spoiled many an opportunity of utilizing the eagerness of Gestapo leaders to derive certain advantages in goods, money or future personal protection, from better treatment of the Jews under their control.

As a matter of fact it would not have been necessary to collect the amount of the ransoms; a simple promise to pay the money would have been enough. But the Westerners would not run even that risk in order to lighten our task at its beginning. It was feared, and is still feared now, to recall our action in Hungary, it is treated as though it were unworthy of being mentioned.

This remark applies especially to the American Joint Distribution Committee. For more than twenty years this organization had done everything to bury in oblivion the most important work it ever patronized and which was effected with a ridiculously small portion of its immense budget. When an undertaking is a grave one, the risks are always great. All the same when it has been successful one does not fear to acknowledge the fact, especially as the greater the risk, the greater the success. Anyway, as far as we are concerned, an enterprise was brought to a happy conclusion – the saving of several hundred thousands of human lives. Since the time of

Moses no comparable success has been obtained by an organization, not even by the 'Joint', although this remark is not intended to disparage the latter's many merits. Out of blind fear of being accused retrospectively of 'collaboration' an effort has been made by some not only to deny the successful results obtained but even to tolerate the accusations of fanatical adversaries, among whom – and this is the last straw – there are many who owe their lives to our enterprise. I am, however, sure that the day is not far off when the American Joint Distribution Committee will at last recognize all the work accomplished in its name.

I could also quote a great deal of testimony from important personages and from institutions that have expressed themselves in favour of our activities. I will mention only the following letter:

Office Palestinian de Suisse   Geneva, 10th August 1945

The management of the Palestinian Office of the Jewish Agency for Palestine, confirm herewith that the engineer Andreas Biss has been known to us for some time.

We know, especially, from various leading Jewish institutions and personages, that M. Biss during the German occupation of Hungary continuously risked his life with the sole object of saving the lives both of Jews and non-Jews from the clutches of the Nazis.

It is in part due to his devoted work in the accomplishment of which he shrank from no danger, that the hundred thousand or so inmates of the Budapest ghetto could be saved. It appears also from different reports that M. Biss collaborated with the Hungarian and Jewish Resistance. In order to save people persecuted and threatened with death, he maintained contacts with certain German officials. The leaders of the Hungarian Resistance must know the nature of these contacts.

After the liberation of Hungary M. Biss continued his social activities. He saved thousands of persons from famine and aided the deportees who returned.

He was entrusted by the Israelite community of Budapest and by other Jewish organizations with the task of arranging the despatch of medicaments, food and assistance for necessitous Hungarians. With this object, during his stay in Switzerland, he entered into relations with different organizations of a philanthropic character.

We know that M. Biss, after having successfully accomplished his mission desires to return to Budapest there to continue his work.

(signed)
Dr. B. Scheps
Dr. Ch. Pozner
Palestinian Office, Geneva

All these spontaneous testimonies of gratitude ceased later on. My friend Rezsö Kastner, a victim to over-excited public opinion, was assassinated.

Chronology

1943

January Creation at Budapest of the secret Jewish mutual aid organization (Waada).

Its aims:

1. To aid in Hungary the Jews fleeing from Poland, Yugoslavia, Slovakia, Austria, Germany etc. Then afterwards to assist the Hungarian Jews.

2. Inform the western countries about the nature of the persecutions of Jews in the Third Reich and in the occupied territories (first reports on Treblinka, Auschwitz etc.).

Committee of management:

Otto Komoly, Dr. Rezsö Kastner, Samuel Springmann and the latter's assistant Joël Brand.

1944

March 19 The SS occupy Hungary.

March 20–31 On Eichmann's orders, the constitution of the Jewish Council.

Members: Counsellor Samuel Stern, Philipp von Freudiger, Kahan-Frankl, Dr. Karl Wilhelm etc. The Waada's members in danger of arrest take refuge in Andre Biss's apartment. Joël Brand hides at a dancing-girl's home. At the last minute Biss evacuates Brand's family from the Hotel Majestic (Eichmann's future HQ) and hides them also at his abode.

April 4 Endre's secret instructions for the rounding-up of Hungarian Jews in the provinces with a view to deportation.

April 5 First contacts of the Waada with *Hauptsturmführer* Wisliceny and Klausnitzer.

Object: attempt to obtain adjournment of the deportations announced in exchange for sums of money.

April 7 Decree ordering the obligatory wearing of the Jewish star.

April 15 Beginning of round-up in the provincial ghettos.

April 19 Kastner and Brand pay 3 million pengoes to *Hauptsturmführer* Krumey and to Hunsche (Wisliceny had been sent to the provinces to deal with the ghettos).

April 25 In Biss's apartment Brand, who is once more united with his family, is contacted by Winninger and Grosz, *Ahwehr* agents, and asked to visit Eichmann.

April 28 Departure for Auschwitz of first train of deportees from Kistarcsa, with Jews arrested during the first days of the occupation of Hungary: among them the Jewish inhabitants of the Hotel Majestic arrested the next day after the flight of Mme Brand and her children.

May 8 Brand with Eichmann. He gives himself out as the head of the Waada and is given the mission of flying to Istanbul there to negotiate the barter of a million Jews for 10,000 trucks. Brand demands to be accompanied by Bandi Grosz.

May 10 Kastner, at the instigation of Brand and Grosz is arrested by the SD. Kastner had protested against the two men being sent to Turkey. Like all the Waada he did not think Brand fit for such a mission. But it was Grosz who was especially criticised. He would compromise the whole enterprise.

May 11 Arrest of the *Ahwehr* chiefs who up to then had maintained contacts with the Waada: Dr. Schmidt, Sedlaczek, Winninger and several others. Bandi Grosz was already an agent in the service of the SD and had turned his back on his old companions of the *Ahwehr*.

May 12 Kastner is freed after having been warned by Clages not to obstruct the departure of Brand and Grosz. And he must not prevent the Jewish organizations from supplying the two men with the necessary credentials.

May 13 The collection of Jews in the ghettos of Transylvania and the Carpathians is finished.

May 14–15 Beginning of deportations from the frontier regions of eastern Hungary.

May 16 Kastner again arrested by the SD so that he might not obstruct the departure of the two emissaries.

May 17 Brand and Grosz, after having received from the Jewish authorities the powers they demanded, leave for Istanbul. Brand and Grosz give their word of honour to return to Budapest in a fortnight. Mrs. Brand is appointed by her husband to represent him with Eichmann. She has to promise not to introduce Kastner or anyone else in her place to Eichmann.

May 22   Mrs. Brand decides all the same to introduce Kastner to Eichmann's staff since the chances of Brand's success were of the slightest and the hope of seeing him come back of his own accord practically non-existent. Kastner meets Eichmann, who he learns, contrary to Brand's statements, had never refused to meet other representatives of the Waada.

May 27   Komoly, Kastner, Mme Brand and Offenbach, members of the Waada, arrested by the Hungarian secret police.

May 30–31   Biss applies personally to Eichmann's staff and to Clages, the chief of the SD – whom he did not know – for liberation of the members of the Waada arrested by the Hungarians.

June 2   Thanks to the intervention of the Germans the members of the Waada are released.

June 3   Eichmann telegrams orders to stop the formation of the test-convoy composed of Transylvanian deportees that was to be sent abroad to support Brand's mission.

June 4   Clages, alerted by Kastner, appeals to Himmler, and Eichmann gets orders to hold up the deportation of the Klausenburg prisoners forming part of the test-convoy and is instructed to have them sent to Budapest where their departure for abroad is to be prepared.

June 6   The Allies land in Normandy.

June 9   Eichmann delivers a quasi-ultimatum of threats to Kastner because of Brand's prolonged absence.

June 10–14   Biss sees Clages about the deportee trains for Auschwitz being rerouted to Strasshof, so that the passengers may be saved from 'selections' and gas-chambers. Himmler permits, to begin with, 30,000 persons being transferred to Strasshof.

June 14   Kastner studies with Eichmann the problem of supplying the 15,000 prisoners at Strasshof.

June 20   First interview between Kastner and Becher.

June 30   The first five trains with a total of 18,000 deportees arrive at Strasshof camp.
  The test-convoy with some 1,700 passengers leaves Budapest.

July 1   Arrest of Waada members by the counter-espionage authorities of the Hungarian army: Mrs. Brand , Mrs. Bis Offenbach, Kastner and Biss are taken to the Hadik barracks but liberated the same day.

July 5–8   Deportations cease in the Hungarian provinces. Provisional stoppage of deportations. Hungarian requests for this.

July 8   Arrival of test-convoy at Bergen-Belsen.

July 8–14   Attempt at a putsch by the Hungarian gendarmerie and the secretaries of State Baky and Endre, supported by Eichmann, to overthrow Horthy. He appeals to his troops and dismisses Baky and Endre. Overbidding between Himmler and the Horthy government as to which has the 'merit' of having stopped the deportations.

July 14   Out of spite against Horthy and to prove that his orders are not valid, Eichmann deports about 1,450 Jewish prisoners from Kistarcsa with the help of the Hungarian gendarmerie. Horthy has Hungarian troops stop the convoy, but he does not liberate the Jews – rather he has them returned to Kistarcsa. This allows Eichmann to form the same convoy again on July 19 and then to deport the prisoners.

July 17   Eichmann informs Kastner that the test-convoy of Bergen-Belsen will be sent to Auschwitz and the total annihilation of the passengers will take place if Brand is not back in a week's time.

July 18   Kastner is kidnapped by Ferenczy's gendarmes.

July 19   Biss visits Clages.

Eichmann's second attempt, this time successful, to deport to Auschwitz the 1450 Jews from Kistarcsa.

July 20   Another visit by Biss to Clages. Stauffenberg's abortive putsch.

July 22   Biss's memorandum, in the form of a note, to Himmler.

July 26   Order from Himmler to stop deportations in Hungary. Clages explains this measure is the result of the memorandum. Order from Himmler to send part of the test-convoy from Bergen-Belsen to Switzerland.

July 27   Kastner liberated. Kastner and Biss together at Clages's office. Kastner then visits Becher.

August 2   Becher, after having met Himmler, comes back with confirmation of the order for the departure of the first 500 prisoners of the Bergen-Belsen group.

August 21   318 deportees from Bergen-Belsen arrive in Switzerland. First interview at the frontier with Saly Mayer. Present: Becher, Krumey, Grüson, Dr. Billitz and Dr. Kastner.

August 30   Himmler recalls Eichmann from Hungary.

September 1   Second interview at the frontier between Saly Mayer, Grüson and Kastner.

September 14   Grüson and Kastner at Bratislava (Slovakia).

September 19 Biss and Grüson at Bratislava with Gizi Fleischmann.

September 20 The Gestapo arrest Grüson.

September 26–30 Conditional 'yes' to Biss's proposals for an agreement telegraphed by Saly Mayer. Kastner's and Kettlitz's third journey to the Swiss frontier. Clages reports Himmler's order to stop the deportations immediately.

October 14 Clages takes part with Skorzeny in the kidnapping of young Horthy. Clages is mortally wounded in the course of the operation.

October 15 Success of Szalasi's putsch owing to total lack of resistance. Horthy is arrested.

October 17 Eichmann back in Budapest at the request of the Szalasi government.

October 20–30 Joël Nussbecher and Perez Goldstein, who were in the military prison, are deported. Joël Nussbecher manages to escape. Hannah Szenes is condemned to death by the Arrow Cross. The sentence is later carried out.

October 27 Kastner, Billitz and Kettlitz go to Switzerland for the fourth time. Becher joins them a few days later.

November 5 Interview at Zurich between Becher and McClelland.

November 8 Becher and Kastner come back from Switzerland.

November 15 Ordinance creating a ghetto in Budapest.

November 28 Kastner goes to Switzerland for the fifth time. Krell accompanies him.

December 2–3 On the orders of Hunsche and Dannecker the Columbusgasse camp is cleared by the Hungarian police.

December 3–4 Quarrel between Biss and Eichmann about the Columbusgasse camp.

December 4–18 Measures to save the ghetto from destruction by the Arrow Cross.

December 7 The last part of the Bergen-Belsen test-convoy (1,368 deported Jews) arrives in Switzerland.

December 18 Eichmann leaves Budapest.

December 23 Becher's departure. Budapest surrounded by the Russians.

1945

January 16 The Russians occupy Budapest house by house. Last interview Biss-Wallenberg. Fighting continues around the city.

June–April Kastner, back from Switzerland, goes to Germany. Budapest is in the hands of the Russians. The Allies liberate the concentration-camps of Auschwitz, Bergen-Belsen etc. Becher, in accordance with Himmler's instructions, sees that the concentration-camps are surrendered without fighting.

April 15 Hitler orders Himmler to do away with all surviving prisoners before the camps are handed over to the Allies.

April 15–30 Becher all the same carries on with his task. Before the Allies' arrival he saves from the extermination already ordered about 110,000 inmates of Mauthausen camp alone – among whom are 28,000 Jews.

Moshe Schweiger is liberated from Mauthausen.

Index

(Compiled by F. D. Buck)

Aczel, George, 180, 181
Adenauer, Konrad, 234
Aguda group, 176
American Joint Distribution Com-
    mittee, 21, 75, 111, 116, 128, 151,
    154, 165, 167, 168, 169, 170, 173,
    176, 187, 189, 190, 191, 192, 206,
    208, 214, 216, 220, 247, 248
  evacuation of test-convoy and, 122,
    124, 126, 127
Arendt, Hannah, 10, 11
Arrow Cross Party, 147, 149, 156,
    174, 182, 197, 199, 200
  Budapest ghetto and, 208, 212, 213,
    246
  in command, 147–56
  patrols, 152, 170, 200, 201, 212, 218,
    219
  seizes power 153, 198
'Aryanization' plan, 186–8
Association of American orthodox
    rabbis, 189
Auschwitz, 10, 21, 61, 64, 67, 74, 75,
    77, 80, 81, 94, 98, 105, 106, 110,
    124, 163, 174, 250
  gas-chambers, 20, 74, 78, 94, 175

Bader, Menachem, 96
Bakay, General, 150
Baky, Lászlo, 100, 104, 105, 171
Bardossy, Prime Minister, 13
Barlasz, Chaim, 96, 122
Batthyányi, 14
Bauer, Emil, 187
Bauvé, 222, 223
Becher, Obersturmbannführer Kurt,
    32, 60, 82, 83, 85, 86, 87, 88, 89,
    91, 147, 154–7, 162, 164, 172,
    175, 179, 183, 184, 189, 190, 201,
    214,
  accused, 203
  activities in favour of Jews, 235ff
  Aguda group and, 176, 177, 178
  Bergen-Belsen convoy and, 142,
    203, 206
  Biss's problems and, 201
  Budapest ghetto and, 207, 208, 209

Columbusgasse camp and, 193
  deportation and, 159, 160
  deposition at Nuremburg trials, 179
  evacuation of test-convoy and
    122–7
  exchange offer and, 182
  Himmler proof and, 128–32 passim
  Jewish Agency and, 116
  Kastner arrest and, 121
  Kastner kidnapping and, 110
  Krumey-Hunsche trial, 179
  McClelland meeting, 159, 160, 164
  on trial, 232
  ransom and, 90, 203, 205, 206
  sees Himmler, 88
  Slovak affair and, 135–8 passim
  Slovakian Jews and, 158
  Weiss works and, 203
Berecky, Albert, 102
Bergen-Belsen, 99, 107, 123, 124,
    128, 195–7 passim, 204, 205 249
  camp, 237, 238, 239
    Kolb on, 237–8
  convoy, 95, 99, 105, 110, 117, 120,
    126, 130, 137, 139, 142, 152,
    162, 164, 167, 168, 190, 204,
    206, 218, 225, 226, 249, 254
Bernadotte, Count, 251
Billitz, Dr., 85, 86, 88, 157, 313
  Aguda group and, 176
  evacuation of test-convoy and, 124,
    126, 127
  Himmler proof and, 131, 132
Billitz-Weiss affair, 85–7
Biss, Andre, 53, 54, 58, 63, 65, 68, 72,
    75, 102, 111, 112–16, 146, 151,
    162, 163, 213, 217, 220–3, 229,
    234
  'Aryanization' plan and, 187–8
  bait for Clages, 83
  Brand and, 230
  Budapest ghetto and, 205, 207
  Budapest 'Joint' and, 220
  Columbusgasse camp and, 191, 192,
    195, 196
  commences service with Waada, 48
  denounced as Gestapo agent, 227–
    228

Biss, Andre—*cont.*
  Eichmann's trial and, 231–2
  Horthy's proclamation and, 148
  Kastner arrest and, 120–2
  Kastner-Becher meeting, 83–4
  Kastner kidnapping, 109, 110, 111
  Osterwell-Kotarba and, 187
  ransom and, 90, 180, 206
  sees Clages, 55, 109
  Slovak affair and, 135, 138
  taken to Hadik barracks, 85–6
  telegram to Mayer, 163–4
  test-convoy and, 73, 103
  Wallenberg's activities and, 171
Biss, Dora (née Brecher), 23
Biss, Dr. Cornelius Samuel, 23
Boda, Dr. Ernst, 32
Bohnekamp, Lieutenant, 240
Born, Friedrich, 181, 182
Brand, Hansi (née Hartmann), 25, 29,
    63, 153, 167, 168, 215
  arrested, 53, 168
  Columbusgasse camp and, 192
  death of, 204
  flees, 67
  freed, 227
  introduced into Gestapo, 49
  Palestine Couriers and, 144, 146
  released, 58, 70
  taken to Hadik barracks, 95–6
  tortured, 58
Brand, Joël, 22, 25, 27, 33, 34, 35–8,
    43, 48, 49, 71, 72, 99, 142, 229,
    232, 233, 234, 247
  arrested in Syria, 98
  Becher and, 233
  Biss and, 230
  counter-espionage and, 28, 54
  'defection', 128, 253
  Eichmann trial and, 232–3
  evacuation of test-convoy and, 123,
    124
  Gestapo contacts, 48
  interview with Eichmann, 43
  Jewish Agency and, 97, 116
  joins Andre Biss, 25
  joins Zionist party, 38
  mission to Turkey, 43–8, 48, 50, 52,
    55
  new beginning in Hungary, 38–43
  provisional agreement, 59, 76
  Palestine, emigration to, 38, 39
  'Trucks Affair' and, 34
  Waada and, 40, 42
  Zionist ambitions, 48–9
  Zionist party and, 39
'Brand case', 232–3
Brecher, Dora (*see* Biss)
Bregenz, 131, 132

Brunner, *Obersturmführer*, 135
Buchenwald camp, 237
Budapest, 92, 165–76, 183, 184, 185,
    188, 213–19, 220–8
  ghetto, 32, 185–7, 202, 205–13, 217,
    218, 246
Bureau of Jewish Affairs, 20, 51, 54,
    60, 65, 66, 68, 69, 85, 89, 91, 110,
    111, 121, 123, 135, 191, 192

Canaris, Admiral Wilhelm, 20, 21, 41,
    42, 70, 71
Chorin, Dr. Franz, 60, 85, 86, 246
Churchill, Winston S., 209
Ciano, Count Galeazzo, 19, 50
Clages, *Hauptsturmführer* Otto, 9, 10,
    21, 32, 43, 45, 54, 55–6, 58, 59,
    61, 69, 71–2, 75, 76, 77, 87, 89,
    90, 91, 120, 141, 142, 143, 150,
    152, 159, 253, 256
  Bergen-Belsen train, 117
  Biss's arrest, 64–7
  Brand-Grosz mission and, 46, 47
  Bureau of Jewish Affairs and, 21
  Eichmann and, 56, 70
  evacuation of test-convoy and, 123
  Gestapo special force and, 42–3
  Himmler and, 104, 127, 128, 129
  Kastner arrest and, 121
  Kastner-Becher meeting, 83–5
  Kastner kidnapping and, 109, 110,
    111, 112
  Mrs. Brand's torture and, 58
  Palestine Couriers and, 144, 145,
    146
  'Provisional Agreement', 98
  Russian attitude and, 119
  Slovakian affair and, 138, 139
  Straashof and, 82, 83
  test-convoy and, 73, 74, 103, 141
  Zionist contacts and, 43
Columbusgasse 'protected' camp, 145,
    146, 173, 174, 191–7
concentration camps, 32, 78, 235–46
  Budapest, 31, 32, 106, 110
  counter-espionage, 43, 114
  Hungarian, 95, 103, 145–7 *passim*,
    168

Dachau camp, 244
Dálnoky, 224
Danielson, 222
Dannecker, Theodor, 20, 58, 81, 172,
    192–5
deportations, 134, 138, 233
Dobkin, Elijahu, 116, 123, 124
Duban, Dr., 216, 217

Eichmann, *Obersturmbannführer* Karl

Adolf, 20–4, 31, 43, 46–8, 50, 51, 55, 59, 70, 75, 77, 81, 82, 83, 88, 107, 128, 154, 171, 172, 173, 175, 180, 183, 184, 189, 191, 193–6, 201, 204, 213, 231, 237, 248
American Joint Distribution committee and, 189
Arrow Cross Party and, 149
Bergen-Belsen convoy and, 157
Biss's arrest and, 67
Brand and, 48, 232
Budapest ghetto and, 202, 208
Bureau of Jewish Affairs and 51, 54, 60, 68, 85, 89, 105
decides to deport Kistarcza Jews, 105
deportations and, 76, 110, 140, 158, 171
evacuation of test-convoy and, 123, 124
Ferenczy and, 104
Fleischmann murder and, 140
Himmler proof and, 127, 128, 130
HQ, 25, 28, 43, 49
Hungarian Jews and, 80
Jewish emigration and, 52
Kastner and, 82
Kastner-Becher meeting, 83–4
Kastner kidnapping, 110
Kastner negotiations and, 48–52, 61
Kastner's obstinacy and, 61
Kovarcz and, 158
Mrs. Brand's torture and, 58
'Palestine certificates' and, 169, 173
'Provisional Agreement' and, 98
ransom and, 28, 32, 33, 89, 90, 180
receives Kastner, 61
sabotages test-convoy, 73
second test-convoy and, 189
Slovak affair and, 134, 135, 136
summons Brand, 43
test-convoy and, 51, 76
transport of Jews and, 62, 91
trial of, 10, 79, 149, 155, 172, 173, 219, 231, 232, 233, 234, 235
Endre, Lászlo, 100, 104, 105, 171
England, news from, 117–22
extermination operations, 20, 158, 172

Fegelein, Herman 244
Ferenczy, Lt.-Col., 104, 105, 171, 172, 181
Kastner and, 120, 121, 236
Fischer, Josef, 49
Fischer, Viki 198, 199, 200
Fleischmann, Gizi, 30, 134
murdered at Auschwitz, 140
Slovak affair and, 135, 136, 138
forced labour, 166, 167, 171, 172

Föutca prison, 201
Freudiger, Philipp von, 31, 46, 92, 153, 233

Garzoly, Lt.-Col., 71, 103, 147
gas-chambers, 20, 74, 141, 157, 158, 163, 171–3 passim, 175, 190, 233, 246
Gestapo, 42, 45, 111, 172, 198, 227, 229, 230, 232, 244, 248
Becher, Kastner and, 236, 237
Budapest ghetto and, 208
Goldberger, 100
Goldfarb, Neska, 200, 201
Goldfarb, Zvi, 200
Goldstein, Perez, 143–7 passim, 167
Görög, Dr. Frederick, 221, 222, 227, 228
Görög, Vera, 221
Grabau, Obersturmführer, 137, 138, 204
Grässler, 174
Grosan, Colonel, 240
Grosz, Bandi, 41, 44–8, 71, 99
Grüson, Hauptsturmführer Max, 88, 107, 136, 137
evacuation of test-convoy and, 122, 124, 126
Himmler proof and, 131, 132
ransom and, 90, 204
Slovak affair, 111, 117, 134–8 passim
Gurion, Ben, 230, 231, 234

Habonium, 147
Haganah, 143, 146, 166, 167, 181, 200
Hain, Peter, 56
Haloutzim, 198, 199, 200
Harries, Colonel, 239, 240
Hartmann, Hansi (see Brand)
Hatz, Colonel, 147
Hausner, Gideon, 231, 234
Hazzalah, 167, 219
Himmler, Reichsführer S.S. Heinrich, 10, 21, 32, 58, 60, 70, 71, 72, 75, 77, 82, 83, 87, 88, 127, 132, 133, 141, 152, 158, 165, 172, 175, 179–180, 182, 184, 230, 236–46, 251
Aguda group and, 176, 178
American Joint Distribution Committee and, 189
Arrow Cross and, 152
Becher and, 155
Becher-McClelland meeting and, 160
Bergen-Belsen convoy, 142, 206, 237, 253
Brand-Clages mission and, 47
Budapest ghetto and, 202, 205–8 passim, 211–13 passim

Himmler—*cont.*
Columbusgasse camp and, 191, 193, 195, 196
deportations and, 158–60
evacuation of test-convoy and, 122, 123, 126, 127
Kaltenbrunner and, 177
Kastner kidnapping and, 110, 111
negotiations and, 119, 120
ransom and, 204, 206
secret order to Tiso, 30
Slovak affair and, 135–9 *passim*
Slovakian Jews and, 158
Stauffenberg plot and, 97
surrenders camps, 238, 239
test-convoy and, 73, 74
Waada, contacts with, 236
Waada, influence on, 247
Wisliceny and, 248
Zionist contacts and, 43
Hitler, Adolf, 11, 19, 23, 45, 100, 133, 134, 140, 180, 209, 236
Horak, 219
Horthy, Admiral Nicholas, 13, 17, 18, 19, 24, 71, 102, 103, 107, 110, 120, 121, 147, 148, 149, 150, 151, 156, 165, 169, 171, 253
asks for Eichmann's recall, 105
Eichmann trial and, 149
saviour of Hungarian Jews, 99–109, 149–50
Horthy, Nicholas, 150, 151
Höss, *Obersturmbannführer* Rudolf, 175
Huber, Professor Max, 224
Hull, Cordell, 100, 209
Hungarian anti-Jewish laws, 14–20, 24
Hungarian Resistance, 181
Hungarian secret police, 227
Hungarian Youth, 197
Hungarian Zionist Union, 139
Hungary: 'Jewish Problem', 20, 31
Hunsche, *Hauptsturmführer* Otto, 20, 31, 51, 54, 55, 61, 81, 104, 106, 172
Biss's arrest and, 65–8
Columbusgasse camp and, 192–5
Hungarian regulations and, 202
Kastner kidnapping and, 110
Hunwald, Simcha, 217

International Jewry, 88, 98

Jewish Agency, 97, 98, 116, 128, 189
evacuation of test-convoy and, 123
Jewish-American Joint Distribution Committee, 9
Jewish Assistance Committee (*see* Waada)

Jewish Committee for Mutual Aid, 59
Jewish Council, 43, 153, 187, 233
Budapest ghetto and, 207, 208
Jewish emigrants, convoy of, 101
'Jewish question', the, 104
Jewish World Congress, 189
Jews, deportation of, 29–30
Juttner, *Obergruppenführer*, 174

Kahan-Frankl, Samuel, 31
Kállay, Miklós, 42, 102
Kaltenbrunner, Ernst, 77, 79, 80, 177, 178, 237, 243, 244, 248
Karie, Ahron, 231
Kassowitz, Dr. Andreas, 204
Kastner, Dr. Reszö, 22, 24, 27, 30, 31, 41, 49, 50, 51, 54, 61, 62, 65, 67, 71, 72, 76–7, 83, 87, 89, 91, 98, 99, 107, 120–2, 144–6, 155, 164, 171, 172, 185, 190, 219, 227, 230, 234, 245
accused by Krausz, 92
activities in favour of Jews, 235*ff*
after liberation, 220, 224, 229
Aguda group and, 177
arrested, 46, 53
Bergen-Belsen train and, 202, 204
Biss's relations with, 229
Brand and, 42, 121–2, 229
Budapest ghetto and, 207, 210
Columbusgasse camp and, 193
death of, 154, 231, 232
deportations and, 51, 59, 76
Eichmann and, 48–52, 78, 82
evacuation of test-convoy and, 122–7
goes to Switzerland, 156–64, 183, 184
Himmler proof and, 127, 129, 131, 132
Horthy's proclamation and, 148
Jewish community and, 189
kidnapped, 108–9
Klausenburg Jews and, 87
negotiations with Eichmann, 78
ransom and, 43, 90, 180, 205
released, 58, 70
Slovak affair, 134–9 *passim*
taken to Hadik barracks, 95–6
test-convoy and, 74, 76, 140
tests Eichmann, 51–2
Zionist groups and, 189
'Kastner affair', 231
Kastner Report, the, 33, 78
Kemeny, Baron, 170
Kersten, Felix, 241, 250, 251
Kertesz, Dr. Eugene, 204
Kettliz, 138, 157, 176, 177, 183, 184, 191, 203, 204
Kirschner, 26

Kiss, Andor (*see* Biss, Andre)
Kistarcsa, 64, 105–7, 110
Klausenburg, 50, 59, 73, 82, 87, 91, 92, 103, 145
Klausnitzer, *Hauptsturmführer*, 31, 44
Kolb, Eberhard, 237–8, 241, 242
Kolleck, Theodor, 234
Komoly, Mrs., 216, 217, 218
Komoly, Otto, 22, 25, 27, 30, 49, 53, 54, 65, 67, 89, 92, 102, 153, 181, 219, 221, 227, 234
  'Aryanization' plan and, 187–8
  besieged Budapest and, 215, 216, 217
  Budapest ghetto and, 210, 211
  death of, 181, 213, 218
  President of Waada, 42
  released, 58, 70
Kossuth, 14
Kovarcz, Emil, 170
  Budapest ghetto and, 208, 212
  deportations and, 158, 171
Kramer, Dr., 238
Krausz, Moshe, 92, 101, 169, 181
Krell, *Hauptsturmführer*, 185, 189, 191, 203, 205, 206
Krem, Joseph, 40
Krumey, *Obersturmbannführer*, 20, 31, 44, 55, 61, 81, 123–4, 175, 207
Krumey-Hunsche trial, 150, 179
Kun, Bela, 17

Levente, 197
Lichtheim, Richard, 189
Lullay, Captain, 181
Lutz, Charles, 101, 168, 169, 171, 174, 181

McClelland, Roswell D., 125, 140, 141, 142, 160, 179–80, 251, 254
  Becher meeting, 159, 160, 161, 164
Maïdanek, 20, 28, 29
Maniu, Iuliu, 50
Mapai, 40, 230
Margitkörut military prison, 200
Marton, Dr. Ernö, 182, 221
Mauthausen camp, 143, 244, 245
Mayer, Saly, 124–7, 134, 157, 164, 183, 184, 189, 194, 225–6, 243, 251, 254
  after liberation, 220, 223, 225, 226, 227
  Aguda group and, 176–8 *passim*
  Himmler proof and, 127–32 *passim*
  Slovakian affair and, 138, 139
  test-convoy and, 140
Mazur, 251
Mester, 102
Molodet, 76

Moscovics, 197
Moson-Magyaróvár, 94, 98
Mufti of Jerusalem, 47
Muller, *Gruppenführer*, 77
Musy, Jean-Marie, 190, 251, 252, 253, 255

Nebe, 56
Neugeboren, *Hauptsturmführer*, 67, 68, 90, 191, 192
Neumann, Dr., 134
Nisson-Kahan, Dr., 32
NKVD (Russian Secret Police), 223
Nowack, 61, 81, 110
Nuremburg trials, 155, 245
Nussbecher, Joël, 143–7 *passim*, 166–8, 181, 200, 223, 229

Olah, Dr., 147
Oranienburg camp, 237
Organization of Jewish Assistance, 189
Osterwell-Kotarba, Dr., 186, 187

Palestine, 101, 143–7, 168
'Palestinian certificate', 168
Palestinian Office, 101, 169, 189
Palgi, Joël (*see* Nussbecher, Joël)
Péter, Gábor, 224
Petö, Dr. Ernst, 31
Pfenbach, Szulem, 53, 70, 89, 90, 93–4, 95–6, 217, 218, 220
Pomeranz, Wenja, 96
Pope Pius XII, 100
Posner, Dr. Haim, 189
Progressive Jewish Community, 46
Provisional Agreement, 96, 97, 98

Ransom money, 31, 32, 43, 51, 82, 137
  convoy held for higher, 88–9
  Times article, 118–19
Raphael, 197
Ravensbruck camp, 237
Red Cross, 147, 162, 181, 199, 215
  International, 101, 173, 181, 211, 216, 218
  after liberation, 221, 223, 225
refugee's children, 186
Rieger, Gerhard, 189
Reiner, Dr. Imre, 32
Reznik, Colonel M., 227
Ribbentrop, Joachim von, 19, 50
  convoy and, 102
Röder, SS Commandant, 202
Roosevelt, Franklin D., 42, 70, 104, 125, 129, 130, 160, 254
Rotta, Mgr, Angelo, 100
Rumanian Secret Police, 37
Russian attitude, 119

Sankt Margrethen, 122–7, 132, 157
Schellenberg, General Walter, 97, 178, 252, 253, 254
Schmidt, Colonel Hans, 239, 240
Schmidt, Dr., 42, 54
Scholl, Hans, 11
Scholl, Sophia, 11
Schröder, 76, 84
Schwabenberg, 110, 121
Schwartz, Dr. Joseph J., 123, 124
Schweiger, Dr. Moshe, 143
Sharett, Moshe, 234
Siguranita files 37,
Silberschein, Dr., 189
Sissu, 128
Skorzeny, Standartenfuhrer, 150
Slovak affair, the, 133–43
Slovak refugees, 199
Slovakian Jews, 158
Solymossy, 171
Springmann, Samuel, 22, 41, 42
Stalin, Josef, 120, 160
Stauffenberg, Col. Claus Schenk, 98, 110, 111
Steger, Alois, 209, 211n
Stephan, Irbirah, 84
Stern, Samuel, 31, 46, 92, 153, 207, 208
Sternbuch brothers, 190
Sternbuch-Musy operation, 190
Sternbuch plan, 191
Stettinius, Edward R., 209
Stöckler, Ludwig, 187, 201
Storch, Hillel, letter, 252
Strasshof Labour camp, 10, 32, 74–81, 94, 103, 130
Szálasi, Ferenc, 103, 148, 149, 152, 170, 208
Szenes, Hannah, 143, 144, 145, 147, 167
Szilagyi, Ernest, 24, 92
Szondi, Dr., 92
Sztojay, Döme, 58, 100

Teheran agreement, 160
Teitelbaum, Joël, 92
Teleki, Tér, 198
test-convoy, 122–7, 189, 202–5
Theresienstadt camp, 21, 61, 244
Tiso, Mgr, Josef, 30, 133
Treblinka extermination camp, 20, 248
Trianon Treaty, 18, 19
'Trucks Affair', 35, 44
Trumpy, 178

Ujszászy, General, 71

Vaida, Dr., 36, 216, 217
Veesenmayer, 56, 58
Vienna award, 50

Waada, 20–32, 55, 72, 102, 106, 107, 122, 162, 166, 171, 182, 201–2, 218, 227
Bergen-Belsen train and, 203
Brand and, 22, 35, 45
Brand-Grosz mission and, 45, 46, 47
Budapest, 125, 131
Budapest ghetto and, 208, 211, 213
Canaris's men and, 22
Columbusgasse camp and, 194
Gestapo black list, on, 22
HQ, 24
Hungarian Jews and, 27
Istanbul, 83, 96, 122
'Palestinian certificates' and, 169
Palestinian couriers, 144, 145
ransom and, 31, 43, 89, 90
Slovak affair and, 136
test-convoy and, 78
trucks affair, 44
Wallenberg, Raoul, 171, 181, 222
War Refugee Board, 141, 160
Warsaw ghetto, 11
Weiner, Zoltan, 187
Weiss, Alexandre, 204
Weiss, Arthur, 217
Weiss, Baron Alphonse, 86
Weiss, Baron Eugene, 86
Weiss, Baron Manfred, 60, 82, 85, 203, 246
Weiss, Rudolf, 187
Weiss-SS agreement, 60–1
Weissberg, Alex, 34, 37
Weisskopf, 219
Weissmandl, Rabbi, 29
Weyermann, Hans, 181 183, 211, 215, 216
Wilhelm, Dr. Karl, 31, 169, 181, 207 220, 224
Winkelmann, General, 212
Winniger, Joseph, 25, 41
Wisliceny, Dieter, 9, 20, 29, 30, 31, 43, 44, 51, 61, 81, 247, 248
Witezka, Lieutenant, 134
World Jewish Congress, 228
Wulf, Josef, 248
Wyler, Dr., 130, 131, 132
Slovak affair and, 138

Yellow Star, the, 63, 64, 65, 68, 184

Zionist Committee for Mutual Assistance (see Waada)
Zionist Congress, 34
Zionist movement, 144